A STUDY OF
DRAGONS
of Eastern Europe

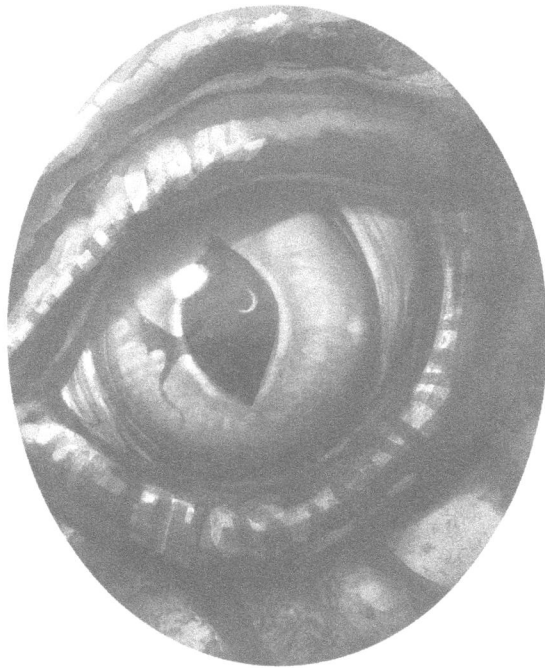

RONESA AVEELA

BENDIDEIA
PUBLISHING

Cover Design by Nelinda, www.nelindaart.com.
Cover Art by Dmitry Yakhovsky, www.entaroart.com © Bendideia Publishing.
Series interior layout design by Nicole Lavoie, www.JustSayingDezigns.com.
Vecna font is used in the book's title. It is available for commercial use from Pixel Sagas at www.pixelsagas.com.

Contents

Editorial Reviews

Ronesa Aveela continues to enchant and educate with the latest installment in the Spirits and Creatures series: *A Study of Dragons of Eastern Europe*. As advertised, the book offers a bountiful amount of dragon lore from Eastern Europe, a topic often overlooked in lieu of Western European dragon tales. From etymologies to protective measures, Ronesa relays a veritable treasure trove of folklore and fairy tales, not only of dragons but also the heroes who fought them. Numerous citations from Slavic sources are included, a feature not often found in English studies. Through examples, accounts, snippets, stories, and poems, the reader is thoroughly immersed in a fantastical world of monstrous beasts both malevolent and benevolent. Ronesa deftly adds breakdowns of the symbolism in tales and offers meanings and morals to stories more complex than they might seem. Folklore told in an informative and engaging way, *A Study of Dragons of Eastern Europe* is a must-have addition to any library of myths and legends!

— David Flora, *Blurry Photos Podcast*
www.blurryphotos.org/podcast/

Dragons are perhaps the most ancient, complex and magnificent of all mythical creatures. They have haunted the human imagination for thousands of years and whenever they appear they herald a significant event, for better or worse.

Ronesa Aveela's wonderful new book introduces us to the fascinating world of Eastern European dragons, a group that is little-known in the West. Meet the snake-like Smok; the shape-shifting Zmey who can transform into an attractive young man to seduce unwary maidens; the Lamia and Hala, voracious female weather demons; and from Romania, the devilish Zmeu and the flesh-eating Balaur who creates precious gems from his saliva.

These dragons inhabit the twilight zone between good and evil. In folk belief, they play an integral part in the human life cycle, both materially and psychologically. They have elemental power. They can destroy the harvest by causing drought, floods and hailstorms, or they can be benevolent and protect the earth's fertility. On the other hand, some dragons can drive you mad. The love of a Zmey, for example, can cause a maiden to languish and pine away – a condition that we might now categorise as mental illness. Dragons can also procreate with humans but the child born of a woman and a Zmey will either become a hero, or in anecdotal accounts, will suffer from physical or mental handicaps.

Well-written, easy to read and comprehensive, including texts that have never before been available in English, this is a real treasure trove of a book. It covers the origin of dragons, their mythological transformation over time, full descriptions of the nature of each species and ways to appease or defeat them, plus an account of bold dragon-slayers from fairy-tale heroes to Christian saints. It encompasses extensive research and fascinating "facts," beautifully embroidered with magical traditional tales, intriguing legends and extraordinary folklore. Did you know, for example, that you can repel a Zmey by challenging him to a pee-ing contest and then tossing his urine over him?

This is not an academic study but it is well-researched and referenced. I have reservations about some of the suggested symbolism, though this is a subjective opinion, and a few of the theories and interpretations that are described are rather fanciful and lack evidence. So keep your critical hat on and decide for yourself whether they ring true or not.

Overall this is an excellent book, a rich voyage of discovery into the mysterious realm of Eastern European dragons. It's full of surprises, fun to read and jam-packed with dragon facts. Yet it touches deeper levels too, for it is also an exploration of the borderlands where human psychology, the natural environment and the mythological imagination meet. There is much here that we may recognise from our own experience of the world, ourselves and others. Read it and enjoy!

— Moni Sheehan, storyteller and director of
A Spell In Time, British-Bulgarian storytelling company
www.spellintime.co.uk

Acknowledgments

So many people have had a part in bringing this book to life. Thanks to David Flora (of *Blurry Photos Podcast*, http://www.blurryphotos.org/podcast/) and Moni Sheehan (storyteller and director of A Spell In Time, British-Bulgarian storytelling company, https://www.spellintime.co.uk/), for taking the time to read an advance copy and providing an editorial review. Additional thanks to Moni for her suggestions for improvement.

A warm thank you to Erin and Alex for being the first to look at early drafts and pointing out areas for improvement.

I'd like to thank Dmitry, Keazim, Valentin, Plamen, and Nelinda for their artistic additions that bring the dragons to life.

Many, many thanks go to the numerous translators involved in this book. I'd like to especially thank Aleksandra Dapkova, for her exemplary work translating numerous Bulgarian texts—old, new, and dialect.

And, always, thank you to our readers! We write these books for you. Be sure to sign up for our newsletter in the "Special Offer" section at the end of this book to receive a free copy of "A Study of Vodyanoy – Water Spirit of Eastern Europe."

Author's Note

Welcome to the third book in the Spirits and Creatures series, where we focus on the mighty dragon. As with the previous books, our intent is not to write a book for academic use. Although many of the sources are from those knowledgeable in the field of folklore, we've also used more controversial material, unsubstantiated references, and general public opinions. It's a book for those who want to learn more about a topic that's sorely under-represented in the Western world. It's easy to discover books and articles about dragons from Western Europe and China, but those of Eastern Europe are rarer, at least in the English language. We've provided an extensive bibliographic list for those who wish to pursue the topic on a deeper level.

In the Beginning Was … the Dragon

In times of old all things were possible.

Etymology

The name "dragon" traces back to the word "serpent," such as the Greek δράκων (*drákon*) or the Latin *draco*, but there's more to the meaning. A study of the Proto-Indo-European word shows that, "[i]f you dig deeper, its root *derk-* (or *drk-*) is the equivalent of 'to see' in Ancient Greek—suggesting that *drk-on* also indicates 'seeing one,' or 'I see' " (Shiau). The possible meaning of this is "the one with the (deadly) glance" (Etymonline .com). Some say this refers to the dragon's extraordinary eyesight (Sheppard Software). But, perhaps it's more sinister. You'll learn later how certain dragons have a "deadly glance," in which they set their sights on a maiden for a bride.

Other sources say "dragon" comes from an Old Norse word, *draugr*, meaning "a spirit who guards the burial mound of a king" (Sheppard Software). It has been interpreted that the idea of dragons guarding treasure comes from this meaning (Radford).

Dragon Eye: A Deadly Glance. Illustration by Dmitry Yakhovsky. © Bendideia Publishing.

The concept of a dragon exists in numerous cultures across many continents. Some scholars in the past believed the creatures had a common origin due to similarities in the dragons' appearance and traits. Dragons of Eastern Europe have aspects common with their western neighbors, as well as similarities to dragons from both the Near and Far East. Besides the well-known common characteristics of having scales, being able to fly and breathe fire, and guarding treasure, some of these traits include:

- Giving/withholding rain
- Guarding water bodies
- Shape-shifting
- Conceiving children with young women
- Creating whirlwinds, floods, and droughts
- Protecting fertility[1]

The origins of dragons have even made it into psychological topics, saying they're impressions of now-extinct creatures that "reflect a genetically encoded memory of dinosaurs from the remote prehuman past."[2]

1

Or, perhaps, yet others have argued, the idea of dragons arose from fossilized bones or eggs of ancient reptiles. Non-animate theories even exist, saying dragons are symbolic of, and evolved from, weather phenomena like clouds, rain, thunder and lightning, and the resulting rainbow after the storm.[3]

Whatever the reason the idea of dragons came into existence—whether they existed physically or only symbolically or psychologically—these mighty creatures have captured the imagination of people for many ages.

Dragon Transformation

In the early stages of tribal societies, the monsters that individuals encountered were enormous fish, snakes, or birds. People believed ordinary creatures could develop into these beasts over extended periods. The actual amount of time required, as well as the conditions necessary for the metamorphosis, varied by country. (You'll learn specific details in the "Origins" section for each dragon referenced in this book.)

Gigantic snakes, in particular, came to represent the concept of dragons. Over time, these snakelike creatures developed into hybrid beasts in people's imagination, often combining various features of birds, fish, reptiles, and terrestrial animals.[4]

Dragons of this sort have fascinated—and terrified—mankind since at least 4000 B.C. A shell cylinder seal from this time period (3509 to 4000 B.C.) is the oldest known object to display an image of what is sometimes called a dragon.[5] This so-called dragon has two wings, a snake's forked tongue, a lion's head and forepaws, and an eagle's hind legs and feet; plus, scaly feathers cover its body.[6] The creature is pulling a four-wheeled chariot in which a god brandishes a whip, while a naked goddess holding thunderbolts stands between the dragon's wings. In front of them, a worshipper pours out libations to the deities.[7]

Early, monstrous images like this represent a destructive spirit whose purpose is to cause disorder or chaos. An interpretation of the seal says:

Cylinder Seal. Internet Archive Book Images / No restrictions.
From: Harper, Robert Francis. *Old Testament and Semitic Studies in Memory of William Rainey Harper.*
Chicago: University of Chicago Press, 1908, p. 362.

> The king is the personification of the sun, the monster or dragon the personification of the storm, the darkness and the abyss. The female figure is the personification of rain, the trident is a symbol for lightning, and the whole scene a representation of the conflict between the nature powers.[8]

Although this is the earliest image found to date of a "dragon," an even earlier record of one exists in Sumerian literature. These people inhabited the land between the Tigris and Euphrates rivers, extending from the Persian Gulf to Bagdad, from approximately 3500 to 2000 B.C. Their Babylonian conquerors used Sumerian stories and legends as a basis for their own mythology.

The prologue to the epic tale about Gilgamesh includes a fragment of their creation myth. In it, Kur carries off a goddess to the netherworld, which causes Enki, the god of wisdom, to set out to avenge her. The prologue is incomplete, so the outcome of the battle is unknown. In the tale, Kur is a monstrous creature, "conceived as a large serpent which lived in the bottom of the 'great below' where the latter came in contact with the primeval waters."[9] In one version of the tale, Kur's actions are described below:

> Against the standing place of the gods it has directed its terror,
> In the sitting place of the Anunnaki it has led forth fearfulness,
> Its dreadful fear it has hurled upon the land,
> The 'mountain,' its dreadful rays of fire it has directed against all the lands.[10]

The mention of "fire" most certainly fits the description of a dragon.

Over time, dragons progressed from these mixed-animal appearances and acquired human features. They either appeared as completely human or had human characteristics, while retaining their reptilian, avian, and animal aspects. Some were portrayed as being able to shape-shift into a different type of common animal (for example, a bear). Dragons could even transform into a natural phenomenon (lightning, clouds, whirlwind) or vegetation.[11]

One researcher describes the possible appearances of the Eastern European dragons as follows:

> To begin with the Snake. His outline, like that of the cloud with which he is so frequently associated, and which he is often supposed to typify, is seldom well-defined. Now in one form and now in another, he glides a shifting shape, of which it is difficult to obtain a satisfactory view. Sometimes he retains throughout the story an exclusively reptilian character; sometimes he is of a mixed nature, partly serpent and partly man. In one story we see him riding on horseback, with hawk on wrist (or raven on shoulder) and hound at heel; in another he figures as a composite being with a human body and a serpent's head; in a third he flies as a fiery snake into his mistress's bower, stamps with his foot on the ground, and becomes a youthful gallant. But in most cases he is a serpent which in outward appearance seems to differ from other ophidians only in being winged and polycephalous—the number of his heads generally varying from three to twelve.[12]

You, however, may be most familiar with the western concept of dragons—fire-breathing creatures with scales, wings, and four legs. Even in this respect, the species varies, including drakes (wingless, four legs), wyverns (winged, two legs), wyrms (legless and wingless), and more.

Early dragons, although scary in appearance, were not the dangerous creatures you may know them as today. Once, they were cosmic mediators, guaranteeing harmony in nature. Over time, during the medieval period especially, dragons were considered dangerous, evil creatures, villains that heroes sought to subdue.

As Christianity emerged, the dragons of Eastern Europe devolved from their role of mediators into the status of demons, transitioning from "the 'time of the dragon,' to the 'time of grace.' "[13] Even the space they occupied expressed this degradation. Once they flew high in the clouds, ever watchful, and lived on mountain peaks like the gods. But as they were vilified, they became "earth dwellers," who lived in forests or who descended into caves.[14]

The formerly benign beings became associated with Satan. Some people have speculated that the snake in the Garden of Eden was, in fact, a dragon. The story of a serpent, entwined in a tree, as an enemy to the world's creator, exists in many ancient cultures, and has "prevailed in the very infancy of the human race":[15] the common theme of good versus evil. This creature tempted humans to do things they should not do.

> It is not always the case that the serpent is in the tree, or that he talks to the woman, or appears as the tempter, yet many of the elements of the story as given in the scriptures are contained in these myths and traditions, and especially that one which represents an antagonism between a monster dragon who often assumes the form of a serpent, sometimes the form of a four-footed, winged creature and whose mission is to work evil. There is no tradition or myth that is more wide-spread than the one that embodies this belief.[16]

After the Fall, the tempter was cursed to crawl on his belly, and so he lost his legs and wings. Some people believe that the same thing could have happened to dinosaurs: perhaps they became "small crawling beings instead of grand, magnificent creatures," stripped "of their grand powers and reduced … to a shadow of their original selves."[17]

Tree of the Knowledge of Good and Evil with Snake and Apple.
Illustration by FoxysGraphic. Stock illustration via Depositphotos.

4

The Biblical creature, as well as dragons in fairy tales, was able to speak. Was this another ability that animals lost from ancient times, or is it merely a fabrication of the tales? It gives one pause for thought, as one blog commenter muses:

> I've also always been curious about the fact that Eve didn't seem surprised when the serpent/dragon spoke. While nothing in the Bible directly says it, I've wondered if some animals possessed the ability to speak, which they lost after the fall.[18]

Although the dragon has lost its original purpose, benevolent dragons still exist throughout Eastern Europe, ones whose purpose is to assist and protect mankind, in much the same way Oriental dragons do. You'll learn more about the good and bad types of dragons in the following chapters of this book.

Creation Myths

Creation myths are an important part of cultures. They're "an effort to explain the origin of the universe, the presence of the gods, and the existence of man."[19] Across the globe, gigantic snakes or dragons are common in these creation myths, in which "the aquatic chaos and the serpent were the primeval state of the universe."[20] One of the many early Slavic beliefs maintains that the world floats on a sea. In the story, Rod, the father of the gods, creates Mother-Earth, but she sinks beneath the water. (Note: This source is probably a reconstruction of Slavic mythology of unknown authenticity.)

> Rod then gave birth to Mother-Earth,
> And fell Earth into the dark abyss,
> Into the Ocean she disappeared.[21]

It takes a duck (born of the gray foam of the ocean) three tries to retrieve Mother-Earth, each attempt taking a year longer than the previous one. On her third attempt,

> Into the Ocean-sea She dove,
> And three years was gone in the abyss.
> As the time passed—ascended from the abyss.
> In Her beak a handful of Earth She brought.[22]

From that handful of dirt, Svarog, the Slavic god of fire, molds Mother-Earth.

> Svarog took the handful of Earth,
> Began to crush in His hands.
> "Warm it, Red Sun,
> Light it, Light Crescent,
>
> Help me, the strong winds!
> We will mold from this Raw Earth
> Mother-Earth, the nurturing Mother.
> Help us, Rod! Lada, help!"
>
> Svarog crushes Earth—Sun warms,
> Crescent lights, the winds blow.
> The winds blew Earth of the palms,
> And She fell into the blue sea.

She was warmed by Red Sun—
Raw Earth became covered by crust,
Light Crescent then cooled it.
Thus was Mother-Earth created by Svarog.[23]

Then Rod creates a gigantic serpent to encircle Mother-Earth and prevent her from crumbling under her own weight.

And so Earth would not again sink into the sea,
Rod gave birth and placed powerful Yusha under Her—
Serpent the marvelous, the strong many times over.
Heavy is His fate—He is to hold
Many thousands of years Mother-Earth.[24]

In a Romanian version of the creation myth, Fărtat, the creator, punishes the mischievous dragon for his many tricks, forcing the creature to coil around the world nine times to prevent floods.[25]

Cosmic Battle

Myths about the cosmos explain not only how nature and the world came into being, but also how universal order was disturbed and then maintained. As the Slavic creation story above continues, giant snakes do more than support the world, and not all these creatures are benevolent. Some are born of fire, or sparks from a god's hammer. These beasts bring chaos into the world.

Inflaming the great flame!
Crept up the Black Serpent to that stone
And struck the stone with a hammer.
Dispersed the black sparks

Across all of the under-Heavens domain—
And thus was born the dark power—
Fierce Serpents [Zmeys], multi-headed,
And all evil-spirits of Earth and water.[26]

Gods, and later heroes, fight the elements to bring balance to the world, while "destructive chaotic disorder"[27] tries to disrupt the harmony and return the world to a state of chaos.

This victory over the enemy is a way to restore the natural order of the annual cycle, indicated by space and time, which they measure by "the movement of the celestial lights (the Sun, the Moon, and some constellations)." As the end of the year approaches, they believe that space and time lose their order and the universe falls apart, and that an unknown threatening force desires "to take over the human world and hold it forever in its sinister power."[28]

In a classic battle of good versus evil, Order fights Chaos (the threatening force), which is described as a fire-breathing dragon.

In the clear field, wide space
Chest to chest the two powers clashed:
Bog Semargl with the Heavenly power

And the monstrous Serpent with the Dark power.
It was not a fiery whirlwind twirling upon Earth—
It was Semargl with the Heavenly power
Taking on the power of the monstrous Serpent!

Began Svarojich to burn the Dark power,
To trample-smash and spear stab the Serpents,
And their heads to throw far into the blue sea.
Scum and the undead the son of Svarog burned,

Spreading through fire in all directions.
As He rode up to the furious Serpent,
The Dark Serpent, multi-headed.
A Serpent with a thousand heads,

A Serpent with a thousand tails.
Svarojich with—a thousand eyes,
A thousand teeth—fiery.
Began here a thunderous battle,

Gathered the black clouds.
Fired-burned the Dark Serpent
Son of Svarog and Heavenly Rod.[29]

This cosmic battle happens at the winter solstice, when Time and Space have shrunk "like the yolk in the egg or the human embryo in the mother's womb." When Order defeats Chaos (or the Supreme God overcomes the Dragon), Time and Space are once again renewed and "rise like a freshly kneaded dough," thus re-creating the world.[30]

Slaying the dragon is not only symbolic of order being victorious over chaos, it's also a triumph of growth over stagnation, of rebirth overcoming death. This cyclical action ensures the fertility myth maintains its magical powers.[31]

From this regenerated world, flow three rivers of fertility: milk, honey, and wine. These correspond to the seasons of spring, summer, and autumn, as well as to the directions of the sun: east, south, and west. Missing are winter and north, indicating that this is when and where the battle occurs: the winter solstice, the transition from the old year to the new one.[32]

World Tree

Prevalent in many of these creation myths is a cosmic tree, or a World Tree, that grows out of the water and supports the land. It's known by various names: "tree of life, tree of knowledge, tree of the Garden of Eden, tree of the cross, Shaman's tree."[33] It's also been called "a golden fruit bearing tree," a "straight tree—tall and lean," and a tree whose branches are "pure silver, dotted with golden bees."[34]

Ancient civilizations considered nature sacred, and they deeply venerated the World Tree as a force of strength and protection. The three parts of the tree symbolize the nature of the universe. Branches represent the heavens where divine spirits reside. The trunk signifies Earth, which is the home of men and preternatural creatures like nymphs and fairies. And roots represent the underworld and the dead who dwell there. Like nature itself, all these creatures live in harmony with one another.[35]

Many illustrations display the serpent coiled at the tree's roots or along its trunk. However, in popular belief, it can also live in the tree's crown as a dragon—thus showing the creature's dichotomy of being both an evil viper and a benevolent guardian. Also inhabiting the branches are magical birds, such as the firebird (the messenger of divine will and the protector of the fruit of life, the magic apple), nightingale, falcon, and eagle (the symbol of light and heaven). Other birds found there include doves, swallows, roosters, and peacocks. Even bees make their home in the tree's branches.

The snake and the bird are the most widespread personifications of a human soul. This belief relates to the shaping of the idea about two worlds of death—one below the earth and another above the clouds. Therefore, the images of snake and bird merge to create the winged dragon.[36]

Over time, the benevolent dragon and the eagle have become interchangeable in folklore, thus associating the dragon with both heaven and earth as a cosmic mediator between the two. And so, from serpent to dragon, the creature becomes connected to all three parts of the universe: the roots and the dead, the trunk and the living, the branches and the divine beings.

- **The Dead**. The World Tree has been called the "Path to the Souls of the Ancestors,"[37] and it symbolizes "the transformation and transition between the worlds."[38] It's a place where the souls of the dead reside, and a place from which one can enter the realm of the ancestors, often called the "other world" or the "beyond." This is a place where not only the dead, but also mythical creatures, live. (You'll read more about the other world in the "Dragon Slayers" chapter.)
- **The Living**. The World Tree has a place in the daily lives of people. It underlines "the inseparable connection between the cosmic balance, life—fertility—marriage—death."[39] Many life-cycle rituals involve trees—especially fruit-bearing trees, symbolic of this World Tree.
- **The Divine**. Among the Slavs, the World Tree is often oak and sacred to the god Perun, wielder of thunder (who in later beliefs becomes St. Iliya or Elijah, who fights against destructive dragons). In folklore, the tree may also be a cypress or sycamore.

  In particular, a *budnik* (a special log burned at Christmas to celebrate the rebirth of the *Mlada Boga* or Young God, when the days begin to be longer after the winter solstice)[40] acts as "a mediator between the heavenly and earthly life." People perform rituals "to magically strengthen the vitality of the World Tree, during the transitional time between the old and the new year, and to further reinforce the equilibrium and order in the universe."[41]

Elemental Connections

In folklore, the dragon's or serpent's role is dualistic. It can destroy or restore balance. Rural people, who survive or perish depending on the success or failure of their crops, believe that dragons and other creatures cause droughts, floods, hailstorms, and more disasters. While you may think dragons are connected only with the element of fire, they actually have an association with all the elements: water, air, earth, and fire.

WATER. The dragon's connection to water is thought to be one of its earliest associations, long before fire became its signature element in many cultures. Within various Eastern European creation lore, the creature preserves world order by maintaining the "balance of water."[42] Every day, it drinks the water surrounding the land, preventing the liquid from spilling over the edge.[43]

Among the Bulgarians, the transformation of the water dragon in folklore begins with it being the master or *stopan* (guardian, owner) of a spring or other water body. It progresses to a *lamia*, a creature that stops water from flowing or produces floods until people sacrifice to her, thus connecting her to water both on land and below it. From there, the dragon becomes a *hala*, controlling water in the air and bringing

World Tree.
Illustration by Dmitrij Rybin. Stock illustration via Depositphotos.

torrential rain and hail.[44] In addition, the *zmey*, a benevolent dragon, also has control over the moisture in clouds. He houses the rain in his mountainous cave, releasing it when crops need water, and restraining it to prevent floods and rotting grain. Among other Eastern European nations, similar creatures with different names perform these same functions.

AIR. Air goes hand-in-hand with water. Hala, for example, is personified as a whirlwind that brings dark clouds that produce devastating rain. In addition, dragons are creatures that can fly, become invisible, and control the movement of the clouds.

EARTH. Snakes are "the earth's brat" according to Herodotus,[45] and they live underground. Since dragons often are thought to originate from snakes, as a result, they, too, have an association with the earth. Dragons reside within caves, which are called the womb of the land, connecting them to the "other world," the land of the ancestors and rebirth. This earthly connection is associated with a "spiritual awakening,"[46] making the snake and dragon both symbols of "empowerment and enlightenment."[47]

In addition, the earth is where minerals are located. Stories often represent dragons as keepers of underground wealth and hoarders of treasures.

FIRE. Besides breathing fire, the dragon has a connection with the sun. Some folk tales explain how the serpent-dragon takes upon itself the duty of maintaining the balance of heat and light from the sun. One day when the sun was thirsty, it bent down toward the seas to take a drink. At this time, the sun had two eyes. The serpent-dragon—fearing the land would get too much light and be scorched by the nearness of the sun's light and heat—sucked out one of the sun's eyes.[48]

In fairy tales, however, the dragon isn't at odds with the sun, but may be perceived as being the personification of the sun itself, which is thought of as a living being. Both "emit light, blaze like fire, shine like gold."[49]

Not least of all is the connection of the dragon's fire with damnation. With the advent of Christianity, a fire-breathing dragon in art appears with its gaping maw poised at the mouth of Hell.

Fact or Fiction?

Belief in dragons was common among the various Indo-European peoples. Creatures like the Bulgarian *zmey* continued to exist among those living in the Balkan area up until the beginning of the twentieth century, and even now places such as Pirin retain their stories (see more in the "Zmey" chapter), while other dragons like the *lamia* remain alive only in folklore.[50]

Some villagers joke that dragons stopped appearing because for a long time their communities lacked girls—either beautiful or ugly.[51] Legends maintain that the creatures disappeared with the invention of firearms, since dragons, as well as other evil beings, fear iron.

But were dragons real in the past? Or did they live only in the hearts and minds of the storyteller? In a folklore study conducted during 1900 – 1901, the author says:

> It is extremely difficult—much more so than folklorists sometimes imagine—in investigating the folklore of a country to fix with absolute certainty where real superstition ends and pure mythology begins. The peasant story-teller, though conscious of the fact that he is narrating a myth, is all the time more than half inclined to believe that the world which he describes is not an improbable world, that in the mysterious "times of old all things were possible."[52]

Perhaps the heading of this section should be "Between Faith and Avowed Fiction" as the above author maintains that "these monsters may be said to dwell in the debatable borderland between the[se] two worlds," that is, they live in a realm that lies between faith and fiction.[53] One peasant's response about the existence of these creatures follows:

> "Why," he exclaimed in accents of triumph, "I myself remember seeing, as a child, monstrous horned snakes swarming on yonder plain (πέρα 'ς τον κάμπο). Where are they now? There also used to be lions and bears; but they have disappeared before modern guns. The same thing must surely have happened to the Lamias and the Drakoi."[54]

Other people, even today, share this sentiment. On Internet forums, you can find comments about the one-time existence of dragons, such as the one below:

> I think dragons and dinosaurs are one and the same. Did legend make them larger than life? or did the curse steal their grandness and seal their doom? I believe we may one day know the truth of it, but for now I'm content with my imaginings. I suspect man and the great reptiles coexisted at one time and they are etched in our histories, but now believed to be made-up creatures of fairy-tale.[55]

Dragon King

In 2004, three paleontologists made a discovery in South Dakota that brought the connection of dragons and dinosaurs closer to reality. Or did they? The bones they found resembled what we today think of as a Chinese or Medieval European dragon, having a flat, spiked head and a long muzzle. They named the dragon *Dracorex Hogwartsia*, Dragon King of Hogwarts. You've got it. It's named after the *Harry Potter* books.

But controversy exists whether this is a new species or not. Some professionals say it's not new; it's merely a juvenile of the dinosaur genus, Pachycephalosaurus.

> What this means is that, as Pachycephalosaurus juveniles grew, their head ornamentation became more and more elaborate, so adults looked very different from teenagers (and teenagers looked very different from hatchlings). What it also means, sadly, is that there may be no such dinosaur as *Dracorex hogwartsia*![56]

Such a shame. It likely won't deter those who believe it's a dragon, or prevent them from hoping someone finds more substantial "proof" of the existence of dragons in the future.

Dragon Relics

Many stories, especially those pertaining to dragon slayers, have "material culture connected with the dragon which confirms the validity of the story, such as the weapon of its celebrated slayer, representations of dragons on tombs or heraldic emblems, the transformation of its body into striking topographic elements or sometimes surviving anatomical elements."[57]

Let's take a closer look at the final item: anatomical elements. Physical "evidence" of dragons—or what people once thought was a dragon—remains in existence: a dragon skull in Karlštejn Castle in Prague, bones discovered in a dragon's cave in Kraków, and an entire stuffed "dragon" hanging from the ceiling in the Old Town Hall in Brno, in the Czech Republic. Today, we recognize the dragon skull and stuffed dragon as crocodiles, while the bones likely come from a mammoth, wooly rhino, and whale.

Some of the so-called dragons mentioned in tales may have been exotic creatures brought from foreign countries. The Church was known to store away treasures and artifacts they considered valuable, including exotic animals. These types of relics, they said, "provided a reminder of the physical presence of the infernal, but also proof that the devil could be overcome."[58]

Dragon People

Talk about the existence of dragons, however, stretches beyond Church treasures or speculation from people who have never studied folklore or ancient cultures. Pianist, academic, economist, and writer Valentin Stamov has a different take on the "dragons of lore." He says they were actually generations of ordinary people who lived deep within caves for 500 to 700 years after a cataclysmic event that happened in the Strandzha mountains thousands of years ago.[59] It was a time when "nature rebelled against humans."[60] A small group of people survived underground where hot and cold springs, rivers, and waterfalls abounded. Their bodies changed due to living underground: their bones became flexible and durable like plastic. They used artificial wings to fly from rock to rock, and they took to the water like amphibians. When they eventually exited their subterranean world, the sunlight made their skin crack and flake like snakes.[61]

And how does Stamov know this, you may wonder. Because, he says, he is a direct descendent of these people. His great-grandfather was one of these "dragons," although their existence has been "exaggerated by fantasy." His father told him detailed stories about their ancestors, and when his life was ending, he vowed to Valentin that everything he had said was true, not his invention, and had been passed from father to son for generations.[62]

Stamov is not the only person who suggests dragons may be real.

> As for believers in the existence of dragon people, the main question is whether this belief is related to a long time ago or is it alive today? And what nourishes or suppresses it?
>
> Here's an honest response recorded in 1997 by an 87-year-old woman in connection with a zmey research in the region of Yugovo village: "There are such stories, but who remembers them, who remembers them?" (Malchev, 2008). Who actually remembers them—the peasant living in isolation from contemporary culture; the uneducated but imaginative person, or the person who, by an unknowable coincidence, has seen, encountered, and communicated with a creature for which he uses the name zmey.[63]

Among some Serbians, it's also theorized that dragons were the "sons of God" the Bible mentions, the ones who mated with the daughters of men.

> Foremost among them was a dragon master who possessed a body that was half dragon and half man. This dragon hero became the Serpent on the Tree of the Serbian Garden of Eden and taught nascent humans many of the mundane and sacred sciences. The other ancient Sons of God that accompanied him were dragons who arrived either within starships from Sirius and other stars, or as flaming balls of fire. They mated with the local women and then built both a pyramid inside of the sacred mountain of Rtanj, as well as a large artificial lake in the shape of a pentagram connected by a network of tunnels to the surface. Those dragons that fell to Earth as balls of fire (the "Fallen Angels"?) are said to have possessed the ability to shape-shift into human males and to then co-habitate with the local women. Their legend was written in some ancient Serbian texts that carbon dating has proven to be 7000 years ago, including The Book of Enoch II.[64]

You'll learn more about how folklore portrays other dragon people in the "Zmey" chapter.

Made by Dragons

Dolmens, chambers formed by large stone blocks, are located throughout Europe in mountainous regions, where sheer cliffs hide a cave. Some of these structures date back 7,000 years, while most are thought to be from the early Neolithic age (around 4000–3000 BC). In folk belief, they're called dragon houses and are said to be proof dragons existed, although archaeologists say they are likely to have been burial chambers.

Other dragon tales explain how geographical sites came into being: rivers, lakes, mountains, and more. Springs at the bottom of a cave or a rock are often described to be tears of a kidnapped girl. The story below relates how one hot spring gained its name.

Many, many years ago, an old zmey ruled the forests between Struma and Mesta [*rivers in Southwest Bulgaria*]. He had two sons, and they were zmeys, which he sent here and there for work.

"And what was the work of the zmeys, Grandpa Marin?" the curious asks.

"Their job," he explains, "was to arrange the clouds, to spread rain, hail, thunder, and lightning."

Once the smaller zmey was flying over the village of Mosomishte. It was Easter, so all the people were at the horo, and among them was the priest's daughter, the beautiful maiden Toplitsa. The zmey saw her from the clouds, liked her, and then came down and grabbed her from the horo before anyone knew what was happening. The poor father asked

Dolmens in Gelendzhik on Markhotsky Ridge.
Photo by Sanexiz. Stock image via Depositphotos.

13

and searched everywhere, but didn't find any trace of her. A long time passed and her parents stopped thinking about her.

One summer day, the priest climbed St. George's Rock to gather wood for fire. It felt like something was pulling him higher and higher, until suddenly he saw his daughter, all in golden clothes and adorned with coins. They hugged each other in tears and the girl said that the young zmey had grabbed her, but his father got angry and drove them away from Alibotush mountain, where his palace was. Now the two lived on St. George's Rock. The zmey's bride was afraid that her husband would meet the uninvited guest, so she quickly sent her father away, but she wanted to give him a farewell gift. She filled up a sack of coins, but since she had already learned some zmey magic, she made the gold light as a feather so that it would not weigh on her father on the way.

She told him to open it when he got home. They said goodbye and Grandpa Priest left with the sack on his shoulder, but something kept irritating him to see what was inside. In the end he couldn't stand it. He opened it and what did he see? The sack was full of onion peels! He got angry, poured out the peels, then took the sack and went home without wood. He decided to shake the sack one more time and what did he see? One coin was stuck inside.

The priest told everything to his wife and she scolded him and ordered him to go back immediately and to bring the onion peels, which were enchanted coins. The priest hurried, climbed back, but it was too late. Right in place of the peels, a large river of hot water gushed out and dragged everything down. When the priest shook the sack, his daughter saw him from the rock and got very scared that the zmey would see and get angry. She began to pray to God for help, and he heard her prayers and made the hot water gush out and take away the onion peels. Since then, they named the river Toplitsa after the priest's daughter.

According to the legend, its warm water gradually cools and when it becomes really cold, the river will dry up.[65]

A few other common places with dragon symbolism follow.

- **Great Stones of Khlyabovo Ridge**. A long time ago in Khlyabovo, Bulgaria, a dragon protected the villagers. In return, the people provided him with animals from their flocks. Some men soon rebelled, saying they would no longer feed the dragon. And so, the dragon abducted and ate villagers to compensate for his abandoned tribute. One boy, Katos, fought with the dragon all day, finally wounding him. When the dragon fell from the sky, he petrified and formed huge stones. Even today, local people say they see flames, the fire of the dragon, coming out of the rocks.[66]
- **Serpent's Wall** or **Dragon's Rampart**. According to folklore, long, tall embankments in parts of Ukraine came into being when a hero tricked a dragon into dividing the land between them. The hero harnessed a plow to the dragon, and the dragon pulled and pulled, mile after mile, deeper and deeper, creating ever-growing embankments. The hero didn't cease urging the dragon onward until the creature died of exhaustion.[67] A more historical purpose of the embankments was as a defense mechanism against invaders, with the dragons being symbolic of foreigners.
- **Balaur Hill**. This hill, named after a Romanian dragon, arose when a gigantic *balaur* fell from the sky and died. A single rib measured twenty-two inches (fifty-six centimeters) in width. His body slowly rotted over a long period of time, forming a great mound.[68]
- **Margarets Hill** and **Latin Well**. A Bulgarian story relates how a Latin man and his daughter Margarita cultivated a vineyard on a hill, which was near a well that dragons and fairies came out of. Near the well, the father built a cellar to store his wine. A young man courted Margarita in the

vineyard, but one day a whirlwind arose and a black cloud covered the hill. The young man, who was a *zmey*, embraced her and flew into the cloud and headed toward the well. As the cloud descended, lightning crackled, and the two young people sank into the well, never to be seen again. The hill and well were named after the girl and her father. Even today, people will tell you, if you part the bushes and grass on the hill, you can see the ruins of the basement by the well. At night, no one goes near, because it's still a *zmey*'s haunt.[69]

Perhaps these examples don't "prove" the existence of dragons, but in the hearts and minds of the people, they did exist at one time.

Smok (Смок)

Why are you so pale, as if a smok has chased you?

Smok (singular); **Smotzi** (plural)

Name variations: tsmok, cmok, zmek, zmok

In its most common usage, Smok is a name for a snake. Some of these creatures, as discussed in the first book in this series about household spirits, are the embodiment of ancestral guardian spirits. They reside in the home, protecting it and the residents. But Smok also refers to a larger version of the snake, one that has become known as a dragon.

Origins

Dragons were once ordinary snakes that grew to an enormous size over time. Since dragons and serpents have "an identical mythological significance,"[70] snakelike dragons, such as Smok, were considered ancestors, or the personification of the soul, in the same way the smaller household variety were.

> The dragon's formation from animals speaks about his totem-related origin. In the Slavic mythology, forests were imagined to be the dwelling places of ancestors, and also as places where dragons live, so this can be seen as a proof that the dragon is a mythical ancestor of the Slavs.[71]

Appearance

Smok most frequently appears as a huge snake. Occasionally, he has wings and limbs, while most times, he remains serpentine.

Getting to Know Smok

The dragon variation of Smok, unlike the household protector, is anything but benevolent and protective. His name invokes fear. One of the most famous of these dragons comes from Poland: Smok Wawelski.

Smok Wawelski

Smok Wawelski, also known as the Wawel Dragon of Kraków or the Dragon of Wawel Hill, lived deep within a cave, coming out weekly or daily to devour cattle. In some stories, he had a preference for eating young girls once a month. If villagers didn't provide the offering, the dragon would attack and consume numerous people instead. The oldest-known version of the story dates back to the thirteenth century. In it, King Krakus sends his sons Lech and Krakus to defeat the dragon.

In an alternate version from the sixteenth century, the king's daughter, Wanda, was the only maiden left, all the others having already been devoured by Smok Wawelski. As was the custom in these types of stories, the king offered his daughter's hand in marriage to anyone who could kill the beast. All failed until a cobbler named Skuba Dratewka came forward. He stuffed sulfur into a lamb's carcass and placed it outside the dragon's lair. When the dragon came for his meal, he devoured the lamb, but he soon had a terrible thirst. He rushed to the river to gulp down water. No matter how much he drank, he couldn't quench

Etymology

Smok comes from an Indo-European word for "swallow" (All About Dragons, "Zmej").

his thirst. On top of that, the dragon's stomach ached and grumbled. Soon, Smok Wawelski swelled and exploded. The humble cobbler then claimed Wanda as his bride. And, in fairy-tale fashion, they lived happily ever after.

The story has similarities to an Apocrypha chapter in Daniel.

> 1 And king Astyages was gathered to his fathers, and Cyrus of Persia received his kingdom.
> 2 And Daniel conversed with the king, and was honoured above all his friends.
> …
> 23 And in that same place there was a great dragon, which they of Babylon worshipped.
> 24 And the king said unto Daniel, Wilt thou also say that this is of brass? lo, he liveth, he eateth and drinketh; thou canst not say that he is no living god: therefore worship him.
> 25 Then said Daniel unto the king, I will worship the Lord my God: for he is the living God.
> 26 But give me leave, O king, and I shall slay this dragon without sword or staff. The king said, I give thee leave.
> 27 Then Daniel took pitch, and fat, and hair, and did seethe them together, and made lumps thereof: this he put in the dragon's mouth, and so the dragon burst in sunder: and Daniel said, Lo, these are the gods ye worship.[72]

Vlechugo, the Reptile

In certain parts of Bulgaria, another snake creature goes by the name of "reptile" (влечуго, *vlechugo*). People likely call it by a generic name, rather than its true name, due to taboos many cultures have against speaking an evil being's actual name. Vocalizing such a creature's name was a way to summon it, and people preferred to keep these creatures at a distance.

The *vlechugo* is overly large and extremely strong. One account from a resident of a village says:

> This animal is a reptile…uh…It looks like it is not a poisonous snake. It is like the so-called smok. And the smok is…I've seen a black smok, but…not such a big reptile. It is huge and with great strength, muscular strength.[73]

Another villager says the creature has wings and can fly from one tree to another. Not only does it have wings, but it also has "a thorn" on the tip of its tail that it uses to strike people.

People believe the reptile lives in "the boundary between the world of humans and the world of demons."[74] They encounter it in all the places demonic creatures congregate: abandoned wells, cemeteries, bridges, water sources, and more. But unlike most demons, the creature attacks humans only when people invade its territory. An older, folkloric belief is that the creature represents "the struggles of the human community with evil spirits."[75] While a more modern interpretation is that the creature attacks as an instinctive reaction to protect its young.

However, the reptile never appears when more than one person is around. It hides if it hears people talking. If you do come across one, don't attract its attention, or it may mark you as a target. When the

Smok Wawelski.
Illustration by Sebastian Münster, 1544. Public domain via Wikimedia Commons.

reptile does attack, it behaves much like a snake hunting rodents: "It wraps itself around them, tightens the muscles of its body, and tries to suffocate them. In one case, it uses the 'thorn' on its tail to hit its opponent and weaken him, causing him additional pain."[76]

Villagers also say, "He doesn't bite. He doesn't poison. But he catches you… He knows how to catch you—where your weakest part is. And he tightens and tightens, be it an animal, be it a man, he tightens until you stop breathing. Such kind of an animal it is."[77]

It's so frightful an experience that villagers have a saying about anyone who is trembling with fear: "Why are you so pale, as if a smok has chased you?"[78]

If the reptile does attack, you may have to kill it in order to survive. But, beware, your survival will be short-lived. It may happen that, without showing any symptoms of illness, you'll die forty days later. Or you may die from an accident; one man suffered fatal injuries when he fell off a wall onto upright wooden posts—again, forty days after he killed such a creature.[79] Villagers consider both circumstances "retribution" for killing the creature: "[t]he reptile is the bearer of the folkloric belief in retribution as a sentence for a life taken."[80]

Buried Treasure

A less-threatening Smok may only protect treasure, instead of harming people. He is said to be the hoard's "jealous guardian," and any human who can outwit him has to be "wily and daring."[81] Among the Albanians, you have the best chance of accomplishing this on a Sunday evening. The guardian snake, who's said to have wings and a human face, is less vigilant at this time, and you'll be able to trick him out of his treasure as you can see in the story that follows.[82]

> A story is told of a shepherd who, when pasturing his sheep in Dibra, saw one day a snake curled up asleep on a great heap of gold. In order to induce him to leave it, the shepherd fetched a pail of milk, which he placed near the snake, and then retired to a little distance to watch his movements. As he had calculated, the snake gorged himself with the milk, and then returned to sleep on the gold heap. But the quantity of milk he had drunk made him thirsty and uneasy, and he wriggled and wriggled and could not rest. Finally he went off to get some water, and, the spring being at some distance, before he returned the shepherd had removed the whole of the treasure to a place of safety. What the snake did when he came back and found his property gone, the story omits to mention.[83]

If you're fortunate, instead of stumbling across the gold hoard, you may discover its location through a dream. If you have the same revelation three nights in a row, grab your shovel and hurry to that spot. You're certain to find the treasure. However, be warned that if you disclose to anyone what you've learned, the gold will turn into charcoal and you're doomed to die.[84]

Among the Russians and other nationalities, dragons "deputize" the common household guardian snake (called the *zmiya-stopan* or master snake) to keep a watch on his treasure, ensuring no one finds or steals it.[85]

You'll discover other interesting facts about dragon treasure in the Balaur chapter.

How to Appease

Since the evil version of Smok has a never-ending hunger, the way to appease him and keep him from eating *you* is to offer him your cattle or sheep. You're certain to end up in poverty, though, if you continue this for any length of time. It's better to find a way to get rid of the beast, so you can live in prosperity and without fear.

To appease the benevolent type of Smok, give him milk. He enjoys it the same as the smaller, household variety does.

How to Defeat

Defeating Smok depends on which variety you encounter. You don't really want to harm the "reptile" type, for fear of karmic payback; if you hurt one, that injury will come back to you in the end. Avoidance works best for this type of snake. It shouldn't be too difficult to accomplish, since the snake generally remains in its own habitat.

For a treasure-hoarding snake, trickery is a good method to defeat it. Again, you don't have to physically harm one; it's easy enough to lure him away by giving him milk to drink. Note: milk works on folkloric snakes, but it's not a staple of any of the creatures you'll find slithering around your yard. Of course, if you do happen to find one that's coiled on top of a pile of gold, who knows if it'll be tempted to drink the pan of milk you've left out for it.

"What about the evil, fire-breathing Smok?" you ask. Unlike other dragons you'll read about in this book, he doesn't normally fall victim to heroes who battle him. The dragon's fire has roasted many a brave knight. It's best to reserve your gallantry for saving damsels locked away in a castle, and use your wits, rather than your strength, to defeat this evil beast.

To succeed, you'll have to use another method: trickery works well here to defeat the gluttonous dragon, although milk won't entice him. This time, your intent *is* to kill the dragon, thereby ending his reign of terror. Getting him to eat an animal, such as a dead calf or lamb, in order to make him explode, has been proven effective. It's not the animal itself that kills the dragon, as you've learned; it's what you stuff inside that'll do the job. Sulfur or lime is a good option. Along with them, you can include kindling, wax, pitch, and tar to make sure a huge fire burns inside the beast. The dragon will get stomach cramps and become extremely thirsty. The water he drinks will activate the sulfur, and *boom*, the dragon will explode.

SCI-FI DRAGON

The story of Smok Wawelski takes on new meaning in a short sci-fi film called "Smok," which is set in modern-day Kraków. The traditional dragon is replaced by a creepy, military-looking thug named Adolf Kamchatkov, who flies a gigantic spacecraft. Instead of consuming livestock and people, he kidnaps beautiful women (Kępa). An unlikely hero comes along when the "dragon" steals a young man's crush. It's not sulfur that the soon-to-be hero has in mind to defeat the monster.

You can watch the film here: https://www.youtube.com/watch?v=1J_Y12RqeLM (English subtitles) (Allegro).

Dragon "Smok" Spacecraft.
Illustration by Dmitry Yakhovsky. © Bendideia Publishing.

Smok Tale

Smok Wawelski

Deep in thought, King Krak sat on the throne in his Wawel castle. A profound sadness tugged at his heart. As soon as he'd managed to save his country from the German onslaught, a new disaster struck him. Now, a terrible monster settled in the depths of the mountain and spread havoc throughout the area. The creature sat all day, hidden in his inaccessible cave, among many caverns. At night, he went out hunting and kidnapped not only cattle, but also people, especially young maidens.

Subjects approached King Krak desperately, begging him for help. They surrounded the castle with a packed crowd and shouted, "Have mercy, King. Save us! Almost everything we own has been carried away by the cursed dragon. Soon, not a single head of cattle will remain in the entire area. All our children will be kidnapped next."

"He's kidnapped my daughter, Zazule, already," said a voice.

"And my only son!" "... and from me, my father!" "... my wife! brother!" ... More people shouted out their complaints, and King Krak's heart bled when he heard them.

Despairingly, he tugged at his gray beard, thinking about how to save himself from fighting the creature. He announced massive rewards to any brave soul who would kill the ferocious beast, but no one responded.

Meanwhile, complaints became more frequent, more terrible.

And, finally, Krak summoned both his sons and said to them, "My children ... you know well how terrible this disaster afflicts our homeland. Nobody has come forward to save our people and fight the ferocious beast. I'm too old to fight him, and I can't think of another way. So you must seek advice and save our country from total destruction. Whichever of you defeats the dragon will be declared my successor, and after my death you will be the ruler of the entire country."

The sons heard their father's words about the dragon, and they promised to destroy the creature.

On the second day, as soon as dawn began to blush, Krak's elder son went to a fairy, who lived in nearby Dąbrowa.

"What do you request of me, Prince Bright?" the fairy asked when he stepped into her cabin.

"Show me how to destroy a dragon, and I'll give you as much gold as you like."

"Okay, kind prince," she replied. "I'll try. Maybe I'll find the way."

She started a fire in the center of the room and sprinkled various herbs on it, which produced a thick smoke.

After a moment, she began to speak, as if in a trance: "Take a large sheep skin, stuff it with sulfur and tar, and throw it to the dragon. When he eats it, it'll turn into fire as it digests and will burst his insides. But you won't get the prize ... I see blood on you ... blood ... a lot of blood ..."

The smoke cleared, and the fairy fainted. When she returned to consciousness, she said to the prince, "You have heard what to do, sir. Go and perform the task you've been told."

The prince returned to the castle and began to act immediately. He stuffed the lamb's skin with an abundance of sulfur and tar, poured fat on it, and set it down at dusk at the entrance to the cave.

The dragon climbed out of the cavern in the evening, caught the smell of mutton, and, rushing at it, greedily devoured the feast. Soon the sulfur burned his guts, so he crawled into the river and gulped water greedily. He drank and drank. The heat in his insides burned more and more, until finally a fire broke out, and the dragon fell dead.

The older prince stared at the creature until the dragon lay dead. He ran out of hiding, cut off the monster's head with his sword and, getting onto his horse, hurried to the castle to present the prize to his father so he would get the promised award.

The young prince had followed him. When the dragon lay dead, envy squeezed the boy's heart. When his older brother, delighted with his victory, passed near him, the younger boy hurled a javelin at his brother. The weapon whistled and pierced the one who had won the prize.

The older brother fell off his horse and died.

The younger boy threw himself at his victim's corpse, ripped away his prey, the dragon's head, jumped on his horse, and rushed to the castle.

King Krak awaited news of the outcome of the fight with trepidation in his heart. When the young king-to-be arrived at the gates, he set his horse loose. He hurried into his father's chamber and laid the captured dragon head at the king's feet.

Joy flashed in the old man's eyes, but some unknown fear gripped his heart. "Where is your older brother?" he asked.

The prince appeared confused for a moment, but soon he regained his cold blood and said, "He fell in battle with the dragon."

"The greater your glory is that seeing the death of your older brother, you did not hesitate to put your life to certain death in the fight against the dragon. You are worthy to be my successor and rule the entire land."

The king proclaimed his second son his successor, but soon sadness and sorrow for his older son overtook him so much that the king died.

The younger son sat on the throne that belonged to his murdered brother and enjoyed its power. His crime eventually came to light, and the elders of the nation assembled and condemned him to perpetual exile. They appointed the sister of both princes, young princess Wandę, to the throne.[86]

Zmey (Змей)

It's as if dragons love her. She hides, withers, loses weight, and fades.

> **Name variations**
> *Bulgaria*: zmey, zmei (plural, zmeĭove – змейове)
> *Russia*: zmey, zmei (змей) (plural, zmei – зме́и)
> *Bosnia*: zmaj (plural, zmajevi)
> *Croatia*: zmȁj (plural, zmȁjevi)
> *Macedonia*: zmej (змеj) (plural, zmejovi – змеjови)
> *Poland*: zmiy, żmij (plural, żmije)
> *Serbia*: zmaj (змаj) (plural, zmajevi – змȁjеви)
> *Slovenia*: zmaj, zmáj, zmȁj (plural, zmáji, zmáji)
> *Ukraine*: zmiy (змій) (plural, zmiyi – змії)
>
> **Related names**: Smok, Pozoj (archaic name used in Slovenia)
>
> **Female**: Zmeitsa or Zmeitza (Bulgarian), Zmeya (Russian)
>
> **Slang**: Zmey and Zmaj are words used for kites that children fly.
> The Milky Way is called Zmej in Ukraine.

Belief in the dragon Zmey was, and perhaps still is, the most widespread across Eastern Europe. In most countries, he's a generic being, one of many of his kind. In Russia, although he bears the same name and has similar traits, he is his own unique personality. He may be Zmey Gorynych, whom legendary dragon-slayer Dobrynya Nikitich battles, or he may be Tugarin Zmeyevich, whom another hero, Alyosha Popovich, slays.

Zmey / Zmaj (or whatever name people call this dragon) has many roles: Lover. Fighter. Protector. Destroyer. Man. Beast. Element.

This dualistic nature is common among creatures that inhabit Eastern Europe. The southern Zmey is mostly benevolent, protecting humans from different, dangerous dragons. In other areas, he's more aggressive, requiring people to perform rituals to drive him away. One thing each has in common, though, is his love for a human bride.

Origins

In the Slavic creation myth you read earlier, you learned that Zmeĭove came into being from sparks that flew off a stone when a god struck it with a hammer. In folklore, however, this dragon species originated from a variety of creatures: snake, fish, bird, or mammal, with the snake being the most common. The transformation depended on the age of the snake and how long it had been isolated from the human world.

- After forty years of not being seen, a grass snake (*smok*) or a carp grows wings and legs and becomes a Bulgarian Zmey. As a person in a remote village today has said: "The big old *smok* didn't die; he became a *zmey*. If he is not seen by a human, he can become a *zmey*. It looks like a huge *smok* with wings."[87]

Etymology

The dragon's name is related to the word *zmiya* for "snake," but it's also used to indicate dragons when referenced in folklore (MacDermott, 65). Additionally, it has a connection to *zemylja* (*zemya*) meaning "earth." This word, in turn, derives its origins from the Indo-European *ǵhdem-* and makes its way to the Proto-Slavic root *zbm-* (Kerewsky-Halpern, 321-322, footnote 14).

- Any *smok* lifted by a whirlwind becomes a Zmey.[88]
- In Ukraine, it takes seven years for the transformation from a snake into a dragon, and another seven years passes before the creature develops wings and two heads.[89]
- A Polish snake must avoid seeing humans or hearing their voices for seven years before it can turn into a dragon—one with seven heads.[90]
- A snake takes longer to develop into a dragon in Belarus—one hundred years.[91]
- In Slovenia, be careful not to cut an Aescupian snake in half. If the front half slithers away into a hole, it'll become a dragon. Even if uncut, it may still grow into a dragon during dry years if no one catches it.[92]
- If it's been a rainy year, you may discover a new dragon streaking across the sky. It develops from an uncaught carp. Fishermen along the Danube have sworn in the past that they've witnessed a carp that's grown wings jumping out of the water; it transforms into a dragon, throwing carp-shaped scales around itself.[93]
- A carp sprouts wings and turns into a dragon if it lives one hundred years without a human seeing it.[94]
- A dragon can come from a hen's egg, if the fowl hides it, then hatches it.[95]
- Among the Slovenes, a dragon can also develop from a ram.[96]

The transformation from snake to dragon appears in both oral accounts and folk tales. The following is an excerpt from one story.

> Suddenly the earth trembled, the sky thundered, and with a great hissing whistling sound a monster dragon flew out of the cavern. It was the old king serpent whose seven years were up and who was now become a flying dragon. From his huge mouth he breathed out fire and smoke. With his long tail he swished right and left among the forest trees and these snapped and broke like little twigs.[97]

Creature transformation isn't the only way a dragon comes into existence, however. The following identify other means for dragons to be created.

- **Second-generation dragons**. Dragons born from Zmey and a woman are more human than creature. In some cultures, these children are always born at night after a twelve-month pregnancy.[98] No specifics have been given about how long the female Zmeitsa carries her infant, but it's likely just as long. If a female dragon does give birth, though, her infant is more dragon than human. You'll learn more about these dragon children later in this chapter.

26

Zmey.
Illustration by Dmitry Yakhovsky. © Bendideia Publishing.

- **Meteor shower**. Many centuries ago, a meteor shower once rained over the Balkans, so the stories go. Dragons fell from inside it, landing in water, on mountains, and within trees. The water-dwelling ones had the appearance of male mermaids: big, round eyes, wide noses, canine teeth. The ones who landed in old forest trees and in the mountains resembled winged serpents.[99]
- **Magic and herbs**. Using magic and herbs can turn a person into a dragon.[100] In one story, a royal son who was enchanted was said to be a boy by day and Zmey by night.[101]
- **Good mother**. A dragon can even be born from a good person, without dragon parentage. If the child develops in the mother's womb for fifteen to twenty months, she'll give birth to a Zmey.[102]

The origin of the female dragon (Zmeitsa) dates back to ancient times. She is often thought of as the creature that coiled around the base of the World Tree.[103] Other folklorists say this was the dragon known as Lamia.[104] The dragon bears different additional names depending on its nationality. The Zmeitsa may even be the snake that wound itself around Mother Earth in creation stories and obtained knowledge from her.[105]

One particular huge snake named Kenhrines has an association with the Thracian Great Mother Goddess. Kenhrines carries with her the concept that, like all snakes, she "originated from the land in which she lives": that is, she comes from the earth itself or the underworld.[106]

Appearance

Some stories describe Zmey the way you likely picture a dragon: a large, winged reptile with four sharp-clawed legs. He may have horns, too, if he originated from a ram. His wings may be leathery and batlike, or they may resemble a bird's wings with feathers. Zmey may have a single head or multiple ones, most often three, although various stories describe him as having seven, nine, or twelve, each of them breathing fire. Some creatures even gain one head a year, as they transform from snake to dragon, ending up with one hundred.

Besides the typical dragon form, Zmey may appear in a variety of shapes: animal, human, and natural phenomenon, among the most common. He can also shape-shift into different types of vegetation and inanimate objects.

Animal Appearance

Since Zmey often originates from various creatures, you'd expect his features to resemble them: part human, reptile, fish, bird, and mammal. Some of the monstrous descriptions people have reported seeing include:

- "[A] scaly snake, with arms, wings, a fish's tail and a human face."[107]
- "With wings, a serpent's head, as it flies, sparks are formed from it."[108]
- "[A] long, thick grass-snake, was covered with scales, had bat's wings and four legs."[109]
- "[A] huge serpent with wings, but it has one eye on its forehead; there is also a tail, three fingers wide."[110]
- "[A] shiny big bird," that "looks like an eagle but blacker than a real bird."[111]
- "[A] large chicken, shiny, white: everything just shines."[112]
- "[H]uge, with a golden mane and a tail."[113]
- "[V]ery rough skin, cut into scales like on a turtle, greenish spots, the head—flat, here on the nose there is a tip up."[114]

Dragon Battle.
Illustration by Dmitry Yakhovsky. © Bendideia Publishing.

- A huge snake with an animal head (sheep, dog, horse) that can fly without wings. It resembles a *krosno* (кросно), a part of a loom that looks like a straight round piece of a tree trunk.[115]
- A handsome young man with a human body and a serpent's head.[116]

Zmey doesn't always appear as a beastly mixture of creatures. In certain areas, such as western Bulgaria, eastern Serbia, and the Rhodope Mountains in southeastern Europe, the eagle is the equivalent of a dragon,[117] due to its connection with the World Tree and its role as a cosmic protector. He may also take the form of a hare, golden goat, fire bird, or ordinary snake, while the female dragon, Zmeitsa, frequently appears as a bear or bear cub.[118]

Human Likeness

Most often, however, you'll see this dragon as a handsome youth. He's highly intelligent and possesses hypnotizing eyes. You may also notice that Zmey has small, sometimes golden, wings under his armpits.[119] The wings are tiny enough that he can hide them beneath clothing. When he disguises his dragon form and appears as a human, people say he "wears his skin inside out."

Sometimes, it may be difficult to tell if that handsome man flirting with you is human or Zmey with his dragon skin on the inside. Mothers, especially those known as sorceresses, warn their daughters to be leery of a man they find loitering in a meadow, saying he just woke up. Mothers tell the girls tales of a dragon who was cursed: "[H]e became a zmey, a smok, that is his body. And when he wakes up, he is a handsome bachelor, but he falls asleep—zmey, smok."[120] Some girls have claimed they've watched the transformation: "And she told her mother how he turns into a dragon, watching him as a bachelor, and becoming a dragon, twisting like a snake."[121]

A sighting of a slightly different Zmey at the Magura cave in northwestern Bulgaria describes him as a naked man with large, rather than small, wings. This being "breaks away from the notion of a monster" and "matches or is very close to the biblical image of the angel."[122]

Other times, the differences between Zmey and a man are more noticeable. The dragon-man may be two heads taller than a human, or his head may be disproportionate to his body. In human form, although handsome, he may have a defect, something unfinished, such as a hole in his nose.[123] His face may look as if it's been burned by lightning. In addition, "[h]is body up to his neck is covered with silvery scales, which shine strongly."[124]

In the folklore story that follows, he has a tail that he doesn't adequately cover.

> According to legends, a zmey lived in the Rusin Kamak cave near the village of Rusokastro in southeastern Bulgaria. Once he turned into a young man and went down to the nearby village, where people were celebrating a wedding in the village square. However, the zmey's tail was sticking out of the stranger's clothes, which provoked the laugh of a girl named Rusa. "Uncle, put your tail away." She laughed at him. The zmey got angry and created a whirlwind, which raised a lot of dust and no one could see anything. When the whirlwind passed, people saw that the girl Rusa was gone. They guessed she had been abducted by the zmey. He settled down with Rusa in the cave.[125]

The female Zmeitsa also exists in ballad songs, where she is portrayed as "a superhuman being who comes into contact with the world of people, in some cases providing help and support, but often bringing threat, illness and death."[126] Bearing the name of Denitsa or Dennitsa, a popular name for Venus, she is the mistress of diseases and lives at the bottom of the sea.

She appears as a tall, thin maiden, with golden-blond hair and a face as bright as the sun.[127] She's a strong woman—both in size and abilities, much like the woodland nymph called Samodiva in Bulgaria or

Vila in other Eastern European countries.[128] Like the woodland nymph, Zmeitsa becomes a hero's *posestrima*, blood sister, and breastfeeds him to give him strength.[129]

Natural Phenomenon

Zmey may appear as a natural phenomenon: mist or fog, a whirlwind, a dark cloud, lightning, a bright light, or a comet. In the latter cases, he glows as bright as the sun and has been described as looking like "a piece of oblong fire" or a creature that "flies in the air in the form of fire, like a long arc."[130] He flashes like an airplane's light at night. The smok-born Zmey produces a series of sparks as he streaks across the sky, while the carp-born Zmey glimmers with a single flash.[131]

In human form, even if he himself doesn't glow, his clothes often do. In the story "Margarita and the Flying Boy," after which Margarets Hill in Bulgaria is named, the dragon who appears to her is a handsome young man whose clothes shine like the sun.[132]

OMINOUS LIGHT IN THE SKY

You may think that light you see in the sky is a comet or a falling star, but it may be a "fiery zmey" as many people in Eastern Europe have believed. He's likely on his way to seduce his chosen love. He flies into the room of a lonely woman when her husband is away. Women seeing the light approach say, "Amen! Fall to pieces," hoping to avoid such a situation (Avilin, "East European meteor folk-beliefs," 114).

Some people say the dragon streaking across the sky carries wealth and good fortune to his mistress or even to a witch or sorcerer. If the light is "fiery and red," he has gold and precious stones; if it's "white," he carries silver; and if the light is "dark and black," he's carrying life-giving grains (Avilin, "Belarussian meteor folk-beliefs," 121).

These lights also have other meanings and warnings.

- *Sparks flying from the dragon's tail indicate a misfortune is imminent: wars, crop failure, starvation* (Avilin, "Belarussian meteor folk-beliefs," 121). In addition, if the dragon flies directly over the village, those sparks are likely to start a fire. It's wise to put a bucket of milk in your yard to appease the creature, so he'll leave your house alone. If the fiery dragon doesn't drink it, you can always use the milk to extinguish the flames. Water won't work on a fire the dragon starts; it will make it burn fiercer. Only milk will put it out (Avilin, "Belarussian meteor folk-beliefs," 122).
- *Every time a person is born, a new star appears; when the star dims, the man, its earthly double, will die* (Avilin, "East European meteor folk-beliefs," 113). The star flies upward when a child is born, but flies "fast and straight" downward when a death is imminent. If it's "not too fast," it means the person suffered illness for a long time before he died a hard death. A "slantwise" star movement indicates a natural death (Avilin, "Belarussian meteor folk-beliefs," 119-120).
- *The star is a wandering soul.* It may be flying to the next world after a person's death. Or it could be a cursed person roaming the earth until he receives forgiveness (Avilin, "East European meteor folk-beliefs," 114).
- *A falling star may indicate a prisoner has escaped.* In order for the person to avoid capture, he must say, "Behind the thorns, behind a bush hide!" (Avilin, "East European meteor folk-beliefs," 115).

Shapeshifter

Zmey is also a shapeshifter, so you can never be sure if one is around. He may become invisible, showing himself only to those humans he favors.[133] The female Zmeitsa does likewise, revealing herself only to a bachelor she intends to seduce. That chill you feel brushing past you may be an invisible dragon lurking, ready to pounce.

Plant matter is a favorite thing for Zmey to turn into when he wishes to avoid detection and possible capture. He'll become a floral wreath like the ones girls wear, or he may turn into a *kitka* (китка), a small bouquet like a corsage that's carried, worn on a man's hat, or tied around the wrist. But, he also turns into inanimate objects, such as a girdle, wrought-iron belt, broom, mop, oven fork, and even a peacock feather—all for the purpose of camouflaging himself. If he and his human wife have a child, the dragon will turn the infant into something else, as well: for example, a crooked feather in his mother's hair or a silver ring on her right hand.

Girls should be wary of picking up any flower, or other pretty objects like a peacock feather, they find lying on the road, near a well, or in a horse's footprint. It may be the dragon in disguise. It's also likely it's something he deliberately dropped there to attract his intended bride. In the evening, he'll find the one who picked it up and seduce her, unless the objects are avoided as in the account below.

> I have an aunt. My aunt once went out, she went somewhere outside the village. She had already noticed something one or two times, but this time it was very strong. A strong storm, and from the storm there were flowers. Where he passed, he left flowers.
>
> Okay, but maybe she knew, my aunt, somebody might have told her, and she was not taking any of the flowers, the flowers that he was leaving. If she took from the flowers, he would have loved her.[134]

Zmey lies in wait for the opportune moment to seize a bride. A villager recounts a tale about a girl named Kalina (Kalya) who was swept away during a flood. A dragon took the form of a pine tree to capture her. This was no ordinary tree, it stood "strangely upright on the water"[135] as it floated down the swollen river.

> And when the water swept her away, there was a pine tree. So this pine was the zmey. That's what people say and that's how we tell it. That the pine, which was in the middle of the river, standing upright, it was the zmey itself, turned into a tree. … The pine was straight, upright, and she caught the pine. And I asked my aunt, "How is that possible? It can't be!" And she said, "Oooh! Your grandmother said that the people saw her when she was holding the pine and she was passing through the village." [She laughs.] So I don't know how true this is, but that is the story.[136]

Zmeitsa can also transform herself into a corsage, often a Bulgarian geranium, that the boy wears on his shirt. Or she can take on other forms, such as trees, when she wants to cause harm to a human. The female snake named Kenhrines mentioned earlier takes the form of a round piece of wood that moves extremely fast when she leaves her cave in pursuit of a shepherd.[137]

Getting to Know Zmey

Let's visit Zmey in his home. Take a look around, but don't linger. He may think you'll want to remain forever.

Although you'll frequently discover him lurking near or within water sources, especially rivers, springs, lakes, and village fountains, this location isn't normally considered his home. However, water bodies are likely to be adjacent to his abode, giving him easy access to these places, which he guards.

Zmey and His River Bride.
Illustration by Nelinda. © Bendideia Publishing.

Most often, you'll find Zmey living in a cave or crevice deep within the depths of a towering mountain. People believe each mountain has its own Zmey and is the place he keeps his hoard of treasure. Or you may discover his home in the forest inside a hollow centuries-old tree, whose roots dig deep into the soil. A dragon popular in Bulgarian songs is called Zmey Gorianin (Змей Горянин), which means "forest dragon."

Another source gives a slightly different interpretation to Zmey's home.

> The summary that the dragon is underground, after mentioning mountains, canals, caves, is also not quite accurate. In fact, it lives inside the earth and in this sense localizes itself in all its hierarchical levels—under (water), on the earth (tree, mountain), above the earth (clouds).[138]

Now that you have a better idea where to find Zmey, you'll want to know a little bit about his habits in the event he entertains you in his home. Those who have researched him say not only can he take on human form, his existence also mimics that of people in many ways: he's born; falls in love; gets married; consumes bread, milk, and wine; and eventually dies. Don't be fooled; it's likely he's grander than humans, and mankind imitates dragons by "eating, drinking, breeding, marrying, [and] dying,"[139] rather than the other way around.

Often, Zmey entertains guests, relatives of his chosen bride, with his fare.

> "Oh you, Zmey Goryanin,
> Where are you, why don't you come here?
> To bring three loads,
> Three loads of pure flour,
> The fourth—honey and butter!
> To treat my brothers,
> And twelve cousins."
> The zmey heard it from the woods,
> And brought three loads,
> Three loads of pure flour,
> The fourth—honey and butter.
> And they treated the nine brothers
> And the twelve cousins.[140]

Zmey has a discerning palate. His drink preference is wine, but it must be squeezed from the largest, ripest, sweetest, and blackest grapes;[141] it must be "the thickest red wine that can be worn in a cloth [*wrapped in a towel*]."[142] To go along with that, you must serve him the best white bread, that's been made from the "purest grains from the field,"[143] and then "minced with flour" and "sifted with the smallest sieve."[144]

He must do more to occupy his time than simply sit around all day, you may be thinking, and you're right. Zmey performs various activities to keep himself busy. He's a self-proclaimed weatherman, a policeman, and most important of all, a lover.

Weather Controller

Zmey acts like a weatherman, not that he predicts what the conditions will be. No, he controls what will happen. He imprisons the wind and rain within his cave, but, not for harmful effects. He sends them out when villagers need to nourish their crops, and withdraws them to avoid floods and rot.

A dragon from another village may also unleash or withhold these powers of nature, however, causing devastating rain and flooding on one hand or droughts on the other. In that case, Zmey does his best to protect both the people and fields from this bad weather by driving away the invader.

Although Zmey has an association with being the guardian of water, fire is his natural element. The fire he breathes may appear as blue lightning in the summer heat or as a bright red ball of a meteor streaking across the sky.[145] You'll know he's up and about when a thunderstorm ravages the land. Sometimes, thunder is the roar of barrels he rolls across the sky. Other times, it means Zmey's having a conversation with another dragon. The variations in the intensity of the booms is the differing timbre of the dragons speaking to each other; older ones speak with "a thicker voice," while younger ones talk with "a thinner voice."[146]

Village Protector

One of Zmey's main roles, especially in the Balkan region, is that of village protector, a remnant of the dragon's role as cosmic mediator in the World Tree. Each village has its own Zmey, who perches in ancient trees, often oaks, called *Samodivsky* or *Zmeyovi* among the Bulgarians.[147] These trees line the cultivated land, so the dragon can keep watch over the crops, protecting them from dark clouds, which indicate an enemy is approaching. While the snake/dragon most often appears at the base of the World Tree, in folklore,

Zmey sits among the branches as storms gather, so he can quickly battle other dragons that seek to steal fertility or devastate the village he protects.

The eagle replaces the dragon in the role of protector in western Bulgaria, eastern Serbia, eastern Bosnia, and Herzegovina.[148] However, in western Bulgaria, the eagle's "function of master and protector [is] intertwined with that of the dragon."[149] It's this bird, and not the dragon, that protects villages. The eagle, which has four invisible wings,[150] builds its nest in an oak, the tree of thunder,[151] or a sycamore, where it awaits the thunderstorm's arrival.[152] When the battle is over and the eagle has defeated the invader, the bird leads the storm clouds away.

In whatever form he takes, Zmey guards the people and land against the destruction and theft from other dragons—whether it be Hala, Lamia, or a Zmey from another territory who invades his domain.

Depending on the region, the dragon himself may perform this role, or it may be Zmey's male child, who was born of a human woman. These children are called *zmajeviti*, dragon men, in some locations. People believe they are invisible guardians.

Whenever a thunderstorm approaches, the human dragon faints, and his spirit ascends to the sky to battle intruders. People believe this is possible because a soul has an independent existence, and it can detach itself from the body and fly off.[153] This trancelike behavior is now believed to possibly have been because "these were persons born with atavistic peculiarities and a particular state of the nervous system which people termed unusual."[154] It's imperative that anyone coming across a sleeping human dragon doesn't wake him. Zmey will die if he returns to where he slumbers only to discover his body isn't as he left it.[155]

The thunder you hear is the battle raging between Zmey and his enemy. Lightning bolts are the dragon's fiery arrows. Sparks fly from his weapons as he hurls them against his dragon foe. In the earliest beliefs from the Stone Age, Zmey used stone arrows to fight other dragons. The classic version of the dragon myth may have emerged during this epoch, when "the principal instruments of labour and means of protection were the stones and arrows."[156] People call these stone arrows by many names: thunder arrows, devil's fingers, Perun's arrows or Perun-stones (after the Slavic god of thunder).

Whenever Zmey fights, these arrows (*streli*) plummet to the land, embedding themselves deep underground. After forty days, they resurface.[157] It's a positive omen when someone finds one of these arrow-shaped stones, because people believe they hold magical power. They break the stones into pieces, grind them into powder, and use them with water for curing wounds and other ailments.[158] A stone arrow that falls into water is useful for treating colic.[159] To bring the implements up more quickly from the ground, people pour milk at the location where lightning bolts have struck.[160]

People also use the stones as talismans in lofts to protect home and outbuildings from thunder and lightning. Or they hang them around the necks of their animals when the creatures act strangely.[161]

Loving Maidens

Zmey's main occupation, however, is that of maiden lover. Even though Zmey can choose a bride from among female dragons, he finds it difficult to suppress his cravings for humans. These girls, called *zmeynichavi*[162] or *zmeyoviti*,[163] cannot escape their fate; they have little choice in avoiding his attention once Zmey loves them.

According to popular belief, Zmey's beloved is his "cosmic twin," someone conceived at the same time he was, or born within months of the dragon.[164] He can't help himself; it's destiny, and his love will be eternal. Even if he never takes the girl for his bride, he'll guard her from her youth onward.

Zmey is also drawn to a girl if her name is connected to a natural resource. Her name may be a "code" to her "true nature."[165] For example,

- Росица (Rosita) comes from *poca* (*rosa*) for "dew."
- Петра (Petra) comes from the Greek πέτρα (*pétra*) for "stone" and signifies health and strength.

34

- Руса (Rusa) comes from *рус* (*rus*) for "blonde."
- Драгана (Dragana) comes from *драга* (*draga*) for "dear," someone who is precious or a treasure.
- Фидана (Fidana) comes from *фиданка* (*fidanka*), which is a young tree that's slim, fragile, beautiful, and flexible.

In folk stories, the girl often comes from a single-parent home, with no father mentioned. The mother or an elderly woman who runs the household is likened to a sorceress, healer, or herbalist, who has great knowledge of herbs and how to outsmart or destroy dragons.[166]

Zmey's chosen bride is often the most beautiful girl, the first to begin dancing the *horo* (circle dance) at village gatherings. She's not only beautiful, she's also personable, outgoing, and hardworking. She's a girl who is characteristic of the "unborn child," a name given to a child (boy or girl) who, even before birth, is deemed to have special abilities, one who will become a hero. In this capacity, the girl, once taken to the dragon's cave, will shine: "a creature that seems to be woven from light."[167]

To find his bride, Zmey disguises himself whenever he's in the village. He may strut around as a handsome youth; he may slink through the crowd, invisible to everyone except the girl he loves;[168] or he may even wander around like a shiny white chicken.[169]

Zmey Abducting Bride.
Illustration by Nelinda. © Bendideia Publishing.

He comes during the warmest months to steal girls from their families, especially on Eniovden, the summer solstice (June 24), and during the harvest on Georgiovden, St. George's Day (May 6), when girls have gathered in the field. Zmey frequents places women and girls congregate: *horos*, *cheshmas* (wells or fountains with naturally flowing water), *sedyankas* (working bees or gatherings of women during harvest time), among others.

One person's account of a girl's abduction from a *horo* follows:

> And the young ones started dancing. [...] At the same time a whirlwind came down. Yes, a whirlwind came down. But the weather was clear and no other sound could be heard but the whistle of the wind and the most beautiful girl on the *horo*, started rising in the air. She was rising and the young men around were trying to catch her, but they couldn't. So the girl disappeared. Till the evening they were looking for her, shouting her name, but they couldn't find her.[170]

In many circumstances, though, the girl is attracted to the handsome, strong, mysterious man who arrives in her village. Some girls are easily swayed by the dragon's tales of his mountain or forest palace and his promise of wealth—for everyone knows dragons hoard gold and precious gems. Such a life, even if she's married to a creature who can appear as a ferocious beast, must appeal to a girl more than living a harsh peasant's life. Oftentimes in the past, the girl didn't have the chance to choose her own husband, so to be desired by a wealthy dragon was a luxury.

In the song below, Zmey tries to quell a young maiden's fear of him. Will he persuade young Ela to come with him? Or will she hold fast to her resolution until she "grows up"?

Zmey Loves a Maiden
Oh beautiful Ela, you young maid,
A zmey came and went around Ela,
Then he spoke to Ela:
"Grow, Ela, until you grow up,
So we two can fall in love [*make love*]."
Then Ela spoke to him:
"I will tell you, Zmey goryanine,
I do not dare to look into your eyes,
Not to say to fall in love!
There are strong sparks coming out of your eyes,
There is a strong flame blowing from your mouth;
When you ride a horse—it is like a mountain,
When you wear your garment—it is like a burning fire."
Then the zmey spoke to her:
"Grow, Ela, until you grow up,
You and I will fall in love,
Do not be afraid of me, Ela."[171]

When Zmey has found the girl of his dreams, he may not win her over right away. He'll often visit her at her home to persuade her.

> In stormy weather he descends to her like a cloud and lightning, cracking and shining. Therefore, the one who knows that the zmey loves her tries to stay alone when thunders

start, and if there is someone with her, she makes him leave, so as not to be afraid because it was scary when the zmey was coming down.[172]

He may also appear as a comet streaking across the sky. He accesses his chosen maiden's house through the fireplace chimney.[173] Once he enters her bedroom, he changes back into a handsome youth. No one but the girl can see him, so it's easy to deceive or confuse her family if they go to check on her as she groans in pain from the dragon's abuse, or moans in passion from his love.

His visits to married or widowed women are also well-known.

> According to other Russian ideas, the meteor-zmey flies to women who pine for their absent or dead husbands too heavily or for too long a time. The zmey takes on the form of the husband, and may even have sex with the woman, but no one else can see him. His voice may be heard in the house talking, or he may even answer questions, and his mistress will grow rich. Such a zmey is usually described as having a head in the form of a ball, a back like a washtub, and an extremely long tail [roughly up to 35 feet] …. When he comes to his chosen place, he explodes into small sparks, and when he flies, he can do so low to the ground.[174]

A sorcerer also takes on the form of a fiery dragon when he visits his mistress while her husband is away.

> The sorcerer flew up to her body in the form of a fiery zmej every night, and every time he came he broke himself up into sparkling fragments, so that the sheep thrashed about in the yard, and the cows lowed. He wailed for a while, then flew away.[175]

Loving Shepherds

While not as prominent as Zmey stories, tales exist about the female dragon, who pines for human men. She falls in love with bachelors—most often shepherds. Like Zmey, she'll cheat on her dragon husband with the most beautiful bachelor, so she can enliven the man's "monotonous life in the open spaces."[176] She never has an affair with a married man; at least no stories of this have been recorded.

Unlike Zmey, she never kidnaps the man, nor hides him in a cave. She always remains in the human world to woo her beloved.[177] If he's out in the field tending his flock, she'll hide among blue mountain stones, waiting for his arrival. If he's gone home for the evening, she'll come out of her dark forest cave and light a fire in his yard. When she has his attention, she'll come inside and lie with him in his bed. She woos him with kisses and helps him around the house by lighting the fire on the hearth, making cheese from sheep's milk, and drying his socks.[178]

She keeps her illicit relationship secret from her dragon husband. Even though Zmey may be pursuing a human bride at the same time, he'll kill his wife and her beloved if he discovers them. If Zmeitsa is a widow, she has nothing to fear except rejection from the one she loves.

Her love is neither gentle nor kind, however, if a shepherd scorns her by choosing a human bride. She'll be vindictive and destroy his flock, bringing him poverty. Or she'll become physically abusive: torturing him, crushing him, breaking his bones, and even killing him by tearing him apart.[179]

> **Did you know?**
>
> The dragon, in the guise of lightning, sucks up bee's honey and cow's milk (Georgieva, 69).

The girl the shepherd loves won't escape Zmeitsa's wrath either. The dragon transforms into a willow by a spring and waits for her rival. She sprinkles a green bouquet of leaves from her branches onto the unsuspecting girl, who becomes extremely ill and eventually dies.[180] Even when a girl isn't a rival, Zmeitsa likes to deceive the girl's mother when she's looking for her daughter. Zmeitsa will deny knowing where the girl is, even though she knows Zmey has abducted the girl.[181]

If a shepherd does succumb to Zmeitsa's entreaties, her love leaves him afflicted, and he'll die if he can't be released from it. The story of Stoyan is a popular one about Zmeitsa's love.

> His mother said to Stoyan,
> "Stoyan,—my son, Stoyan,—
> Whilst thou wert my son, with thy mother,
> Thou wert fair and ruddy.
> Since thou hast parted from thy mother
> Thou art a pale yellow,
> Like a yellow orange,
> And like a green bush.
> Hast thou, my son, evil companions?
> Or are the shepherds rude to thee?"
>
> To this the son replies that he has no bad associates, nor is he ill-treated by the shepherds, only at night a she-bear comes to him and calls him her sweetheart.
>
> To Stoyan his mother said,
> "This is not a savage bear;
> It is Elka, the she-dragon."[182]

Maladies of Love

While people believe a light shines within a girl who joyfully leaves to live with Zmey, they say the one he loves who remains at home loses that light. She's quiet, sad, and depressed; she often cries or mumbles; and she suffers from hallucinations. Her skin becomes dry, pale or colorless, and withered. She has sunken cheeks and watery eyes.

She suffers from a curse, a disease called *oblachka otrama* or *ograma*,[183] which refers to a cloud (*oblak*), one of Zmey's disguises.[184] This leads to maladies of the mind that today we'd call mental illness. Even nowadays, people say, "A dragon loves her," as a way of indicating someone has gone mad.[185]

Zmey is an obsessive, controlling, jealous lover. He "possesses the girl's consciousness and she remains forever his captive."[186] The girl who pines for him avoids social gatherings, especially the *horos* and *sedyankas* she once loved so much. While at home, she idles her time away, forsaking tasks she used to enjoy. She neglects her appearance, neither brushing her hair nor washing herself. People say the dragon doesn't let her dress well and that he steals all her energy. Many women have claimed that Zmey lies to them about his love. Instead of being an adoring suitor, he "comes every night and tramples and tortures the one he has chosen."[187]

A woman who a dragon loves has a short lifespan. During a thunderstorm, she sleeps heavily, while her lover invades her dreams. Her face becomes sickly yellow and is covered with bruises, which is a certain sign a dragon has made love to her. Some say he drinks the pooled blood,[188] or he sucks milk from her breasts, making her grow weaker daily until she dies.[189] Even if she remains healthy, she doesn't dare tell anyone about the dragon and his love, because he informs her she'll die if she breathes a word of it.[190] Unable to tell loved ones, she keeps the secret so bottled up that it may drive her to commit suicide.[191]

Shepherdess Falls in Love with Zmey (Залюбил змей овчарка).
Illustration © Keazim Issinov. Used with permission of the artist.

In the poem below by Pencho Slaveikov, you see how a dragon's love distresses the girl called Yana. Although she manages to tell others of her affliction, she believes she has no hope of redemption.

Zmey's Beloved
Shy stars darkened in the sky;
So early the roosters crowed…
Late harvesters return to the village.
Pretty Yana's girlfriends are so eager:

"Yano, what is this change of yours?
You were happy and laughing before—
Why do you walk so worried and miserable?
Maybe you have some secret sickness?"

"I am sick, my friends, an evil sickness is beating me,
I am shivering, I am dizzy,
A whirlwind is coming, and the night is dark…
Who knows if tomorrow I will wake up!"

The clear moon sank behind a cloud;
A whirlwind came, and bent the trees…
Yana was staggering down the road, bending her body;
As a Veda [*an evil female creature who roams at night*] she was—neither dead nor alive.

The harvesters around her were in wonder;
Beautiful Yana's friends were eager:
"Yano, where are you going, why are you bending your arms?
Where is your memory? What is happening in your heart?"

"My heart is sick and my memory is lost…
My unfaithful friends, the zmey loves me.
God damn all the dark herbs.
Oh, these black clouds are not in vain!"

Dogs started barking far in the yards,
The dark sky split into two—
And arrow-shaped lightning flashed;
Suddenly thunder crashed.

All the elements flew at the ground with a crash:
Male and female zmeys with golden chariots—
The whole family of the zmey Ognyan [*from the dialect word* ognyan *for fiery*],
Gathered for the wedding of beautiful Yana.

They turned around and flew to the sky.
Only for a moment, the timid harvesters saw them,
How the beautiful Yana and her beloved
Disappeared behind the clouds.[192]

Even if Zmey doesn't sprint his beloved away, he won't let her get married to anyone else,[193] despite the fact the girl's parents try to force her to wed.

> They were making them get married, matchmakers came, boys from here and there wanted them, the girl refused, she did not want to get married. The parents were pressuring her because good boys were coming, rich people, they already wanted to marry the girl. But the zmey told the girl that if she allowed the marriage, he would eat her, that he would kill her. And the girl was crying and didn't want to. And then, because they were insisting a lot, she revealed herself to the mother and the father, she told them that it was like this, and like that, that there was something, it came every night, at midnight, when a rooster didn't sing.[194]

The girl may also be so under Zmey's control that she doesn't want to escape his love. If her parents force her into a marriage, she loses the desire "to have sex with a human because of the dragon's huge potency."[195]

There's a chance she can escape her fate and return to normal, however. If the dragon leaves the area for any reason and is gone for nine years, the girl will be free from his love.[196]

One story describes an eighty-five-year-old Bulgarian woman who was the recipient of a dragon's love when she was young. He lived the life of a human and one day had to go off to fight in a rebellion. He left her with a message: If a spring in the village dried up, she would know he'd been killed. If it continued to flow, he would return to her. The day the water stopped running, she knew he was dead and would never return. She married someone else and had children. However, she was never happy with her husband; they quarreled constantly. She was unable to love anyone, because she had once had a dragon lover, someone from the "other world," and so she could not be happy in the human world either.[197]

Did you know?

When a dragon knows his death is imminent, he buries his treasure and leaves a *talasum*, a spirit, behind to guard it (Aveela, *Household Spirits*, 82).

Even some girls who are swayed by the dragon's promises of love and wealth live to regret it. Love for and marriage to a dragon often have fatal results as you'll discover in the tale below.

> A legend tells that people organized a yearly fair in a small village in Thrace. One day, a lass named Ruzha, from a village nearby, set out to visit the fair with her mother and father. After walking for some time, the girl felt thirsty and asked her father's permission to go to the Dragon's well and drink some water.
>
> "Don't go," said the father. "Wait until we get to the village! This is a bad place."
>
> But the girl didn't listen to him and went to the well.
>
> As she bent down to drink water, a dragon came out and asked her to marry him. "You will be rich, very rich," he said.
>
> But Ruzha ran away frightened, caught up with her parents and continued to the fair without telling them what happened. At the fair, all other girls were singing but Ruzha looked sad—she was thinking about the dragon's proposal. She was not sure if she did the correct thing because she wanted to be rich and live in a palace. When the fair ended, she left her parents and went back to the same well, saw the dragon, married him and started living in the dragon's palace.

Many years passed. Ruzha felt more homesick as the days passed by and decided to asked the dragon to let her visit her family. The dragon agreed and took her to the same well where they met.

All was good, but during the years she had spent with the dragon, Ruzha had grown a dragon's tail. She decided that she couldn't go to her folks looking like that and decided to first get rid of it. She turned and tried to bite it off, but she couldn't, then she turned to the other side and tried to catch it but failed again. Then she started throwing herself from side to side but to no avail.

Suddenly she heard songs of girls, *lazarki*, who were coming back from the fair. Horrified that her friends would see her this way, she tried once again to get rid of her tail, but her heart didn't hold out against the pressure and burst.

The girls found her dead and buried her. From that day on, every year they gathered around the well and danced a *horo*, not in a circle but the *buenetz*, a snake-like form, in order to remember young Ruzha, the dragoness.[198]

If Zmey's words aren't enough to persuade a girl to leave with him voluntarily, he'll abduct her. Her negative reaction to him may anger him so much that, instead of taking her as a bride, he'll keep her locked within his cave as a servant. Even a dragon doesn't want to wed someone who's going to battle his will all the time. Some studies of Zmey say those with a zoomorphic image have "a different mental characteristic," which includes abducting girls who have angered them.[199]

The girl's delusions of a palace and wealth fade when she discovers his home is a dark cave and his wealth is only the majestic stalactites and stalagmites. Whether she's an unwilling bride or a reluctant servant, you'll know her sad fate when you see "a spring at the bottom of a cave or at the foot of a rock that arose from the tears of a kidnapped girl."[200]

Another story discusses a stolen girl the dragon guarded so she couldn't escape.

You also have to go to the Serpent's Hole. She was stolen by the dragon we have been calling the Serpent Hole. And he kept her in the hole, encircling her in the morning with stones, with trees there, so she couldn't come out and escape, he went out and collected various fruits to feed her and brought her through the Dragon's hole. There are deep roots there, right here close to my house there are such small holes in the Red Wall. He took her out from the cave to let her watch how they perform the horo in Yugovo.[201]

If you think all is hopeless, don't worry. You'll find remedies to cure a dragon's love later in this chapter.

Dragon Weddings

Dragon weddings are highly spectacular, dramatic events, but only the bride-to-be can see the arriving procession. Whirlwinds. Fire. Thunder. White horses. Golden chariots. The groom tells the girl to be ready for the wedding party. Washed, clothed in ornamented wedding attire, hair braided according to customs, she waits in the yard for him to come in the night to whisk her away. With tears in her eyes, she turns and says a final "goodbye" to her mother, for she may never see her again. The song below provides a glimpse into the dragon's arrival.

Radka and Zmey
"You are arranging a wedding, mother, you are getting me engaged,
But you are not asking me, mother

Zmey Wedding.
Illustration by Nelinda. © Bendideia Publishing.

Whether I want to get married, or not?
A zmey loves me, mother,
A zmey loves me, and a zmey will take me!
Every night he comes
He will come tonight as well:
Male zmeys—with well-fed horses,
Female zmeys—with golden carriages,
Small zmeys—with painted carts.
When they walk through a forest,
The forest will lie down without wind;
When they pass through a field,
The field will tremble without fire;
When they come home,
The house, mother, will catch fire,
From the four corners—
Don't be afraid!"
Radka was just saying that,
When a thin rifle shot,
The boxwood door opened,
And the yard got full of
Male and female zmeys.
The female zmeys were telling Radka:
"Rado, you beautiful maiden,
Undo your thin braids—
We are going to braid them our way,
Our way, Rado, the zmey's way!"
And they braided Rada's hair,
Then sat in the golden chariots.[202]

When the dragon flies above a house or enters it, it bursts into flames.[203] It's not so much that it's intentional. Remember, dragons are personifications of lightning. As the dragon flies overhead, he "shakes the air very much and releases strong sparks"; these ignite everything he passes, "especially hay, chaff, sheaves, and more."[204]

The burning of the house in the wedding song has a deeper meaning, though. At some point, mythology ceased to be understood only as an explanation of natural events, and it became closely tied to ritual life. The stories began to function as a way "to regulate and maintain a certain natural and social order."[205] A dragon kidnapping the girl—and the subsequent burning of the house—disrupted the harmony of the patriarchal society.

> The burning of the home, as a symbol of the violation of the harmony of the patriarchal cosmos, is an extremely important moment for the folklore pattern. This harmony will be restored when Radka lights hay with herbs in it and thus gets rid of the zmey.[206] [*You can read the rest of the poem describing this later in this chapter.*]

Dragons, like the gods of old, exuded potency and sexuality, common characteristics of beings who have a connection to fertility. This was especially true in agricultural societies. And what better rite to propagate fertility than that of marriage? Dragon weddings, therefore, were once a common way to offer a girl of marriageable age as a sacrifice to a dragon to ensure crops flourished.[207]

Stories about dragon weddings are full of symbolism. The suggested symbolism within the stories and villager recollections that follow varies and may not agree with academic study.

The Story: Abducted from a Sedyanka

The tale of Rada and the dragon is popular in Bulgaria. (You can listen to a narrated version of the full tale in the sidebar "Rada, a Zmey's Beloved.")

The story begins with *sedyanka*—the girl states that no one can "lie" to her, i.e., make her marry him. The zmey, a handsome young man, hears her and comes "with a six-winged horse" or on foot and abducts her by enchanting her with the melody of his kaval. He takes her to his home—a cave in the mountain, puts on her iron shoes (*opinki*), and tells her that she can return to her mother once she breaks them.

The zmey's sister feels sorry for the girl and tells her how to break them faster—in the evening bury them "in clear embers" and in the morning water them with cold water. After three months, the zmey's bride breaks the shoes and holding a child in her hands she goes to her home together with the Zmey. The mother manages to separate them with the help of some herbs and the Zmey turns into a green wreath.[208]

The Symbolism
- **The cave**. This is the portal to the dragon's realm, in the "other world." A cave is a common place where initiations take place.
- **Iron shoes**. When the Zmey puts the iron shoes on his bride, it signifies her new sexuality as a woman; she's now ready for marital consummation.
- **The child**. Signifies fertility, that the initiation process has been completed.

PODCAST:
RADA, A ZMEY'S BELOVED

In the Folklore Podcast, storyteller Moni Sheehan and musician Ivor Davies, from the British-Bulgarian group "A Spell in Time," present the story of Rada, a girl bewitched by a Zmey's promise of wealth if she'll become his bride. What she discovers is deceit. But she finds a way to trick the dragon who deceived her. You can listen to the podcast here:
https://thefolklorepodcast.weebly.com/season-5/episode-68-zmey-performed-by-a-spell-in-time

The introduction to the tale states: "Bulgarian traditional tales have ancient origins and are largely unknown in the west. They are magical and deliciously dark with a dash of humor, archetypal characters, thrilling narratives, and exquisite images, combined to conjure the intense world of dreams and a mythic age of long ago when anything was possible."

Source: **The Folklore Podcast**. "Episode 68 – ZMEY. Performed by A Spell in Time." January 29, 2020. The episode is closed by special musical guest Polly Preacher.

To support the Folklore Podcast on Patreon and access exclusive extra content, please visit: www.patreon.com/thefolklorepodcast

A Spell in Time: https://www.spellintime.co.uk/

Zmey Bride.
Illustration by Nelinda. © Bendideia Publishing.

The Story: Bitten by a Snake

Songs performed on Easter and Midsummer's Day tell stories of a maiden going to the forest and being bitten or swallowed by a snake, which represents the most archaic idea of Zmey.

The maiden in the songs is "bitten" or "eaten" by a character with the appearance of a snake or who wears a snake mask. What follows is her symbolic death, from which the maiden returns as a woman with the right to marry. The initiation is connected with the idea of temporary death, after the resurrection of which the maiden has a new social status.

Many ancient cultures perform a similar ceremony with a ritual loss of virginity, often performed by a priest or a person with a high position in the society. In more recent times, this has remained symbolic, but its roots can certainly be traced back to archaic practices.[209]

The Symbolism

- **Swallowing or eating**. Symbolizes death for initiation.
- **Being bitten**. Loss of one's virginity.
- **The forest**. Signifies "the other world," that is, the afterworld.[210]

The Story: Kidnapped near Water

Although Zmey may abduct a girl through a well, it isn't because that's where he lives. He's its guardian, and so you'll often find him near wells and other water sources.

The following is a re-enactment of a pre-wedding ritual.

> On a green meadow in the woods there is a gathering on Holy Sunday [*the last day of the week after Easter*], at which all the girls and brides gather, and the bride of choice goes with her brother-in-law / brother. The abduction takes place after "the *horo* rotates three times" on the third day of the *horo* or after they step on the stone bridge in the field.
>
> Suddenly there is a whirlwind, a storm or a strong wind that throws dust in the eyes of the bride and blinds her, messes up her hair, dirties her face and clothes, takes her feather to the "swamp of the samodivas" and grabs her headscarf. She asks her brother to take her to a well, lake or swamp to wash herself and her clothes. When she's done and she stands up, there is a yellow zmey above her, claiming that she belongs to him:
>
> "Whether you wash yourself or don't / You are mine and only mine."[211]

The Symbolism

- **Washing person and clothes**. Signifies sexual maturity. The dragon can seize the girl even if she has performed the marriage rites, as long as she "has not undergone marital initiation," that is, consummated her marriage.[212]
- **Water**. Another gateway to the "other world," a place to meet the dragon.
- **Dirt and blindness**. Signs of the "other world."
- **The bridge**. The path that leads to the "other world."
- **Whirlwind**. Zmey personified.

The Story: Abducted through a Chimney or at a Gate

When the dragon streaks through the sky as a comet, he's on his way to someone's house, most likely to visit his sweetheart. If her parents have found her a husband, the dragon will try to convince her to run away with him. But, to travel there, she'll need a new wardrobe. And so, he tells her:

> "I will give you a dress decorated with silver and gold,
> I will make you iron shoes,
> I will make you a clover hat,
> I will make you a bracelet,
> I will bring you wine in the bucket."[213]

The Symbolism

- **Gold**. An object from the "other world," and so wearing gold (or its folkloric variants of silver and iron) is necessary in order to travel across realms. A woman's wedding attire consists of gold coins strung around her neck, some can be like a bib of coins, resembling Zmey's scales.
- **Iron shoes**. Mentioned earlier, these indicate the woman is mature enough to consummate her marriage.
- **Clover hat**. Symbolic of a married woman's headscarf.
- **Bracelet**. Wrapped tightly around the woman's wrist, it's a symbol of a relationship.
- **Wine**. Zmey drinks "the densest and finest wine."

FILM:
BUTTER ON THE LATCH

A Bulgarian folk song comes to life in the film *Butter on the Latch*, which is set at a folk song and dance camp in modern-day California. In the lyrics, a dragon takes a bride: "[T]he dragons descend on the girl, / And entwining themselves in her hair, / Carry her away, burning the forest as they go" (Imdb).

Without understanding dragon folklore, you may not appreciate the depth of the film. The dragon's dualistic nature is evident throughout the story: fire and water, abduction and seduction.

An in-depth review of the film states:

> After Steph leads her over a fallen tree over the river, crossing a threshold together to their future, he brings her to a desolate part of the forest, its swampy green heart that both shelters and isolates them. Close-ups follow one another with rapid cuts, shoulders, locked thighs, hands scratching skin, clothes falling off. We are promised a sensual sex scene, yet the swiftly changing camera angles effect in a dizzy spell: from above, then below, cut to the side, tilts, horizontal is exchanged for a vertical shot, until the bodies are cut off at the very edge of the frame, blurred beyond recognition. Is this the dragon taking his bride?
>
> … [V]iolence prevails, as Steph forces Sarah deeper into the water. Her swollen red lips share the same tint as his neck, scarred by Sarah's nails, while both their bodies glisten in pale whites. The assault is conveyed by such details, ultimately trading its stark representation for disrupted images and lack of sound, yet it echoes more prominently. In the visual dissonance, it remains ambiguous who has harmed whom and we cannot help but root for the woman, rather than the dragon (Petkova).

The story leaves you wondering: Who is the dragon and who is the victim—the man, Steph, or the woman, Sarah? A description in the summary says, "When reality and fantasy collide, Sarah finds that the dragons she's visioning may be inside her" (Imdb).

Sources:
Film: Imdb. "Butter on the Latch." May 9, 2013. https://www.imdb.com/title/tt2252304/.
Song: "Жениш ме, Мамо" (Zhenish me, Mamo), https://soundcloud.com/blackseahotel/zhenish-me-mamo.
Review: Petkova, Savina. "#DBW A Dragon's Wife: Rewriting the Folklore Tale in Josephine Decker's 'Butter on the Latch.' " September 1, 2019. https://screen-queens.com/2019/09/21/rewriting-the-folklore-tale-in-josephine-deckers-butter-on-the-latch/.

The Story: Abducted through a Dream

In the following poem by Geo Milev, the girl reaches the dragon's world through a dream. The poem shows the passion—and fear—a girl feels when a dragon tries to seduce her. Phrases such as "wild, ferocious arms" and "burn me with the blazing bait of your kisses" show the girl's "love ecstasy,"[214] a wild passion that a dragon's love evokes in her.

Zmey
Leave me!
A fiery zmey is my lover!
Amidst flames, whirlwinds, and thunder
There are zmeys with white stallions,
Female zmeys in golden chariots—
With wings
Spread
Wide
Every night
He comes to me.

Come!

Hold me tight with wild, ferocious arms
To your scaly chest full of red stars,
To your beastly heart,
Soaked in purple blood:

Take me, burn me with the blazing bait
Of your kisses—
Grab me from here and
Fly
Bring me
Far, far away—
Beyond woods, mountains, steep abysses, and cemeteries,
To your kingdom with no name
Oh, dream! Oh, monster!

Where there is neither day, nor year, nor morning, nor evening:
There!
Oh, I know:
You are Him!
Don't reject my single request,
Fulfill my only wish—
Ah…stop!

After a fiery and scary fight,
Unconscious, without knowing—
I will be fading—naked—
In the obscene sweetness of your hug

No, no, no!—
I am falling down
Together with you—
We fly
Through fire and smoke and stars,
Green snake twirls,
Edgy spears,
On invisible steep roads—
Crash and dust,
A scream and a bell;
No, no, no!—
Ah!

Awakening:
The bell's ring.
At the dawn of a deserted land
I am mourning on my soft knees
The monstrous
Corpse of my dream.[215]

A Dragon Loves Me, Mother.
Illustration by Nikola Kozhukharov, 1922. Public domain via Wikimedia Commons. This work is licensed under the Creative Commons Attribution 2.0 Generic License: http://creativecommons.org/licenses/by/2.0/.

The Symbolism

- **Dreamworld**. When a dragon abducts his bride, he takes her to the other world—beyond the human realm, to a "kingdom with no name ... where there is neither day, nor year, nor morning, nor evening." In this poem, the abduction takes place within the realm of the girl's subconscious, during sleep: "Oh, dream! Oh, monster!" It's here that "there is a fervent, ecstatic desire for contact with the other world. Both the dream and the ecstatic love for the mythological person are a way to achieve temporary death or temporary intercourse with the beyond and a change in social status."[216]

  Unlike folklore abductions you've already read about, in which the beast steals the girl from a dance or field, here, he's "in the very consciousness of his chosen one."[217] The events occur in the borderland "between dream and reality, between reality and super-reality, between myth and everyday life," and "between life and death."[218] In mythology, the dreamworld or the near-death state of unconsciousness was a way "a person could travel to the other world and still return from there alive."[219]

Dragon Children

Even though male dragons (Zmeĭove) have females of their own species (Zmeitsi), a reproduction crisis may have prevented both male and female dragons from creating offspring together.[220] Therefore, in order to keep their race from becoming extinct, they likely procreated with humans.

Most often Zmeitsa doesn't want to have children with a human. Perhaps this is due to fear of what her husband, the Zmey, will do if he finds out. When she does have a child from a human lover, she gives birth in a deserted cave, not the one where she lives with her husband. She keeps her infant concealed there while she feeds it.[221]

In folklore, it isn't considered immoral for a woman to have a child by a dragon. The child born of the union between Zmey and a female is always male and has a strong voice, extraordinary beauty, great physical strength, invincibility, and wisdom. He is fated to become a hero. Historical heroes, in fact, have often been given the nickname of "Dragon" in folk poems.

A dragon's offspring has small wings beneath his arms the same as his father, although the appendages won't be visible to everyone—only to those who are "just and righteous,"[222] or to those born on Saturday, according to Bulgarians.

> **Did you know?**
>
> Zmey in human form can uproot the largest tree with a single breath (Georgieva, 60).

The child must wear a special shirt to hide his dragon wings. At his birth, nine old women, or twelve maidens, must make the garment in a single night. In silence, they create the shirt from scratch: spinning the yarn, weaving the material, and sewing the shirt.[223] The story of Rada, who gives birth to a child in Zmey's palatial cave, tells more about this shirt.

> Then the dragon went in the dead of night to the village, and he brought in secret twelve maidens to weave a shirt for the dragon child, so that he could walk unnoticed in the human world and none would see his dragon nature except the pure at heart.[224]

The actual function of the shirt is unknown. Perhaps it helps the child grow or protects people from the child's dragon nature.[225] Another suggestion is that the shirt gives the child extraordinary strength and power so he can become the village protector like his father and defeat evil dragons, like Hala and Lamia[226] (whom you'll learn about later in this book).

SYMBOLIC CAVES

In folklore, a girl's contact with Zmey begins in the physical world. The dragon takes her—willingly or not—to his cave, which is a portal to the other world. Maidens captured by dragons were considered to have died—literally and symbolically. You can find physical proof of this death, they claim, in the fossilized images located outside a dragon's lair. A dragon in one story turned a girl into stone because she wouldn't leave her beloved to be with him. At other times, this visible evidence may be only a petrified portion of the abducted girl's body, such as her hand, head, or hair. Or it could be part of her clothing, like a woolen dress, belt, or a *kosatnik*, a hair piece decorated with flowers and coins (Simeonova, 75).

Although she's dead in terms of the human world, she's not completely gone, because she lives on in the cave, that is, the other world. When a girl succeeds in convincing her dragon husband to allow her to visit her family, it's a way to extend "her life in the world of people" (Simeonova, 66). In folklore, she can return from this "death"—temporarily or permanently—if certain conditions are met. In the story where Zmey takes Rada to his cave and she becomes his bride, he makes her wear iron shoes, and tells her she can visit her home when they wear out. She discovers the secret to making this happen. She must bury the iron shoes in the burning embers at night and in the morning sprinkle them with water. Within three months, rather than a lifetime, her shoes wear out, and Zmey takes her to visit her mother.

This transition from life to death and back again is called the myth of "eternal return." It portrays time as a circle and conveys the idea that "[n]o event is irreversible, no change is final" (Hristov). It speaks of the restoration of time and the rebirth of people. Life and death are intertwined with the concept of fertility and regeneration.

Caves reflect the notion of conception and rebirth, as much as they do the concept of death and the afterlife. They not only receive the souls of the dead, they also are where those souls are "reborn to new life" (Genov, 2860). Caves are considered "earth wombs." Their natural structure resembles a womb, and its features are suggestive of reproduction, from the "phallic looking forms of stalactites" to the "forces of the water" (Genov, 2681). In addition, much like a mother's womb, which shelters the unborn child, caves were mankind's earliest shelters (Genov, 2859).

The silvery flakes of a dragon's skin have also been said to be similar to a garment. Zmey's wife can acquire one "by pouring 'dragon fire' on her body," a transformation associated with "a feeling of great power."[227]

Even if the child's wings are hidden, you'll know he's a dragon because he has big eyes, and his head is larger than a normal child's. Villagers describe his head as being like a *shinik* (a round, wooden bushel basket).[228]

A boy child born from a female dragon and a man also has wings under his arms, but instead of the rest of him looking human, he's more snakelike. He may have a snake's head that's as large as a human child's head. He'll have fiery eyes[229] or even one eye.[230] He may even be a beautiful boy from the waist up, while a "colorful smok" (snake) from the waist down.[231] A girl child won't have a human appearance; she'll be a Zmeitsa like her mother.[232]

Most often, folktales tell how a dragon abducts an unmarried girl and brings her to his cave, where she bears a child who becomes a hero. But other research provides conflicting results; the type of child born depends on the woman's marital status and where the offspring is born.

- An unmarried girl taken to a cave will have male and female children who are dragons (Zmeĭove and Zmeitsi).
- A married woman who remains in her home, while conducting her affair with a dragon, will give birth to "snake-men, heroes, with wings."[233]

Although in folklore, children of a woman and Zmey are considered heroes, in oral accounts, these children have a sadder fate. Any girl who suffers from *oblachka otrama*, a dragon's love, and is unable to rid herself of her suitor, will birth a winged child.[234] Not only that, but the infant will have physical and mental handicaps. He'll be ugly, abnormal, and weak or even stillborn. If born alive, he always dies soon afterward. A girl who's a dragon's lover is thought to be evil or even a witch, and she'll become ill and die, as well.[235]

In other instances, a child can become a dragon if he's orphaned before he's born.[236] That is, the mother dies before she gives birth. By being stillborn, the child has a connection to "the other world." The child's attachment to the worlds of both the living and the dead "makes him related to the serpent, and in the eyes of humans, identifies him with the zmey."[237]

Protection from Zmey

Don't despair. If an amorous Zmey has taken a liking to you, ways exist to protect yourself from his advances. Obeying ritual taboos, performing various springtime rituals, and using herbs are the best ways to succeed.

Ritual Taboos

It's not always beauty and personality alone that attract a dragon to a girl. Her failure to follow strict ritual taboos like the ones listed below can jeopardize her safety.

- *Don't sleep in any place where food waste and swill have been thrown away.* This is an unclean place in both a physical and a spiritual sense. People consider places like this that are "external to human habitation" to be symbolical of the world in which dragons live.[238] And so, in these places, Zmey can easily discover—and, ultimately, fall in love with—the girl.
- *Don't go outside for the first forty days after giving birth.* The first forty days after a child's birth are a critical time for both mother and child. They are vulnerable to evil forces, attracting Zmey being one of these risks.

The woman described below disobeys this taboo and brings Zmey's attention to herself by singing.

> My grandmother Minka, who was Todor Mazarov's great-grandmother—was reaping. And while she was reaping, she was singing. And she had given birth three days ago. She was in the fields with the baby. And she was singing something, she was humming—it wasn't something extraordinary, but she was humming. As soon as she sang, immediately something like a snake appeared, like a big snake.[239]

Even though the woman leaves the field after encountering the creature, she discovers she cannot escape Zmey.

> And when she left, in the evening she went to the cellar to get something. There a very shiny thing appeared to her—and everything shone in the basement. And a man appeared to her, and he said: "My name is Petko." And he began to make love to her—to lie down

with her, to chase Grandfather—like he was with a woman. She would no longer be afraid. He was coming every evening.[240]

- *Don't venture outside on a foggy day or during a thunderstorm.* Both these weather conditions mean a dragon is lurking nearby. Zmey often waits until a thunderstorm's brewing in order to seize a girl for his bride or servant. Whomever he sees as he flies overhead, he grabs before she has a chance to run or scream.
- *Don't go outside at night, even if it's not stormy.* If a dragon has landed in a tree, performing his duty of protecting the village, the girl may inadvertently make eye contact with him. That's all it takes for him to fall in love with her.[241]
- *Don't drink, wash with, or look into water left uncovered during a thunderstorm.* As the dragon flies overhead during the storm, he may look into the water, leaving his image there for the girl to see. And as in the previous statement, just one look is all it takes for him to become enamored.

Additionally, Zmey's reflected image is likened to his very soul left in the water.[242] In a way, the reflection brings the girl closer to the dragon, making her "like" or identical to him,[243] because she can see him as he can see her. And so, he falls in love with her.

If anything falls into the water in a vessel that's left uncovered during a thunderstorm, that, too, is dangerous. The dragon may have dropped it there to attract the girl. Throw the object away immediately.[244]

The water's surface acts like a mirror, and so, in the same way, a girl has to be wary of mirrors, especially if she finds one along the road. Mirrors establish a link from her world to the dragon's realm.[245] Any girl who looks into a mirror faces the probability that a dragon will see her from the other side and, therefore, fall in love with her, with dire consequences as the story below demonstrates.

> We were still little, and this woman was our relative, my husband's cousin. Once they went to dig in the fields, and she found a mirror and looked in it. And when she looked in the mirror, the woman got sick. And she wasn't lying in bed, but she was fighting back, and she wanted to go out. She was shouting:
>
> "Let me go to the zmey! He is waiting for me there!"
>
> And her brother-in-law was holding her, her husband was holding her, everybody was holding her, and they couldn't calm her down. And when they opened the door—she was like a bullet on the road. She was hiding, dressing up, not on the road, but at her place, she was hiding, getting dressed, and walking around the yard like insane. And if they didn't let her go, she was going to the fireplace, looking through the chimney, and shouting:
>
> "Let me go. I'll get out of here!"
>
> They believed that the woman got sick because she looked into a mirror that fell from the sky.[246]

Lazarovden Rituals

Although in the distant past, societies may have offered their daughters to dragons as brides, in more recent human history, people have tried to prevent dragons from taking the girls.

Those most susceptible to a dragon's love are girls who have not yet performed the ritual of *lazaruvane*, a procession of young, marriageable girls through the village. It's a celebration where girls (called *lazarki*) proclaim they are old enough to fall in love and get married. At one time, girls were forbidden to marry until they had participated in this ritual.[247]

These springtime rituals are dedicated to love and fertility, with the customs varying by location. A *lazarki* game called *kumichene* is a way to symbolically protect the girls from dragons. The girls dress in

Zmey Bride with "Dragon Scale" Bib.
Illustration by Nelinda. © Bendideia Publishing.

wedding attire, each piece being symbolic of fertility. In certain locations, the jewelry they wear on their chest resembles a dragon's scales. The girls also bake ritual bread called *kukli*, "dolls," which have snakelike (that is, dragon) designs on them.

One of their ritual games determines who will be the *kumitsa*, the leader of the girls. The chosen one's job is to protect the other *lazarki* from dragons until Easter. The girls toss wreaths or pieces of their dough "doll" into a river. Whichever girl's wreath floats the fastest to the other side, or whose doll surfaces first, is the winner. This ritual is symbolic of the girls' victory over the dragon.[248]

Part of the *kumichene* games includes the *buenets* dance. While many of these traditional dances are fast and performed in a circle, this dance is slower, the steps resembling the slithering of a snake. (You can watch a *buenets* performance here: https://www.youtube.com/watch?v=_K9es1WS4ew.)

After girls undergo these rituals, a dragon is not supposed to be able to kidnap or fall in love with them.

Researchers have suggested the custom is an "initiation into death."[249] This symbolic death is typical of initiation rites that transform youths (adolescent girls) into adults (sexually mature women).[250]

> In traditional culture, the ritual is played out, with the initiate dying symbolically and going to the beyond world, after which she returns to the world of the living, acquiring new knowledge and skills and with a higher social status.[251]

With the "death" of a girl's old self and rebirth as a full member of the community, she is now ready to undertake marriage.

The rituals get their name from St. Lazarus, who, as you may know, was the man Jesus raised from the dead. In sainthood, one of Lazarus' characteristics is that he personifies the boundary between life in this world and that in the next, and celebrations on his day are symbolic of nature's revival as it changes from winter's deathlike state to the rebirth of spring. This transition is a period of chaos, a time when people believe the dragon rules the world and gains control of fire and water.[252]

Herbs

In folk songs, the most common and effective way to rid yourself of a male or female dragon's love is with various types of what are called "Zmey's grass," in particular, herbs like tansy, meliot, and gentian varieties. These are called "separate herbs," because they have the "power of separating lovers,"[253] or "hateful herbs," since the dragon ends up hating you or falling out of love with you as the herbs separate you from his love.

Wormwood is another herb that's always good to have on hand. It's effective against dragons and other spirits and creatures that may try to harm you. Leaves from the walnut tree (*oreh*) are also useful for banishing dragons.[254] Other protective herbs and plants are hellebore, iris, primrose, yarrow, spiny rest-harrow, birthwort, yellow pheasant's eye, shepherd's lemongrass, and more. In folk medicine, many of these herbs are used as sedatives because they have "a calming, beneficial effect on the nervous system."[255] Before you begin any treatment, though, it's best to check with someone who knows the correct combination of herbs to use for a specific situation.

As with other magical, healing herbs, these "separate" herbs will be more powerful if you pick them at sunrise on special days, usually between May and September when the weather is favorable. Popular times are Eniovden (Midsummer's Day, June 24), from St. George's Day (May 6) through Spassovden (Ascension, forty days after Easter), between Mary's holy days (August 15 and September 8), or during Rusalka Week (also called "Green Week," approximately six or seven weeks after Easter).[256] And, if you can pick the herbs from special places, all the better.

"Separate" or "Hateful" Herbs.

Tansy (*Tanacetum vulgare*): Johann Georg Sturm (Painter: Jacob Sturm), 1796 (Bulgarian: Вратига, *Vratiga*).
Yellow sweet clover (*Melilotus officinalis*): Franz Eugen Köhler, Köhler's Medizinal-Pflanzen, 1897 (Bulgarian: Жълта комунига, *Zhŭlta komuniga*).
Great yellow gentian (*Gentiana lutea*): Franz Eugen Köhler, Köhler's Medizinal-Pflanzen, 1897 (Bulgarian: Жълта тинтява, Zhŭlta tintyava).

[Public domain], via Wikimedia Commons.

Common methods for applying the herbs include 1) wearing them, 2) burning them and spreading the smoke like incense, including burning hay in a field that contains the herbs, or 3) soaking them in water, then sprinkling the water on the victim or the place where the dragon resides.

Wearing Herbs

You can make a small bouquet or corsage (китка, *kitka*) of flowers. Bulgarians like to include a geranium (здравец, *zdravets*) among the flowers. Its leaves smell nice and protect against the evil eye, and bring health and strength to the wearer. Men often pin the *kitka* onto their shirt, while girls make herbal and floral wreaths to wear in their hair.

Another option is one my grandmother prescribed. Put a bit of yarrow under your pillow before you go to bed at night. Not only will it keep Zmey away, but it also provides a pleasant aroma, helping you fall asleep.

Burning Herbs

Burn herbs as incense to "fumigate" yourself if you've become a dragon's beloved. Have someone light the "separate" herbs in a dish and wave the smoke all around you. It's especially important to ensure the smoke reaches your hair,[257] which holds a wealth of symbolism in wedding customs.[258] The smoke from burning herbs will protect and purify you, and its smell will sicken Zmey so he'll no longer come near you.

It may even kill the dragon. If you've become unwell yourself because of his relentless pursuit, the smoke will help you recover from the illness.

If you forget which herbs are effective, you can trick the dragon into revealing which ones will drive him or her away. The dragon is not likely to suspect you intend to use them against him or her, as you'll discover in the continued story about Stoyan, in which his mother tells him to tell the dragon he wants to make a "certain Turk" hate his sister. The dragon tells him the effective herbs, and Stoyan's mother boils them at midnight.

> It was not the sister of Stoyan she anointed,
> But Stoyan himself.
> When even came,
> Lo! the she-bear came,
> She came from afar and cried out,—
> "Stoyan, dear Stoyan,
> How easily you have deceived me,
> And separated me from one whom I loved."[259]

When you can't trick Zmey or Zmeitsa into telling you which herbs work, you can try setting a field on fire, hoping that the right herbs are there. (This really isn't a good idea, so I wouldn't suggest it unless you have someone nearby who can put out the flames after the dragon leaves.) Radka, in the earlier poem, lit hay filled with herbs and escaped from being Zmey's bride, even though he was already carrying her away in his golden wedding chariot. The rest of the poem you read earlier continues below.

> They were passing through a green forest,
> And after that through a wide field—
> Toward them, five carts were coming,
> Five carts, full with sheaves and hay.
>
> Radka was telling the zmey:
> "Oh zmey, fiery and flaming,
> As you are so fiery and flaming,
> Could you light this hay,
> This hay, and also these sheaves?"
>
> The zmey was telling Radka:
> "Radka, you beautiful maiden,
> The sheaves, Radka, I can light,

> The hay, Radka, I cannot,
> That there are all kinds of herbs,
> *Kuma*, *komuniga*, and *tintyava*
> If I light the hay,
> I will part with you."
>
> Radka was cunning and clever,
> So she lit the hay herself,
> And she parted with the zmey.
> The zmey was telling Radka:
> "Radka, you beautiful maiden,
> Why were you so cunning and clever,
> And you played me so cunningly,
> And you parted with me!"[260]

Since Zmey can change into a wreath, sometimes the best way to get rid of him is to throw that foliage directly onto the hearth or into an oven. The item won't smoke, and the dragon doesn't burn up; instead, he'll return to his dragon form and abandon the one he loves.[261]

Herbal Water

Sprinkling or pouring magical herbal water on you purifies you and protects you from a dragon's advances. One method is to boil the herbs on an abandoned hearth, then "water" or sprinkle the concoction onto the afflicted person. Here's one woman's account of how to manage the process.

The zmey turns into anything. And he can thunder, light up, drag girls and women, love them, and then turn into something else. And if a zmey comes to you, pour yourself with the zmey's grasses—there is one zmey grass, windy grass, it is exactly for that, but you will also put *vratika* and *komunika*. You will boil them on Tuesday night and you will go somewhere to pour yourself, somewhere where nobody goes, because if someone steps on these decoctions, they will get sick.

One woman poured herself like that, but she entered someone else's garden and the other woman got sick, then the water answered [*probably meaning water magic, as a result of which the disease returns to the one that caused it and causes their death*], and the first one, the one that poured herself, died. Don't go to people's gardens, but go to the small river or to a crossroads. And you will get better—he will be defeated and he won't want you for his wife anymore.[262]

The steam itself from herbs boiling in water is enough to drive away Zmey. In the account below, fortune tellers (врачки, *vrachki*) and healers (баячки, *bayachki*) work together to accomplish this task. In Bulgaria, "fortune teller" and "healer" are rather synonymous, although a fortune teller mainly diagnoses the problem, while a healer provides the treatment. Often, however, both discover the disease and treat it: their rites have both a cognitive and a healing function.[263]

And then all the grandmothers, fortune tellers, old healers gathered and consulted there, they knew, they took herbs in the woods, they picked herbs, all kinds of herbs and they said to themselves: "Now one night you will go to bed to sleep."

And they took a big cauldron and put it on the hearth, on the fireplace like that. In the old days, there was a big cauldron full of water, they were putting all these herbs and they were boiling them, and with that, a zmey was driven away. And so they did. And in the middle of the night, something started to smoke, to smoke, as if, she says, something was breaking the tiles and snoring. But the grandmothers kept going—that cauldron was boiling intensively and the steam was coming out, and he couldn't come because of the steam. They did so for three nights in a row and they say that they drove the zmey away.[264]

You can also use herbs to make humans fall out of love with one another. If your mother-in-law is jealous of you, beware. She may go to a gypsy and get advice about how to get rid of you. Don't worry too much, though. A lot of conditions have to be met before the remedy she receives will work. First of all, she must place the "separate" herbs in a new clay pot and pour over them water that no one has touched. She can't do this any time; it has to be on a Friday night, before it turns into Saturday. Then, she'll have to get you to go to a deserted house. And you must be naked and bareheaded before she can pour the water over you.[265]

If she accidentally pours this herbal water on her son instead, she'll be in for a fright. He'll turn into a colorful Zmey from his waist downward. He'll slither off to his father's meadows, where a Zmeitsa is likely to fall in love with him. The human woman who loves him will have to find him and douse him again with the "hateful herbs." This has several effects: the Zmeitsa falls out of love with the man, he becomes fully human again, and he's more handsome than he was before.[266]

Be extra careful if you collect water from the village fountain or well, even if you're bringing a gift for the guardian spirit, which is the customary thing to do before you take water. You'll want to make sure you're protected before you venture out, and always tell the dragon the truth. Zmey stands guard by the water, ready to seize his bride. In the case of Rada in the song below, she's accustomed to bringing him gifts, but this time, it doesn't go the way she planned.

Rada Carried Off by a Dragon

Rada went to fetch some water
From the Fountain of the Dragons.
As she homeward was returning,
On the way she met two Dragons,
Two fierce Dragons, flaming creatures.
One goes by and harms not Rada,
But the younger stops fair Rada,
Slakes his thirst from out her pitcher.
Then he Rada thus addresses:
"Rada, Rada mine, my dearest,
Every eve you've come to see me
You have brought a brighter posy
Than the one you bring this evening."
Rada answered thus the Dragon:
"Dragon, Dragon, flaming creature,
Let me go my way, O Dragon!
Sick in bed my mother's lying,
Sorely does she pine for water."
Said the Dragon unto Rada:
"Rada, beautiful and youthful,
You may lie to any other,
But you'll not deceive a Dragon,
Soaring in aerial regions,
With keen eye the ether piercing.
I've just passed above your cottage.
There I saw thy mother sitting,

Thy wise mother, the enchantress.
She for thee did sew a garment,
To it divers herbs she fastened,
All the herbs which love do hinder,
Souls divide, and hatred kindle.
So that I may hate thee, Rada,
She has witched the woods and waters;
She has ta'en a living serpent,
In a cauldron new she's placed it,
Fire of thistles white she's lighted.
In the cauldron writhed the serpent,
Writhed and hissed he in his fury
While her spells thy mother chanted:
'As this serpent writhes in torture,
For the love they bear to Rada
Thus may writhe both Turks and Bulgars,
And the fiery Dragon hate thee,
So the Dragon, hating, leave thee.'
Since her spell has not availed,
Hence with me I now will bear you."
Hardly had the Dragon spoken
Than he seized upon the maiden,
Bore her up unto the welkin,
Bore her to the mountain summits,
Hid her in the darksome caverns.[267]

In a variation of this song, Zmey lets Rada bring the water home to her mother, and he waits for her promised return. After waiting for three days and nights, he realizes she isn't coming back, so he goes after her.

The Zmey jumped over
Into Rada's garden,
And he grabbed the white Rada,

So Zmey took her
Right into the deep caves.[268]

Similar to how to remove Zmey's love, you can collect special "hateful" herbs to make Zmeitsa fall out of love with a man. Some of these are cattle sweet clover (*komuniga*) and shepherd's lemongrass, which you can find at a gypsy campsite. Once you've boiled the herbs, you must pour the water over Zmeitsa and the man she loves. First, you have to wait until the two of them are hiding within the branches of a thorny, rose hip bush.[269] Good luck with that.

In the village of Pirin, in southwestern Bulgaria, where the ancestor of the famous Pirin dragon still lives, villagers reveal a harsher side of dragon lore. Since a dragon can love a girl from birth, it was common practice to douse her with herbal concoctions if a family suspected a dragon loved her. This remedy, when applied to infants in real life, however, often produced disastrous results.

In the early nineteen twenties, villagers will tell you, a bright light lit the room where Nikolina was sleeping in a cradle. It was the dragon Gincho coming from the mountains to lay claim to his future bride. As she grew, she became the most beautiful girl dancing at the *horo*.

ZS [Zlata Stoimenova]: And she was very pretty, Nikolina. The most beautiful maiden on the *horo* was her. And as she was dancing the *horo*, she started sleeping. So the zmey came there, above the *horo*, to take her. And she left, and her mother went after her to check what was going on with her daughter.

VB [Vihra Baeva]: So she left the *horo*? As she was sleeping, she went somewhere?

ZS: Yes, she left. She came home and went to bed. And the mother came to her and saw that one head was lying next to her, a handsome man, a blond head. Lying next to her, she was sleeping. And then her mother went down to the neighbor and said: "What are we going to do with our girl? A zmey loves her. What can we do to make her give up on him?" And she said to her, "Let's pick one herb, named *stovraz*. Let's boil it and sprinkle your girl with it. And he'll give up on her." And the mother agreed. They picked up that herb, boiled it, and poured it on the girl. And she became incapable, incompetent, and not good at anything.

VB: And was it because of the herb or because of the zmey that loved her?

LB [Lyubimka Biserova]: Because of the herb. She scalded her, the mother.

ZS: And the zmey didn't come anymore?

A View to the Pirin Village in Bulgaria. Photo by Deyan Vasilev (Dido3).
ShareAlike 2.5 Generic (CC BY-SA 2.5): https://creativecommons.org/licenses/by-sa/2.5/legalcode.

VB: He never came close to her again.
ZS: We remember that Nikolina.
LB: As children.
N [Aunt Nedyalka]: We were students.
VB: What was wrong with her?
LB: She was burned whole, withered.
N: She had scars.[270]

Nikolina lived, to be tormented by the other children because of her deformities. She sang long, strange songs, the tune echoing around the otherwise quiet village. She died in 1966.[271] She is said to be the last love of the Gincho Zmey of the mountains.

Another mother at that time did the same for her baby girl, Maria, hoping to make her ugly so the dragon would leave her alone. Maria was burned so badly she didn't survive the "cure."[272] Whether the herb used in these cases was poisonous or the liquid was too hot is unknown.[273]

Other Remedies

Besides using herbs or making sure you participate in the *lazaruvane* spring rituals, you can try some of the following remedies to deter Zmey.

Dragon's Eye or Scale

Wearing something that came from the dragon's body, like his eye (змеино око, *zmeino oko*) or a scale (отриш от змей, *otrish ot zmeĭ*), is one method of protecting yourself from him. You may have to dig into the ground to find his eye. It embeds itself there during a thunderstorm. The old folks like to say: "It happens that the zmey somehow pulls out his eye, he hits himself and it falls. It's as big as a walnut. They soak it in water, and wear it like a necklace around the neck, under the garment."[274]

Even more difficult to find, they say, is a dragon scale. It's small, like ones on a fish, but remains hidden under the dragon's feathers. Sometimes, a scale falls to the ground when it thunders.[275] Other times, you can find one in the river, where a dragon bathes in the spring and changes his scales.[276] It's easier to find a female dragon's scale, because it'll multiply after it's fallen. If you find one, you can tie it in a rag with wax and an old coin. Then sew it into your clothing for protection.[277]

> **Did you know?**
>
> If you kill a dragon and eat its heart, you'll gain the dragon's strength (All About Dragons, "Zmej.").

Bodily Substances

Another way to repel Zmey is with various bodily substances—both human and animal. In folk medicine, saliva, tears, urine, feces, and menstrual blood are widely used to treat ailments and protect against evil forces.[278] Some actions you can take are:

- Smear the girl with human excrement.[279]
- Pour a black bull's urine on Zmey (or where you think he's lying, since he'll be invisible). You'll hear a whistling noise; that means the dragon has disappeared.[280]
- Toss Zmey's own urine on him to discern if he's human or a creature.

The story below demonstrates how Zmey's urine can reveal his identity. A young man had been keeping a girl in a cave, but she pestered him to let her go home to visit her mother, until he finally agreed. He, however, said he'd wait for the girl in a meadow overgrown with shrubs while she visited her mother.

Zapryan Dtsmchev: … He looked like a young man, not like a zmey and the girl had never seen him in another shape, he always looked like a man. So he said, "I am staying here. You go now to meet your mother! Once you are done, come back here at the turn of the road and start singing, then I will meet you and we will go home!"

Konstantin Rangochev: Which song?

Z.D.: No matter which one. Okay, then she came here, to her mother who was living in the upper part of the village, I don't know which house exactly. She came to her mother who was kneading bread dough at that time. When the mother saw her she started thinking weird things, because you know at that time people believed in such miracles. So the mother felt scared, but the girl reassured her: "It is me, mother, do not be scared!"

And she told her the whole story. Then her mother said, "Well, looks like a zmey loves you." The girl answered, "That's not true. He is a wonderful young man. He is not a zmey." And her mother said, "Listen now. A zmey loves you. If you don't believe it"—she gave her a pair of *terlichki* [*shoes made of thick woolen fabric or thick woolen yarn*]—"do not wear *tsarvuli* [*leather sandals with blunt tips tied onto feet with long cords*] or shoes! Take these *terlichki* and walk silently from here to the meadow, it is not far to get there. Go and see who is sleeping on the meadow! Just check and come back!"

So the girl went and indeed there was a big zmey sleeping in the meadow. She walked back wearing the *terlichki* and said to her mother: "Indeed, a zmey loves me."

The old woman, the mother, was some kind of a witch, so she did what she did and gave the girl one *masurka*. I don't know if you understand what *masurka* is, it is made of reed, with a hole in the middle, a hole in the middle.

K.R.: Uh-huh.

Z.D.: And the mother said: "Take this *masurka*, dress up and go, when you reach the turn of the road start singing! Then the zmey will meet you. Hug him and flirt as young people do, then tell him: "Now let's compete peeing!"

"What do you mean to compete peeing?"

"To see who can pee farther, me or you. To pee through the *masurka*. Through the *masurka*. Argue with him until you make him pee first because he is a boy! Make him pee first. Don't agree to be first! When he starts peeing, take in your hand some of the piss that comes out of the *masurka* and splash it in his face! Then see what will happen!" And she did like she was told. She went there and they started flirting, then he agreed to pee first. When he started peeing she splashed some piss into his face and he exploded, flared up and burnt out in the walnut forest. And everything around burst into flames and burnt out, and since then they call the place The burnt walnuts. You can ask all the people in Yugovo where The burnt walnuts are, they are there. And the story ends here. It ends.

K.R.: What was the zmey like?

Z.D.: Well, he exploded, he…

K.R.: No, I mean his body, what was it like?

Z.D.: She did not see him. She could not see him as a zmey. She was always seeing him as a man, as…

Rosen Malchev: But he was sleeping in the meadow, right?

> Z.D.: She saw him as zmey, but…a monster lying there, I don't know, she is a girl, she got scared or something, so how it was exactly, I cannot say. So since then the zmey is no longer in *Zmeeva dupka*, many people have been there.[281]

An analysis of this Zmey account follows:

- Zmey remains outside the village, because to enter it poses a threat to his life. Even so, he meets his death at the border between the human world and the world beyond.
- The mother is a type of sorceress, knowledgeable in life's secrets and the ways to identify and destroy evil beings like the dragon. She stays within the human realm, signifying she is a hearth, a pillar that sustains the village.
- The girl acts as a mediator between demons and humans. She can pass from one realm to the other, because of her ability to conceive, which puts her in an in-between state, between life and death. She signifies purity and human energy.
- Silence is a characteristic of the other world, while singing and whistling are inherent in the human world. And so, Zmey makes the request of the girl to sing as she approaches, while the mother advises her to be silent in order to deceive the dragon.[282]

Implements

To ward off dragons, you can use things like yokes, pails, *kavals* (shepherd's pipes), and wedding cups made from magical trees, such as sycamore (*yavor*) and ash (*yassen*).[283]

Animals

Ride a horse if you need to travel any distance, especially at night. Besides the fact that a horse is a faithful and loyal animal, a dragon can't harm anyone riding on such a creature. A horse can sense danger and gallop away to keep you safe.[284]

Listen to Dreams

A village man named Petko was unfortunate enough to have a dragon love his wife. He was at wit's end what to do, until an old man came to him in a dream. The man told Petko to make his wife walk nine days. So together they left, walking where they chose. Upon returning, the wife was healed; the dragon no longer came to love her. The wife didn't appear to appreciate her husband's efforts, and said, "God! This dragon comes at night and does not leave me alone, but Petko, my husband, sleeps!"[285]

Cart Ritual

In some villages, people continue with their old traditions for curing a dragon's treacherous love.

> The parents took the girl on a cart without the sides and took her outside the village in the direction of the sun. When they reached an incline, they disassembled the cart, and parts were thrown to different sides. This was done by strangers many years ago when it was suspected that a girl was in love with a snake.[286]

Violence

If all else fails, you can attempt to destroy the source of the problem—Zmey himself. If he's been sneaking into your house through the chimney, you can set a cauldron of boiling water in the fireplace.[287] When he makes his way down—in a manner similar to the wolf trying to eat up the three little pigs—*Splash!* He'll burn up. Problem solved.

MOVIE:
HE IS DRAGON

In olden times, to keep their village safe, people offered their daughters as brides to a dragon, called "the darkness." They dressed the girls in wedding attire, set them afloat in boats on the lake, and sang an ancient wedding song to summon the beast. Little did they know the actual horror that awaited the girl in the dragon's den.

In the Russian village from this movie, the wedding tradition continues as a "charming old custom," because the dragon is no more. The Dragon Slayer vanquished him ages ago. Or did he? Watch for yourself as the tale of Mira and Arman unfolds.

Sources:
Movie: Siamashka, Volha. "He is dragon (English Version) HD." April 2, 2018. https://www.youtube.com/watch?v=K9yi_DzmNy4.
Review: The Idle Woman. "I Am Dragon (Он – Дракон) (2015)." August 12, 2018. https://theidlewoman.net/2018/08/12/i-am-dragon-он-дракон/.

Castle on the Water.
Illustration by e71lena. Stock illustration via Depositphotos.

An even more drastic measure is to find the hollow beech tree he lives within. To rid yourself of your infatuated beast, set the tree on fire. You can then make a suet using his ashes. This will repel the amorous advances of any future dragons.[288]

How to Defeat

While you'll do everything you can to protect yourself and your family from Zmey's amorous advances, you really don't want to defeat your own Zmey. When he's not chasing the lovely ladies, he's fighting other dragons in order to protect your village. Nonetheless, he does have enemies who desire to destroy him, like Hala, whom you'll learn about later in this book. Even though he's stronger than she is, Hala has a nasty habit of being able to wound or kill Zmey with a sharp fragment from a broken *podnitsa*, an earthenware tray used to cook on coals. In the same way that stone arrows have been the dragon's weapons since ancient times, this clay type of baking dish is "one of the most primitive implements for preparing food." As it was readily available when our ancient ancestors lacked other weapons, the *podnitsa* became "a chief weapon in the war on the dragon."[289]

> ### Did you know?
>
> Zmey bones are poisonous, and their sting causes death (Baeva, 151).

You'll want to give Zmey all the help he needs whenever a thunderstorm approaches, because that's the signal that Hala is on her way. Put every *podnitsa* away. If you've broken one, even if a storm isn't imminent, grind the pieces into dust, to make sure Hala has no weapon to strike Zmey with. You'll want to go to that extra trouble, because if your guardian Zmey is wounded, the weather in your village is going to get nasty. Expect torrential rainstorms or hail that will destroy your crops. In certain cases, Zmey can reverse the situation and use a piece of a *podnitsa* to defeat Hala—if the clay for the tray was kneaded on St. Jeremiah's day (May 1).[290]

Chasing the Zmey

When a Zmey other than yours settles in your village, because your Zmey has been unable to defeat him, you'll want to drive away the intruder. He's not there to protect anyone. You'll know an evil foreign Zmey resides nearby, because he'll "lock up" the water in all your sources: wells, springs, rivers, and even the clouds, and your land will suffer from drought.

One way to get rid of him is by cutting down the tree he resides in. Beware, however, doing this will soon afterward also cause the death of the person who cuts down the tree.[291]

A more effective way is to perform a ceremony called "Chasing the Zmey" (Гонене на змей, *Gonene na zmeĭ*). Drought, however, may occur due to other reasons, so before you undertake this action, make sure Zmey really is the one causing the problem. To do this, first perform other rain-inducing rituals: the Peperuda (Пеперуда) and the Herman (Герман).

The Peperuda is a word that means "butterfly." This is a rain-calling ritual that young girls perform. The group covers one girl with greenery and pours water over her as they lead her around the village. She waves her arms as though flying like a butterfly.

The Herman ritual is also performed by girls in order to bring rain. They make a mud or clay figure of a man, with a large phallus. Crossing his arms to look like a dead person, they put him into a coffin and mourn him. They bury him near a river or crossroads or throw him into a river.

The failure of these rituals to produce results (that is, rain) means one thing: Zmey is causing the drought. And so, he needs to be chased away from the village.

Two variants of the "Chasing the Zmey" custom exist: expulsion and erotic. Both have aspects of initiation and restoration of fertility, but the importance between the two functions varies. The expulsion version focuses on initiation; it's called the classic or serious version and is described as "nocturnal," "not provoking laughter," and "beyond" (referring to the world of the dead). The aspect of fertility is more prominent in the erotic version, which is referred to with the words "day," "laughing," and "festive." What they have in common is that the ritual of "expelling the dragon" is a way to "restore the equilibrium" of the village when drought has disturbed its harmony.[292]

Expulsion Version

The most common practice, the dragon expulsion, is a ceremony for unmarried men only, regardless of their age. As long as they're strong and healthy, they can join the ritual. However, the rest of the village shouldn't know who's participating. No one should even look at the men or watch the night's undertakings. If you try to sneak a peek, you're doomed to be hit by a bell or other object one of the men carries, because he may mistake you for the dragon. It's better if you pretend you don't hear anything and stay out of the way. Widespread knowledge of the partakers means the night's activities will fail.[293]

The village herald travels to every house and yells out the date the ceremony will take place. Everyone then knows to leave their doors open that night, so the men can enter. It's also a warning to girls, brides, and really any women to remain hidden, so the dragon doesn't come after them and carry them away to his cave. Everyone else who's not involved should hide inside, too, because the men chasing the dragon may accidentally beat anyone who ventures outside.[294]

The men gather by the river at midnight and strip off all their clothing and foot attire. Their leader, an old man called the *palich*, lights straw and walks around the group waving the fire like incense to "drive

Silhouette of Giant Monster.
Illustration by zeferli. Stock Image via Depositphotos.

the devils out of them."[295] After their ritual cleansing, the young men jump into the river and bathe, without making a sound. They believe the power of the water carries away all the evil energies the smoking straw released from them.[296]

When they've eradicated the evil from around them, the *palich* leads them throughout the village. They make sure they walk around the entire yard and visit everyone's home, outbuildings, watermills, beehives, and every niche they can find. In a small village, all the men will stay together. However, in a larger place, they may form several groups.

They must walk in complete silence. If anyone makes a noise, Zmey is certain to hit the offender, who then suffers a severe illness—or even dies. Although the men themselves don't speak, they make as much of a clamor as possible with the implements they carry: axes, clubs, iron pokers, thick sticks, shepherds' crocks, tin cans, bells, rattles, whistles, buckets—anything to show the dragon they mean business. Of course, this clatter gets neighborhood dogs riled up, and they join in the cacophony.

The men beat iron vessels and drag sticks along fences. They poke their weapons into every place they think the dragon can hide: gardens, piles of hay, and even weeds in the yard and shrubs along paths to the village. Some men wave their weapons threateningly in the air, while others overturn chests, barrels, and troughs. Inside the homes, the men shake their hands toward each corner and possible place the dragon may hide. They do whatever they deem necessary to frighten the dragon so he'll run away from the village.

Zmey remains invisible throughout the night, so it's important that someone born on a Saturday attend the ceremony. These people can see supernatural creatures. Once the men find the dragon, the one who can see him ties up the creature with a horsehair or goat's hair rope.[297]

When the men have finished their route around the village, the *palich* leads them to the cemetery, where he lights a new divine fire. Until this point, no fires can be lit inside or outside the homes, and no water can be left uncovered. The other participants in the rite circle their leader, drive their sticks into the ground, and howl like wolves. The *palich* jumps over the fire, and then pours water on it to put it out. Not any water will do. He uses water he left uncovered overnight by the cemetery fountain.[298] In Poland, they drive Zmij toward a fire they've built outside the village, and continue their dance. Insulted, the dragon runs away to torment another village.[299]

The ceremony concludes at dawn with the men returning to the river. They throw the *palich* into the water, grab their clothes, and run home before he drags himself out of the river.

A resident of a village provides a different account of the ceremony that happened in the past in his community.

> Chasing a zmey is done when there is a drought everywhere. There are snake herbs, but you can't chase a zmey with them. The chasing takes place the night after the Pemperuga [*Peperuda*]. It's done by bachelor boys. They gather in their neighborhoods first, but then at night it is done in the whole village. The bachelors go out somewhere around one or two o'clock—at "a secret time" they go. They go only in their underpants. They undress at home and go in their underpants. They wear pokers [*ръжен, razhen, a tool for poking the embers and logs in order to stir up the fire*] and ogribkas [*огрипка, an iron spatula used for scraping the wooden trough in which bread was kneaded in the past, or for scraping the burnt parts off of bread*] and make noise with them. They walk only on the streets, they don't enter the houses. And with pokers and *ogribkas* they rattle. They walk around the wells and the small river and make noise there, so that the zmey doesn't hide there. They do not bathe, only rattle. And they mutter. They do not dare to speak. The one that speaks will fall and die. They just mutter.
>
> Grandma Yana told me that before the bachelors used to go with iron forks, so if they met a dragon, they would stab it. Later on they started using pokers and *ogribkas*.

In the village no one makes any noise and does not speak. They won't even watch. They pretend not to hear anything. If anyone sees the bachelors, everything will fail. A girl should not go out at this time, not be grabbed by the zmey while running.

Some bachelors are engaged with the chasing, some watch. If they see light far away, then it is the zmey, they have chased away the zmey.[300]

Those who participate in the ceremony resemble Zmey: naked, silent, and invisible to others. Do they become like the dragon so they can fight the beast? Or does the ritual have a deeper meaning?

In the past, this ceremony wasn't meant to persecute the dragon by having Zmey hunters chase him, but it was a way to remove an old Zmey and replace him with a younger one. It was a rite of passage for boys, one that symbolically turned them into Zmeĭove themselves. The *palich*, the old man, represents the old dragon. He demonstrates to the younger ones how to light and extinguish a new, living, divine fire. A younger boy (or perhaps even several) then passes through the fire and water. After the ceremony, the old man is tossed into the river so the younger one can become the new dragon.[301]

Erotic Version

The second variant of the Chasing the Zmey custom has more of an erotic nature. It's performed by both single men and single women. The males are between fifteen and twenty years old, and the females are between eighteen and twenty years old. Although its purpose is still to bring rain, it's not a somber occasion and has been called a "laughing" festival. The young people gather in the village square, each attired in old clothing, not the normal festive clothing worn for many rituals. One male and female are chosen to represent the dragon. The male dresses in women's clothing and the female in men's clothing.[302]

The following is how a villager describes this ceremony.

They walk and the others after them are saying:
"Well, well, well, well, well! You, zmey! Well, well, well, well, well! You, zmey!"
They go from the lower end along the river to the end of the village, then across the river, and back down the river. They pass through the fountains and splash themselves with water. Everyone is laughing. The others splash the two, who represent the dragon, with cups, kettles [*котле, kotle, a copper water vessel*]. Everyone has taken a kettle and has dressed in tattered clothes. It starts after dinner and continues until eleven-twelve o'clock. They hit tin cans to scare the zmey. Some people go out of their houses and are splashed with water. All have to be wet. *Jumbush*! [*Джумбуш, merriment, entertainment, a joke*] Well, bachelors can pinch a maiden! They can kiss her! *Jumbush*! Donkeys are rolling on the maiden doors.[303]

Such a laughing festival, with its gaiety, pinching, and kissing, is said to raise "the erotic status" of the young people within their social and cultural setting.[304]

How to Appease

Remember that Zmey protects your village and water supplies. In return, you can do things for him to show your appreciation. Bring him an offering when you come to the village fountain to get water, as Rada did in an earlier song you read.

Every eve you've come to see me
You have brought a brighter posy
Than the one you bring this evening."[305]

Be careful you don't overdo your gifts if you're a girl, or Zmey may get the wrong idea and think you want to be his bride.

Another occasion when you can cater to him is if he becomes wounded after a fight with another dragon. Take care of him until he can fly again and make the sky friendly. If you recall, his favorite food is fine white bread, but he also enjoys honey. His favorite drink besides wine is milk.[306]

One tale tells of a woman who tended to a fallen dragon.

> In a sheepfold, an old woman fed a dragon wounded by a whirlwind on honey. On the fortieth day, it told her to leave the door open and flew out like a big fire. The old woman's bin was never empty as the dragon filled it up secretly.[307]

Another story relates how three elderly women regularly bring fresh milk to their Zmeĭove, two brothers, who lived in their area. The women pour it into a clay bowl, glazed green inside, the type of vessel traditionally used to cast spells.[308] The women leave the offering in the branches of an old dogwood, where the Zmeĭove live. Whenever it empties, they fill it again, hoping it makes the dragons meek.

One of the women describes the dragon she saw when she was bringing the milk:

> I heard something in the field screaming like a small child. I stopped in the field and I saw the zmey lying in the rye. Half—from the waist up—a man, and from the waist down—a fish with scales, scales like silver.[309]

Unfortunately, a goatherd killed the other Zmey after the man found the dragon drinking milk from his goat. Misfortune befell the man because of this, and two of his children died soon afterward.

If you bring Zmey bread, you may want to perform a ritual similar to one that women in the Sakar mountain region do.

> Three widows knead the dough and bake three loaves of bread [*кравай, kravai, round ritual bread with a hole in the middle*]. While doing this, they are naked and observe ritual silence. The next day after sunset, they leave the bread, which is smeared with honey, under a "zmey's tree". At the root of the tree they slaughter a black hen. The sacrifice is for the zmey, which must protect the village from natural disasters and diseases.[310]

A popular story exists among villagers about a deer that came every year to voluntarily be a *kurban* (blood sacrifice) to appease their Zmey. People gathered to dance the *horo* and hold festivities in a meadow.

> The roe deer was always coming on its own; they were slaughtering it and making the *kurban*. Then dividing it between everyone on the *horo* and going home. All good, but one year the young came there and danced the *horo* until the sun went down, but the roe deer did not show up. Usually when the roe deer was coming, they had to leave it first to lie down and rest. After resting for some time, they could slaughter it and cook it there for the *kurban*. But the last time the roe deer got there very late. It was all wet and covered with foam; most probably it had been chased by an animal, a wolf or another one. So the roe deer came late and fell on the ground. And because it was already very late and the sun was going down there was no time to wait for it so they slaughtered it right away. And they put it into the boiling pot. And the young ones started dancing.[311]

The result of this failure of the deer to arrive on time was that Zmey came in a whirlwind and captured a girl instead.

Zmey Cave.
Illustration by Nelinda. © Bendideia Publishing.

On the Dark Side

While Zmey among the Balkan Slavs is mostly benevolent, the same species of dragon among the Eastern Slavs is seen more in a negative context.[312] People in this area have often sought the services of a dragon slayer, because when their Zmey captures or demands maidens, it isn't to satisfy the dragon's amorous desires; instead, blood lust drives him. This type of dragon is called Lamia in some locations and will be covered in more detail in that chapter.

Besides requiring maiden sacrifices, the evil Zmey causes destruction of land as in this folk song.

> Its soul brings a torrent down,
> Its wings crush the forest,
> Its feet trample down the forest,
> Whenever it passes, everything withers away,
> Wherever it stands, everything dries up.[313]

This type of dragon is also called Hala in various regions and will be discussed in more detail in that chapter.

Zmey Tales

A Zmey and a Peacock Love a Maiden

A dragon may find himself in a situation where he has a rival for a girl's affection. A peacock and a Zmey once wanted the love of pretty girls. Instead of fighting over them, they decide to wait at the village fountain and throw items to attract the girls.

Note: "Le" (ле) in the song below doesn't have a particular meaning; it's used to emphasize the name or title of the person addressed.

Peacock, colo… bird
Peacock, colorful bird,
Zmeyo le, goryanine le!
The zmey tells the peacock:
"Peacock, you colorful bird,
Do not come to my territory,
Do not love the woman I love!"
"Zmeyo le, goryanine le,
It is not good to have a quarrel,
It is not good to be angry!
Wait tonight,
Tonight at the fountain,
Where girls pour water
And young brides wash fabrics,
There we will compete.
You will throw small pearls
I will throw small feathers.
The maiden that collects pearls,
That maiden will be yours,
The maiden that collects feathers,
That maiden will be mine!"
So they stayed and waited,
And the young maidens gathered,
The young maidens on the fountain.
The peacock throws small feathers.
The zmey throws small pearls.
All the maidens collect feathers,
Only Yana collects pearls
And she goes crazy,
She goes crazy, she goes wild.[314]

73

The Pirin Dragon

You've read about how women in the village of Pirin unintentionally maimed and killed girls with boiling herbal water to protect them from being loved by a dragon. The story that follows is a well-known tale about their ancestral dragon.

Accarding to legend, a dragon in Pirin seized a pretty girl named Stana, who was dancing at a *horo* on Easter. He took her away from the village and brought her to his home, called Dragon's Hole, where she became his bride. After some time, she bore him a son named Gincho, who was unusually large and had wings beneath his arms.

One sunny day the zmey stretched and yawned in front of their cave. He said to Stana, "I think I'll take a nap. Sit down next to me, and I'll lie on your lap. But be on your guard and protect me. If you see even the smallest cloud coming from the Belasitsa mountain range, wake me up immediately."

"Very well," she said.

And the zmey lay on Stana's lap and fell asleep. After a while, Stana saw a small cloud forming in the mountains, but she didn't want to wake up the zmey. The cloud got closer and was growing larger. As it passed the village of Katuntsi, the cloud grew even larger. She shook her husband, trying to wake him, but he continued to sleep soundly. Stana started crying because she'd waited too long, disobeying the zmey's command to let him know immediately. Her tears fell on him and he woke up. When he saw the cloud approaching, he entered the cave to get his mace. It was too late. Another zmey exploded out of the cloud, broke into the cave, and killed Stana's husband.

The widow Stana left the mountain with her child and returned to her father's home. This boy had extraordinary strength. By the age of three, he was so strong he went with his grandfather to the mountains to gather firewood. When the boy was thirteen or fourteen, he helped his grandfather to dig for coal, as his grandfather was a coal miner. They went to a place called Tsvyatkov Grob, where there was a lake. Today it is dry, but then it was a lake. The boy kept walking around the lake, but the grandfather didn't pay much attention to that.

A few years later, when the boy turned sixteen, he said, "Grandpa, listen. I'm going to tell you something, and I want you to do exactly as I say."

"What is it, son?" he said.

"Buy a ram and kill it."

"Why do you need that?"

"Don't ask me now," the boy said. "Just choose one with a lot of fat."

After questioning the boy for a while, the grandfather finally agreed. He bought a ram and slaughtered it.

"Now take the fat," the boy said, "and form it into tallow balls."

The grandfather did as he was told.

The boy said to him, "The zmey that killed my father is in the lake. I'm going to go inside and fight him."

"Don't go. He's too strong," the grandfather said. "He'll kill you, too!"

"Don't be afraid," the boy said. "Just listen carefully, and remember what I tell you. When I go into the lake, the water will get stirred up as we start fighting. If you see a blue flame come up, throw a ball of tallow into the water, so I can eat it to increase my strength. And if you see a red flame, don't throw anything in. Don't forget!" [*The giving of tallow is suggestive of ancient sacrificial practices to the serpent master.*[315]]

The boy jumped into the lake and fought with his father's killer. The water rippled, and a blue flame shot out. The grandfather threw in a tallow ball. When a red flame erupted, he held onto the balls. Every time, he saw a blue flame, he tossed in a tallow ball, until they were gone. Finally, the boy emerged from the lake, carrying his opponent's liver and heart. The lake dried up, its water ran out and now it is called Dried lake (Сухо езеро, *Suho ezero*).

"Well, Grandpa, I defeated him. It was so tiring. I need to sleep now," the boy said. "Make a shish kebab with the heart and liver and roast it for me. But be careful not to taste it."

"Not to worry," the grandfather said, "I don't want to eat a liver from a zmey!"

So, the grandfather lit the fire, cut the meat, made the skewer, and started roasting it. But when he turned the meat over, he scalded his hand and unwittingly licked it. When the meat was cooked, the grandfather hung the shish kebab next to a pine tree.

Soon, the boy woke up and said, "Well, Grandpa, what did you do?"

"Yes, I baked it."

"I can tell you ate from it, when I told you not to."

"No, I didn't."

"You didn't, huh? I know you ate some," the boy said. "Go and push that pine tree."

The grandfather pushed the pine, and it toppled to the ground.

"See, Grandpa, you lied to me," the boy said.

"I didn't intend to." He told the boy what happened.

"Okay. Come here and spit on my hand!"

The grandfather spat on the boy's hand, and the boy licked the spit.

"Now, Grandpa, go push the other pine."

The grandfather did, and nothing happened.

Then the boy said, "Well, Grandpa, we have to say goodbye. I'm now the new zmey."

The boy flew away and settled on the Chaushka Rock. When the weather is clear, villagers see a small white cloud visible on the top of the mountain. The zmey protects the land of Pirin the way his father once had. He even helps people build their houses, carrying huge stones weighing a half ton to use as the foundation stones. From time to time, the zmey takes his due and comes to the village to select the best girl for his bride.

And this is the legend.[316]

Hala (Хала)

Let the hala break it like a tree!

Name variations
Bulgaria: hala, khala (хала) (plural, hali – хали)
North Macedonia: ala (ала) (plural, ali – али)
Serbia: ala (ала) (plural, ale – але)

Related names: Lamia, Aždaja, Kulshedra

Slang: Gluttonous people are called hali, while those who work hard are said to work like a hala. Used in oaths or curses: "Hala to break you," "Hala to blow you,"[317] or "Go to the halas!"[318]

Hala is a female dragon or weather demon found in Bulgarian, Serbian, and Macedonian folklore. The serpent-like Hala surfaced in the area after the Slavs immigrated to the Balkans.[319] The creature has been influenced by the Greeks and Turks, but it's thought that a being possessing these characteristics, but going by another name, existed prior to the influence of these nations.[320]

She's Zmey's sister. Like him, she's mainly a generic creature. However, she has earned herself a personal name in some stories: Smiljana, Ogršćana, Kalina, Magdalena, Dobrica, Bugarka, Jevrosia Ruskinja, Dragija, Zagorka, or Ilenka Rumunka.[321] She appears more often in "the figurative world of songs (heroic, mythical and ritual), fairy tales (magical and humorous), legends and myths," than she does in the oral accounts of witnessed events.[322]

Origins

You've already learned that dragons evolve from regular snakes and other creatures when certain conditions have been met. When an ordinary snake lives for forty years, it can become a Hala; from that point onward, it lives in the sky as far away as the stars, rather than residing on land.[323] However, this isn't always where their development ends. They also transform over time. Different dragon species have an association with various realms: Zmey with the underworld (and also the heavens), Lamia (and others) with the land, and Hala with the air.[324] And, it's in this order, some say, that the dragon has evolved: from under the land, to a creature of the land, to a being belonging to the air.

> According to popular knowledge, "... the dragon after many years becomes aloof and no longer lives on earth, but in the sky and the stars. And the stars that are seen flying in the sky are nothing but *hali*." … This spatial journey from the underworld to the sky is possible when experiencing the appropriate age—from 40 to 100 years for the conversion of the snake / fish into a *zmey* and then "long years", unspecified in number, for the transition to another status—*ala*.[325]

As mentioned in the Zmey chapter, people also believed that a human child born with a large head and small body, or with wings under the arms, was considered a dragon. A girl was called a Hala or a Lamia, while a boy was a Zmey.

Etymology

Different views exist on the original meaning of the word "Hala." Various dictionaries say it comes from the Turkish word *àla* for "snake" (Markov, N., 213).

Many etymologists disagree with this. Some believe the word has Thracian roots, coming from *ala* (*hala*) for "whirlwind" (Markov, N., 214, footnote 17). Or perhaps it was adopted from Hellenized Thracians (MacDermott, 64), or *hala* comes from the Greek word χάλαζα (*cnalaza* or *khalaza*) for "hail" (Baeva, 399).

Others say it originally stems from the Proto-Slavic **xal-*, which represents elemental fury; the original meaning meant disaster or storm, which was associated with a storm-causing demon whose attributes included enormous size, strength, and gluttony (Bjeletić, "Јужнословенска лексика," 144-145). From this meaning, all other word associations developed: rage, madness, excessive size, gluttony, and so on (Bjeletić, "Јужнословенска лексика," 144).

Additional thoughts about the name say the initial "h" in variations of the name is linguistically difficult to explain. With this reasoning, they say *hala* has a basis in the Indo-European *holiti/haliti*, meaning "to throw" (Markov, N., 214).

Hala may not always have been considered evil. As you've learned, snakes and dragons portray dualistic symbolism, embodying both life and death. While Zmey gained the beneficial characteristics of snakes, Hala and other female dragons like Lamia took on the creature's destructive, antagonistic qualities. These negative attributes merged with those of terrifying and bloodthirsty female demons existing in the Balkans, and the image of an evil Hala (and Lamia) emerged.[326]

According to ancient legends, Hali have a Greek beginning. They're daughters of the supreme god Zeus and one of his dalliances, Lamia. Hera, Zeus's wife, slaughtered most of Lamia's offspring, but some managed to escape. Another account says their father was not Zeus, but a giant who lived north of Greece.

Regardless of their parentage, they came to live in the Balkans, they were grateful to the wild tribes living there for sheltering them. In return, they stole grain from neighboring people and gave it to their own tribe. As time went on, they mingled with demons in the Balkans and created a new breed of Hali. These were less powerful, but more vicious. They imbided too much beer and fought each other, uprooted trees, and made terrible noises. In the process, the once-kind creatures began to hurt people.[327]

Appearance

Hala's features are not clearly defined, nor are they consistent across the locales where she's found. Most often, people associate her with weather phenomena. The gathering storm clouds you see may be Hala herself, or the clouds may be the smoke she exhales while fighting other dragons.[328] It's also possible she's that strong wind blowing the clouds onward. The wind itself has a shape among the Slavic stories: large lips, puffy cheeks, tall stature.[329]

She may even take on an indistinct shape, hidden from view. That sparkle you see within the darkening clouds is likely her shooting off fire. If you look closely, you may glimpse her huge wings and powerful tail. They appear as a black cloud of "sticks" or "stripes," those evenly spaced, straight, narrow streaks of clouds that look like a field plowed for sowing. Often, she's entirely invisible. As she leads the clouds forward, only her hissing, whistling, and roaring let you know she's around.[330]

People have described her as follows:

- "[S]ome kind of black and terrible creature in the form of the wind that kills people with its breath."
- "[A] black wind that goes on the ground. Wherever it passes, a wind must blow, which spins like a drill."
- "[T]he hala is the one strong wind that carries everything in front of it and brings great devastation."
- "[H]uge, dark as a cloud being, a strong whirlwind that destroys everything around."
- "[A] whirlwind that breaks trees with roots and demolishes houses."[331]

Often, she creeps over the land as heavy, dark-gray fog, lying in fields, ravines, and valleys for days or weeks.[332] She also frequently makes her presence known as a black, frightening whirlwind that terrorizes the land, sweeping everything away as it rotates like a drill, before it disappears underground.[333] A song describes this event as: "Up to three angry halas came out, / Nine hours of not blowing." This indicates a rare phenomenon, meaning "three fierce winds that have not been blown for nine years."[334]

As Hala grows extremely old, she becomes too huge and powerful for Earth to contain. She must then leave the planet and head out into the atmosphere, where she becomes a falling star or a comet.[335]

Hala.
Illustration by Dmitry Yakhovsky. © Bendideia Publishing.

People also describe Hala as a huge snake, lizard, or dragon-like creature. She breathes through only one nostril, because if she did so through both, she would devastate the world. A traveler who saw one variety of this creature said she lacked a tongue. He insisted the beast did have a huge mouth and sharp teeth, though.[336] She also has a huge head, her arms and legs are stunted, and she has a long snake-like tail.[337]

In this form, she's so enormous she drags her tail along the ground while her head hides among the clouds. Not only that, but her gaping maw stretches from land to sky. This creature may bear a single head or multiple ones (usually three, six, seven, nine, or twelve) with sharp teeth. Instead of stunted limbs, she may have four legs with strong claws, and she can sport six wings and twelve long tails that may end with a giant horn shape.[338]

In Bulgaria, farmers have caught glimpses of her among the dark clouds and whirlwinds, describing her as having huge wings and a thick, sword-like tail. Shiny yellow, scarlet, or golden-red fishlike scales cover her entire body.[339]

Other descriptions of her dragon-like appearance include:

- "[A] snake-like creature with a horse's head."
- "[A] large and rough snake with large wings."
- "[H]uge sea beasts that cause waves and eat people."[340]

She can transform into other animals as well. That raven following you or joining with its flock to steal your crops is possibly Hala. An eagle flying in front of the storm may be her. Hala chooses that form to impersonate Zmey,[341] who can appear as an eagle to battle Hala and lead the storm away from the area in order to protect its nest.[342] Disguised as an eagle, Hala can accomplish her nefarious goals more easily. Or she may appear as a furless, horned, black bull, a snake with a horse's head, a boar, a black wolf, or some other zoomorphic form.

Finally, disguising herself as a human is one of her tricks. When she's an old woman, she'll cause your house to shake when she enters.

Getting to Know Hala

Hala lives in remote, hidden locations such as impenetrable caves and mountain crags, as well as inside hollow old trees or on top of tall ones, and within forests, whirlpools, springs, and lakes. Hordes of gold, silver, and precious stones sparkle inside her home.

Air is the domain she roams, but it's the water in the air she controls. People describe her as a creature that "comes" and "goes," rather than a phenomenon that "happens."[343] She withholds rain, guarding it deep within her cave, as Zmey does. However, that's where the similarity between the two ends. Hala keeps rain constrained, for the simple reason that people need it to nourish their crops.

This malicious, demonic creature is hostile toward humans. She's bent on destroying harvests by stirring up gales. Not only that, but she uproots trees, hurling them high into the sky, and she tears off the roofs of houses and barns in her rampage. Many songs, like the one below, describe her anger and its destruction.

> It echoes, it roars,
> With its soul it carries torrents,
> With its wings it breaks a forest,
> With its feet it plucks up a forest.
> Where it passes, everything withers,
> Where it steps, everything dries up.[344]

Hala Hiding within the Clouds.
Photo by minervastock. Stock Photo via Depositphotos.

She leads dark clouds over fields to soak them with torrential rain and hail. She may also morph into fog and cover the land; the lack of sunshine prevents corn and other crops from growing or ripening.[345] These actions make this evil creature much feared by agricultural societies whose livelihood depends on what they produce.

Insatiable Appetite

Hala is called "the insatiable."[346] Instead of destroying crops, she may steal them to satisfy her voracious appetite. In the guise of dense fog, she "drinks" the crops[347] with her huge mouth, devouring everything in her path: wheat, corn, grapes, and more. Or she quickly scoops up the harvest with a large wooden spoon she holds for that purpose. People say Hala, the fog, has come "to eat white wheat and to bite white grapes."[348]

Sometimes, she'll steal the land's fertility from one village to deliver it to another, carrying it tucked inside the flaps of one of her gigantic ears. When she arrives, she'll shake her ear, releasing the captured fertility to scatter across the land.[349] In this way, she behaves like Zmey, choosing a location and people as "hers" to protect and provide for.

She'll also devour cattle—and more—as you'll discover from a villager's account below.

In each sea and in each lake there is one hala. Therefore, when it thunders and shakes, it is very bad and ugly near the lakes. When it explodes and lights up, the water just splits there, it crashes and disappears again. This ala is like a bull with horns and a naked shin like a man. She has been hiding in the water all day, and when a cattleman brought his herd to a watering hole, she attacked and ate the strongest ox. Sometimes the hala fertilized cows and then they calved a naked calf like a human. When cattle did not pass by the lake, the hala remained hungry, then it lurked on the shore, grabbing and dragging a man or a child to the bottom. The halas that live in the seas are even bigger and uglier. They also overturned ships.[350]

Her appetite extends to drinking milk, especially from sheep. Villagers recall a story of a man who found Hala in his barn. He provided her with eight gallons of milk a day, which she scooped into her huge mouth with a large wooden spoon.[351] Another Hala that stayed with a man not only drank a lot of milk, she also enjoyed eating three kinds of bread: "black bread made from the crops she gathered in the morning when it fell over the fields like a mist; green bread made from wheat harvested before it bears fruit and white bread from ripe wheat."[352]

Hala's voracious appetite occasionally takes her to new heights; she flies high into the sky to devour the sun and moon. Soaked in their own blood, the heavenly bodies turn red with each bite Hala takes. The scars on the moon are a testimony to its many battles with the dragon.

People wept and suffered from depression when they were left in complete darkness, thinking the end of the world was upon them. Only when the sun, or a friendly dragon like Zmey, slew Hala did the light return. People would help the process along. Men shot guns into the sky toward Hala, women cast spells, and other villagers rang bells to frighten the beast.

Earlier, you read that a snake once sucked out one of the sun's eyes when the heavenly body got too close to the earth, in order to prevent its heat from scorching the land. Other stories say there were once ten suns, and a snake (that is, dragon) sucked up nine of them to regulate the generated heat.[353]

Dragon Devouring the Sun.
Modified Illustration by grandfailure. Stock Image via Depositphotos.

Afflictions of Mind and Body

Although Hala and Zmey are siblings, Zmey is quick to drive her away. He plays the role of the "protector dragon," while she is the "wrecker dragon,"[354] symbolizing both the dragon's creative and destructive duality in nature.[355] In the midst of battle, Zmey spits fire at his sister. Hala lowers her tail into a lake to collect water and hurls it at her brother, trying to put out his fire. This clash between fire and ice creates torrential rains and hailstorms and uproots trees.

Compelled to fight, Hala may never reach her destination and is forced to drop her stolen goods to defend herself. Wherever this fertility lands, the soil below becomes blessed from that point onward, while the place Hala steals from turns unproductive.

If the battle turns against Hala, she'll look for a place to hide: a tree, a container of water, or cattle. Any bird that comes across Hala in the clouds will go mad, diving to the ground to kill itself. A creature that eats the possessed bird also loses its mind.

Not only animals, but a person becomes insane if he happens to see her head peeking out from the clouds as she looks for a place to hide. If she sees you, she'll take up residence in your body and control your mind. Such a person is said to be *alosan*, that is, "Ala-possessed."[356] Once she's made herself at home there, you'll act strangely, like an insane person, and you'll exhibit Hala habits: your appetite becomes insatiable. If the affliction isn't too severe, your mind will merely be "confused" by Hala; you'll become dizzy and lie in bed for a long time.[357]

A legend tells how Hala crept inside Tsar Simeon (Nemanja), who then couldn't get enough to eat. St. Sava, fortunately, recognized the symptoms and removed the demon from the ruler.

> Stories go that Nemanja was *alovit* [ala-like]. St. Sava came across a coastal place where lunch was prepared for "Emperor Simeon" (Nemanja). As they were roasting oxen, rams, wild boars, and so on, he asked: "Who are you making this lunch for?"
>
> "For Emperor Simeon."
>
> "He'll eat all of that alone?"
>
> "Yes, because he's *alovit*."
>
> Then St. Sava invited Emperor Simeon for a walk by the sea, a boat trip. Once they'd gone far into the sea, Emperor Simeon started insisting that they go back because he felt hungry.
>
> St. Sava knew why this was happening, so he deceived him by repeating: "We'll go back in a moment."
>
> Soon, the ala inside Emperor Simeon became agitated. He fell under the boat, and the ala jumped from his mouth into the sea.[358]

Coming in contact with Hala not only affects your mind, it also affects your physical well-being. The three-headed dragon carries afflictions in her huge mouths, as a portion of a spell below indicates.

> In one mouth she bears fairies and winds,
> The second mouth—infirmity and bad diseases,
> The third mouth—spells, curses.[359]

Spells and curses are evident in the problems they can cause when a knowledgeable being casts them, but what about the other calamities Hala carries? In the first line, you see fairies and winds. Fairies (*vilas*) have many similarities to Hala. They appear in whirlwinds and cause diseases of both mind and body. Winds can also cause diseases and rage. People called these natural forces by many names: evil, raging, fairy, or disturbed winds.[360]

WAYS TO PREVENT HAIL

When summer clouds bring devastating hail instead of nourishing rain, agricultural societies fear for their welfare. They devise solutions to disperse or avert the hail. Shooting a gun (or larger weapon like a hail cannon) into the clouds, which are deemed to be Hala herself, is one method. The "scientific" idea behind this is that if the charge is strong enough, it will reduce the hail to rain or slush, thus causing minimal to no damage. The theory has yet to be proven, but it's still a common practice in many areas.

Other folk methods for preventing hail also exist.

- Place an axe with its blade upward, so it "cuts off the hail."
- Kill a lamb and place its shoulder in an eagle's nest (MacDermott, 64).
- If you're an old widow, you can raise your feet toward the clouds or watch them through a sieve while you cast spells.
- Bargain in secret with twin brothers, who are plowing their field at night with twin oxen.
- On St. George's Day (May 6), bury in a field the first egg you colored at Easter.
- Mix the shells of Easter eggs into the soil along with the first grains of wheat when you sow fields.
- On Palm Sunday (Vrabnitsa), have your priest sanctify bundles of willow sticks in church, then place one stick on each windowsill in your house.
- Drive your sanctified willow sticks into your field.
- Leave white laundry to dry outside between Holy Thursday (Veliki Chetvurtuk, the Thursday before Easter) until Ascension (Spassovden, forty days after Easter).
- Every Thursday, from Easter until Ascension, don't work in the garden or vineyard.
- On St. Urban's Day (May 25), don't dig in your garden.
- Don't throw apples upward until after St. Peter's Day (Petrovden, June 29) (Markov, N., 221).

Hala not only carries items that cause affliction, she herself can cause infirmity and diseases. Your best chance for staying healthy is to avoid "unclean" places she frequents. Don't go near crossroads at night, especially on major holidays. All kinds of evil creatures gather there, including Hala. This is where she has her nightly meal. If you step on her table, she'll make you go blind, deaf, lame, or mute.[361] Even if you don't disrupt her meal, if she smells your presence, she'll chase you off the road and torture you, often riding on your back as if you were a horse.

It's also a good idea to stay away from walnut trees, where Hala likes to sit. From there, she's known for spewing out all kinds of diseases.[362]

A wounded Hala is potentially dangerous as well. She'll crawl away and die in a cave, as happened once in the town of Golubac, Serbia. Every spring, bloodsucking black flies (*Simulium colombaschense*) breed on her carcass. These insects create no end of torment for your livestock, and soon you'll be left with dead animals. The insects also bite humans, transmitting diseases to people as well. If too many of them bite you, you're likely to end up with anemia. Worse case, they can cause blindness.[363]

Hail Cannon in Banska Stiavnica (Slovakia) Old Castle.
Probably designed by Julius Sokol.
Etan J. Tal, CC BY-SA 3.0 <https://creativecommons.org/licenses/by-sa/3.0>, via Wikimedia Commons.

How to Appease

Hala has an occasional soft spot for people who respect her. Talk to her. Promise her you'll take care of her and provide her with plenty of milk and grain if she becomes wounded in battle. Carry on a good relationship with her, and she'll reward you. She'll become your personal guardian, providing you with wealth and safety when trouble arises. Instead of eating her ill-gotten crops, she'll be sure to dump everything she stole from other villages onto your fields, making them lush and fertile.

If you happen to meet Hala, it's best to be courteous. One girl, chased from her home by her stepmother, found herself at Hala's house. The girl called the dragon-lady "mother," picked lice out of Hala's hair, and fed the "livestock": owls, wolves, badger, and others. Not once did the girl make a fuss about how strangely Hala lived. Therefore, Hala rewarded her with a chest full of gold.[364]

How to Defeat

More often than not, you'll want to get rid of Hala. Sometimes, herbs may work to expel her from your community, in the same way you drive out Zmey. You'll have to pick special herbs in unclean places that Hala visits, such as levees and locations where a plow turns around on a field.

Another method is to shoot into the clouds when you hear her approaching—not to kill her, but to force her to leave. If Hala is devouring the sun or moon, you can also aim your gun in that direction, while other people in the neighborhood ring bells to frighten her. A woman who's knowledgeable with magic can also perform a ritual while chanting the following spell to send Hala away:

Did you know?

Grass snakes were once streams of rain that stayed on the ground after a storm rather than running away (Avilin, "East European meteor folk-beliefs," 113).

Not hither, ala,
A mightier, bareheaded ala is here.
Off into the mountain, cloud,
Where no rooster crows,
Where no dog barks,
Where no cows bellow,
Where no sheep bleat,
Where *slava* [*ritual to honor family patron saint*] is not celebrated.[365]

Another activity that works wonders, especially when Hala is devouring the sun or moon, is to make a lot of noise: beating pots and pans, firing pistols, ringing church bells, and beating pigs and hens until they squeal and squawk.[366] And don't forget to say your prayers or chants. It may take a while, but little by little, you'll see her retreating, and the heavenly bodies will return.

You can try shooting the dragon while she's transforming from one form into another, but think twice before you decide to kill her. If you do, you'll have to suffer from those bloodsucking flies that feed off her carcass.

Some people believe ordinary humans can't kill Hala, so if you can't drive her away with the previously mentioned methods, you'll need help from someone who can ascend to the sky. An eagle (especially one with a cross marking on its back)[367] or Zmey is a good choice as already mentioned. Zmey battles her with his fiery arrows, creating a thundering disturbance in the sky. Oftentimes, many dragons die or are wounded in the battle against Hala. The cunning female manages to twist out of the way, and Zmey's weapons fall to the ground with a great crash. They may destroy the crops and fields they fall on.

Hala can be tricky, too, as she's dodging these arrows. She'll circle around a "sinful" person, then dart out of the way. Zmey's arrows will strike the unintended victim and kill him.[368] Even if you don't consider yourself sinful, if you're caught out in a storm, avoid standing under a tree, because Hala likes to hide there. Zmey will send his fire toward it, to burn the tree and everything around it, along with Hala—and you. Instead, find shelter under a small bush or some place where there's a cross.[369]

If no Zmey is nearby to help, you may have people in your community who can perform the task of defeating Hala. Like the *zmajeviti*, who battle dragons where Zmey predominates, people in Serbia called *aloviti* protect their community from Hala. They can be male or female, old or young, but boys tend to be the most challenging to Hala. These people also fall into a trance to ascend to the sky, and their spirit leads storm clouds away from their village. At other times, they'll fight Hala to drive her away. Be warned, however, that while they're in a trance, any wounds they receive while their spirit fights will also appear on their sleeping body.[370]

These people originate in a similar manner to other dragon people: they're children born from a dragon and a human woman. Another way humans can become *aloviti* is if Hala blows on them, and they survive what should have been her lethal breath. A side benefit of this is these people gain exceptional strength.

A song tells how a village youth, called the "good hero," battles Hala, the dark cloud. Emboldened by wine, he takes on the villainous beast, who calls out to him, "Come out, come out, good hero. Let the two of us fight." The battle lasts "two days, three days, exactly three weeks" before the dark cloud defeats the hero and drags him away. The youth begs his enemy to spare him, saying his mother will ransom him with the three cities she owns. In one version, the mother refuses to give up her cities, even if it means her son will perish. In another account, she's kinder, and pays the price. In the latter story, the hero is a young Zmey, rather than a human.[371]

In another village, crops were failing, because a terrifying Hala living in a lake consumed them. The people sought to kill her by nailing metal spikes into beams and placing them facedown onto the surface of the lake. After that, their harvest was no longer stolen.[372]

Dark "Stick" Clouds.
Photo by alexkich. Stock Photo via Depositphotos.

On the Dark Side

If you renege on your promises to protect Hala, watch out. She'll become vindictive and cause even more destruction to your property than she would have in her normal fits of rage.[373] Make sure you stay hidden, so at least you'll escape with your life.

Even more terrifying, though, is Hala's wrath when you become too inquisitive about her lifestyle. The dragon gets testy when you keep mentioning things that make her different from humans, as you can see in the following Serbian tale.

Yesterday, the woman went to the ala's house with her child, the ala's godchild. Upon entering the first room, she saw a poker and a broom fighting; in the second room, she saw human arms; in the third, she saw human legs; in the fourth—human flesh; in the fifth—blood; in the sixth—she saw that the ala had taken off her head and was delousing it, while wearing a horse's head in its place.

After that, the ala brought lunch and said to the woman, "Eat, *kuma* [*godmother or godchild, depending on the reference*]."

"How can I eat after I saw a poker and a broom fighting in the first room?"

"Eat, *kuma*, eat. Those are my maids: they fight about which one should take the broom and sweep."

"How can I eat after I saw human arms and legs in the second and third rooms and human flesh in the fourth?"

And the ala told her, "Eat, *kuma*, eat. That is my food."

"How can I eat, *kuma*, after I saw the fifth room full of blood?"

"Eat, *kuma*, eat. That is the wine that I drink."

"How can I eat after I saw that you had taken your head off and were delousing it, having fixed a horse's head on yourself?"

The ala, after hearing that, ate both the woman and her child.[374]

Hala, in this old woman human form, is similar to Baba Yaga, the witch who terrifies and eats children. The witch is depicted as a huge woman, with a large nose and protruding chin. On occasion, she aids people, but she also has a nasty habit of eating children. Like Hala, the witch has been called a demon of stormy weather. Baba Yaga's connection with dragons will be covered in more detail in the Lamia chapter.

Hala Tale

Nikola and Hala Semdndra

There was a thunder, a crash,
A letter from God fell down
To Borovanska mogila,
In the letter it was said:
The villagers should gather,
Villagers *borovachani* [*people from the village*],
To slaughter a barren cow,
To cook all kinds of dishes,
Because hala Semendra would come to them.
After they read the letter,
The peasants gathered right away,
They slaughtered a barren cow
In Borovanska mogila.
All the peasants gathered,
They didn't call Nikola,
Nikola the bastard.
When Nikola heard,
He came uninvited.
When the villagers saw him,
All of them got up,
To shake hands with Nikola
And gave him cups,
Cups to drink.
Nikola drained the cups,
Two of them until the bottom.
As they were sitting,
There, the hala was coming.
She was scary, God kill her!
How slowly she was walking,
She was turning trees and stones upside down.
When the villagers saw her,
Everyone stood up,
Only Nikola did not.
The hala shouted:
"Peasants, village mayors,
When you saw me,
You all stood up
To give me honor,
But this child did not get up!
Is he young and stupid,
Or old and insane,
Or a strong hero?"
Then the villagers said:
"He is neither a strong hero,
Nor old and insane,

But he is young and stupid."
Nikola shouted himself:
"Hala, you maiden Semendra,
I am neither young and stupid,
Nor old and insane,
But I am a strong hero!
Let two of us fight:
If you, hala, prevail,
You can take my blond head;
If I, hala, prevail,
I will cut all three of yours!"
When the hala heard that,
She stretched herself,
And took Nikola from the table,
Then they started
The heroic fight.
They fought on a summer day until noon,
They dug holes until their knees,
The hala was soaking in white foam,
And Nikola in white and bloody one.
Then Nikola shouted:
"Mother, you old stepmother,
Give me water to drink,
To cool down my heart,
Cause this hala will kill me!"
When his mother heard that,
She took a green jug,
She poured water from the well,
She put poison in the water,
To poison Nikola.
When she gave him the jug,
The hala turned him around strongly,
Nikola dropped the jug
On a sharp stone.
Then the stone broke
Into forty pieces.
Nikola got very angry,
He hit the hala into the ground,
With his right knee he stepped on her chest,
And cut off the three heads.
And he said to his mother:
"Mother, dear stepmother,
What you deserve from me,
May you receive it from God!"
Thus Nikola destroyed the hala.[375]

Lamia (Ламя)

The child has been strangled by the Lamia.

Name variations
Bulgaria: lamia, lamya (ламя) (plural, lami – лами)
North Macedonia: lamja, lamna (ламја) (plural, lamji – ламји)
Serbia: lamnia, lamija (ламња) (plural, lamnje – ламње)

Related names: Hala

Slang: "To eat like a Lamia" is a saying that means someone has an insatiable appetite.[376]
Lamia's greedy appetite is also the basis of sayings such as "word of mouth."[377]

Lamia, like Hala, is a female dragon found in Bulgarian, Serbian, and Macedonian folklore, predominately appearing in songs, fairy tales, legends, and myths, more so than in oral accounts. She's often interchangeable with Hala, and is also considered Zmey's sister. In some locations, the creature has the name of both dragons: Alamunja.[378] However, she does differ from Hala depending on specific location, sometimes both dragons existing within a community: "The foreign borrowings of the names lamia and hala do not predetermine their identical images in the folklore of different peoples."[379] You'll discover these differences in the pages that follow.

Origins

While you've learned that dragons often originate from snakes, Lamia has a rather unique way of coming into being. If a snake's head gets cut off and an ox or buffalo is nearby, the snake's head may become stuck on the animal's horn as it grazes. After forty days of being stuck there, the head and horn grow together and become a Lamia.[380]

Another way for Lamia to come into existence involves humans. While a good person can give birth to a Zmey if the child remains in her womb for fifteen to twenty months, a bad person will deliver a Lamia under these same conditions.[381] And a child with unusual features (large head/small body/wings under the arms) can be a Lamia, as well as a Hala.

Appearance

Lamia is the creature who most resembles the fire-breathing, human-eating monster you may be familiar with. She's described as winged, horned, and multi-headed (three, seven, or nine). Her body resembles a yellow or scarlet scaly serpent or a lizard-like creature. She has dog heads, sharp teeth, huge eyes, webbed wings, four clawed legs, and a tail that ends in a horn. Her mouth can open so wide that she can swallow a human or buffalo whole. She may also appear as an old or young woman, or even a beech tree.

Getting to Know Lamia

Lamia lives in all the usual dragon places located on the fringes of human society: caves, mountains, forests, and trees, but most often, you'll find her in or near water sources like lakes, wells, and springs. Stories describe her as protector of the marvelous World Tree and also guardian of the "living water."[382]

Etymology

The term "Lamia" for a dragon is likely derived from a creature in Greek mythology, whose name may originate from the Proto-Indo European stem *lem-*, from which comes the word "nocturnal spirit" (Mallory, 538). In Greek mythology, Lamia was a Libyan queen who conceived children with the god Zeus. In a fit of jealous rage, Zeus's wife, Hera, killed the children or forced Lamia to do the deed. This Greek Lamia had the upper body of a woman, and the lower body of a snake. She became a gluttonous being who ate children, and so her name "shows that its main distinguishing feature is its greed and insatiability" (Baeva, 399). The dragon Lamia also resembles the Lamme from Sumeria, creatures who ate the flesh of children (Jobes, 968).

Like Hala, Lamia is associated with causing devastating storms, and she can appear as clouds, fog, or wind. She, too, is linked to water, but while Hala controls moisture in air, Lamia's connection is to the water on land and beneath the surface.[383]

However, Lamia has another side, a fiercer, crueler, bloodthirsty one. She kills and eats cattle and people alike. A child's sudden death is often attributed to her cruelty,[384] and from this comes the Greek proverb: "The child has been strangled by the Lamia." She also scorches crops, steals light, and stops water from flowing, which ensures widespread droughts across the land.[385] She requires human sacrifices before she'll release captive water.[386] While battles with Hala take place in the sky, those with Lamia occur on the ground, water, or in the other world. Among the Bulgarians, she's the dragon Saint George slays in epic battles.

Guardian of Water

While Zmey uses his guardianship of wells and springs as a pretext for scoping out future brides, Lamia is a more sinister protector of these sites. She prevents the water from turning and flowing in the opposite direction,[387] or stops it from flowing altogether.

In folk poetry, a water serpent or dragon, such as Lamia, is often blended with the concept of a spirit-guardian of the well. People believe that one such protector lives in every lake, spring, and fountain,[388] much like other spirit-guardians protect every field, forest, and valley, and all require gifts to appease them.

The poem that follows talks about one such guardian of a well.

The Haunted Well
Four and five, nine brothers,
Eighteen cousins, lads of little luck:
A message came to them from the King, bidding them
To go forth and fight in the far-off land of the Franks:
"Thy blessing, mother, that we may go forth!"
"May ye go forth nine brothers and come back eight;
May John the youngest never return."
They set forth, and as they crossed the vast plain,
They lived forty days without bread,
Forty-five more without water,

Victory Over Evil (Победа над злото).
Illustration © Keazim Issinov. Used with permission of the artist.

And then they found a dear little fount; but 'twas a spirit-haunted well:
'Twas thirty fathoms in depth; in breadth twenty.
"Halt, dear brothers, and let us cast lots,
He on whom the lot will fall, let him go in."
The lot falls on John, the youngest.
They bind John and let him down:
"Draw, dear brothers, draw me out,
Here there is no water; but only a Spirit."
"We are drawing, John, we are drawing; but thou stirrest not."
"The serpent has wound itself round my body, the Spirit is holding me.
Come, set the Black One also to help you."
When the Black One heard, he neighed loud,
He reared on his haunches to draw him out.
When he drew out his arms, the mountains gleamed.
He draws out his sword also, and the sea gleamed.
They drew out John together with the Spirit,
They lifted their knives to cut it asunder,

93

But instead of cutting the Spirit they cut the rope,
And John falls in together with the Spirit:
"Leave me, brothers, leave me and go home,
Do not tell my dear mother that I am dead,
Tell her, brothers, that I am married,
That I have taken the tombstone for a mother-in-law, Black Earth for a wife,
And the fine grass-blades all for brothers and sisters-in-law."[389]

This water spirit takes her due, but more often, the physical being Lamia requires a much greater sacrifice for the use of her water, or for the return of something else that's valuable to the community. A common theme in stories is one where the dragon demands a human sacrifice before she'll release the water, such as the following excerpt from "The Three Wonderful Dresses."

"Alas! noble stranger, mine is a sad fate. In this country a terrible dragon has made his abode, who lives on human flesh and blood. This spring is the only one in the land, and the monster will allow no one to take water unless a maiden is given to him every day. Fate has willed that to-day my turn came, and I am here waiting for the frightful dragon with seven heads to come and devour me."[390]

The Feminine Connection

Lamia bears the name "Lamia bitch," not in a derogatory sense, but due to her dog heads. This connects her to the Great Mother Goddess, a huntress who is depicted with small dogs. Dogs, in many ancient mythologies, act as mediators between the dead and the underworld gods; they guard the border between our world and the "other world."[391]

If we look more deeply into the folklore texts, we will find that they have preserved relics of the archaic past of mankind, according to which the lamia / hala has the characteristics of a deity from the early cosmogonies—multifaceted, many aspects. It is a chthonic (underground) and solar (sun) symbol, it is associated with death and life, it is a destroyer, but it is also a guardian. She lives underground, but has wings and flies in the sky. She is the master of the earth's interior and underground resources. Cosmologically, it represents the primordial ocean from which everything originates and to which everything returns, the primary undifferentiated chaos, the archetypal feminine principle.[392]

That isn't where her connection to deities ends. Lamia, as well as Hala, bears similarities to Baba Yaga. This witch was once a minor deity, but more often has been considered a storm demon, who merged with a demon of the local people when the Slavs entered the Balkans. She has a penchant for eating children. Baba Yaga lives in the forest in a hut that stands on a chicken leg (sometimes two legs). Surrounding her house is a fence made of the human skulls and bones of those she's devoured.

Similarly, Lamia bears the malicious feminine traits of a cannibalistic witch in many fairy tales she appears in. She also performs activities associated with women in patriarchal societies: cleaning, cooking, making bread. Her family includes one or three daughters, or perhaps three or thirty-nine sons and one daughter. One daughter is often beautiful and the hero falls in love with her; she, in turn, assists him in overpowering her mother. Once defeated, Lamia, like Baba Yaga, assists the hero as he continues his quest.[393]

How to Defeat

You can use metals to rid yourself of Lamia. Iron has often been used as a weapon against any demonic creature. Lamia is no exception. Villagers have been known to put iron on the tips of a bull's horns so it can fight the dragon as she emerges from the water, ready to devour the animal.[394] People have claimed that after a battle, the bloody water proves the dragon has been defeated. This may have an adverse effect, however. That water source soon dries up and reappears as a spring in another village. The dragon has taken its water with it as it relocates to a new site.[395]

Silver is also commonly used to kill monsters, such as werewolves and vampires. It can also be used against dragons like Lamia. The metal is associated with the feminine, much like other things are considered feminine: the moon, night, water, and roe deer. Therefore, "like destroys like," and silver will kill the female demonic creature.[396]

In an interview, a villager tells a story that was passed down generation after generation, about an animal, "something like a lamia," that was terrifying the community. This beast guarded a bridge along the road, rather than a waterway, and she killed anyone who ventured there in the dark.

This place was on the outskirts of the community, which was the dragon's "own outer space," something that separated her from the realm of the human world. One brave man (called a *zmeeborets*, someone who fights monsters in the form of snakes) defeated the creature.

> All the people, it was killing them, so the people knew not to go out during that time. They knew and they didn't travel. My mother, my father, and my grandfather, it was so long ago this thing. But before there were weapons, and people knew how to kill this kind of animal. He had one [pistol, rifle] with ammunition, well, but there was special ammunition with silver inside. Only silver could kill what appeared in the evening.
>
> When he was passing from Yugovo down, the people said: "Hey, Pichuf (he was named Pichuf). Hey, Pichuf, where are you going at this time, that animal will kill you!"
>
> And he said: "It's all right, there is no danger."
>
> And the man left. At that time he loaded the weapon with the silver bullet. And when the man came near, it came out.
>
> And he took out the weapon and shot it, and then that animal started speaking: "Shoot me one more time."
>
> He said: "No, my mother gave birth only once, I also shoot only once!"
>
> And that was it. There were blood and firm skin, and the blood ran out. And it's gone, all is over.
>
> And the man returned to the village and said: "You don't need to be afraid anymore. I killed it. It is over."[397]

The *zmeeborets* is no ordinary person. He has knowledge of the proper way to destroy the beast.

> Belief in the magical power of silver bullets when shooting at demons and people with demonic characteristics is widespread in Bulgaria. The motive is that the fighter with the evil creature must strike him once (shoot him with one bullet), because the second blow (bullet) restores the vitality of the demonic character. A constant feature of the texts that develop the motive is the dialogue—the demon's request for a second blow and the emphatic refusal of the victorious man. He knows. That's his strength.[398]

You can also defeat Lamia similar to the way clever people have defeated Smok Wawelski, as the person's account below indicates.

> Eighteen years ago, my grandfather used to tell my father and my uncle that the Chepino valley was once a lake. In this lake, there was a sea animal called lamia. This lamia had to eat one man every twenty-four hours. At that time it was the turn of a girl to be eaten by the lamia; she was engaged to a shepherd. To save his fiancée, the shepherd collected a load of tinder and loaded it onto his donkey, then set it on fire and took the donkey to the lake to drink water, where the lamia immediately swallowed the donkey together with the burning tinder. As the tinder was burning in the lamia's stomach, the lamia couldn't stand still in the lake because of the great pain; she tried with all her strength to break through the mountains around the lake, and finally, she made her way between the two mountains of Karkaria and Smilyuvi skali, from where the whole lake ran out. The lamia remained in a dry place on the Pazardzhik field, where the dogs were eating it for a whole three years. That place, where the lamia broke through and the lake ran out, is still there, and until now the Old River flows through it; it's called Eli Dere.[399]

In fairy tales, though, only heroes can kill Lamia. Battles with Lamia in epic tales are only one episode in a hero's exploits. He encounters many dangers and has numerous adventures as he seeks his fortune or sets out on a godly quest. However, in the end, he is always victorious and defeats the beast.

How to Appease

No satisfactory way exists to appease Lamia, unless you desire to sacrifice your children to the beast. It's best to be on the lookout for a hero to defeat her instead.

Lamia Tale

The Story of the Prince and the Eagle

Here begins the tale. Good evening to you.

Once upon a time there was a king who had three sons. The youngest was the bravest and handsomest of the lot. A time came when the king was taken dangerously ill. He was at the point of death, and the doctors said that, in order to recover, he should eat the fat of a male hare. He called to himself the princes and said to them:

"My children, I am dangerously ill, and the doctors have said that, in order to recover, I must eat the fat of a male hare. So I beg of you to go out to hunt and to bring me a male hare."

"Very well, father," said the boys and, having taken their bows and clubs, they set out on their way to the far-off forests, in order to find hares.

The two elder sons did not succeed in killing one, but the youngest killed three. Unfortunately, none of them were male. His brothers began to be envious of him, because he had proved abler than they. Next day they went out once more to hunt, and again the same thing happened. The two elder ones failed to do anything, while the youngest killed two hares, and one of these two hares was a male. Their envy grew thereat, and they said one to the other:

"Let us kill him and then say to our father that robbers came and slew him."

Close by there was a well, a very ancient well with marble slabs round about, and the water issued forth from within and flowed over the marble slabs. When the younger brother joined them, they said to him:

"May we not drink some of the water of this well, especially as we are so thirsty?"

"Right," answered he, "let us drink."

"We must, however, drink in due order," said the eldest. "First one, then the other, and next after him the third."

So first drank the eldest, next the second, and last of all the youngest. He put his club and his bow under his arm and laid himself down upon his face, in order to drink of the water which flowed over the marble-slabs. Then one of them seized him by one foot, and the other by the other, and they flung him into the well. So the prince fell in, and his brothers fled and returned to the palace. When they got home, they took the hare to their father and said:

"Father, behold, we have succeeded at last in finding a male hare; but we have lost our brother"—and they pretended to be overwhelmed with sorrow.

"What! what did you say? how has that happened?" asked the king, rushing out of bed; for he loved his youngest son more dearly than the others.

"What can we say, father?" answered they. "As we were hunting, suddenly a band of robbers came, and they meant to destroy us all: we two managed to escape; but our poor brother perished."

Then great wailing arose in the palace. The king and the queen put on black, and wept bitterly.

Now let us leave those wailing, and let us go to the prince. The well into which they threw him was exceedingly deep. He fell for three years before he touched bottom. After three years he set foot on the ground and came out at the other end. He opens his eyes and sees that he is in another world: it was the Nether World. Far, far away he espies a light. He walks on and on and at last arrives at a cottage. Within there was an old woman kneading dough in a small trough, in order to make a cake. The prince noticed that the old woman had no water, but only wept and kneaded the flour with her tears, and she also spat. And as she wept and spat and kneaded the dough, she sang a sorrowful dirge.

The prince wondered greatly at seeing her spitting and weeping, and took pity on her.

"Good evening, grandmother," said he.

"Good be to my child," said she, and she looked at him in amazement; for he was a big, brave-looking youth and carried the club in one hand and his bow on his shoulder. "Whence comest thou, my son? Thou art not one of these parts. Art thou perchance come from the Upper World?"

"Yes, I come from the Upper World; but how did you find that out, grandmother?"

"Oh, we have no such men like thee here. It is easy to see that thou art from above. And how didst thou get down here?"

Then the prince told her everything: how his brothers had thrown him into the well and all the rest.

"But wilt thou not tell me," he said to the old woman, "wherefore dost thou not get some water wherewith to knead the bread, but thou kneadest it with tears and saliva, and wherefore dost thou weep and wail?"

"Ah, my son, water we have none in these regions. There is a well; but it is guarded by a Lamia, a monster with four legs and three heads, and it demands every month a maiden to devour, in order to let the water issue forth. This month the lot fell upon my only daughter Maruda, and she is now bound with chains to a plane-tree. To-morrow the monster will come out and eat her. Therefore do I weep and wail."

When the Prince heard these words, he said:

"I will kill this monster and rescue both thy daughter and the whole country. Only give me a morsel of this cake, when it is baked."

"Ah, my son, how canst thou kill the monster, since even the king of this city and his army have been fighting it so many years and have not prevailed?"

"I will kill it," answered the Prince.

"Go thou not, or it will devour thee also."

"I fear it not. Either shall I destroy this monster, or I will die."

As they were talking, he suddenly heard a cry: *Kra, kra*. He turned his head round and saw a great bird standing in a corner of the cottage. It was an eagle golden like an angel. He asked:

"What is this bird?"

"This bird my husband on dying left to me. It is now a hundred years since then. I have reared it, till it grew and became as thou seest it."

"And that she-buffalo, what is she?"

"That buffalo also my husband left me, a hundred years ago, and I reared her," says the old woman.

So she gave him a morsel of the cake to eat, after having baked it, and the Prince set forth, with his club and bow, to go where Maruda stood bound, waiting for the monster to come out and devour her.

When he got there and saw her, he said:

"Wherefore art thou here?"

"It is my destiny. The lot has fallen on me and I am waiting for the monster to come out and eat me, in order to let the water issue forth."

Then the Prince drew his sword, cut the chains asunder, and said to her:

"Fear not, I will rescue thee."

She, seeing a youth fair like a star, as he was, took pity on him and said:

"Flee far from hence, or thou also wilt perish as so many others have perished. Look, yonder is the graveyard where lie buried all those who have died these many years past in trying to rescue the country."

"Be thou easy in thy mind," said the Prince, and he turned and looked, and saw the whole plain covered with graves. But he was not daunted. And as they were talking, there came a fearful din like thunder, and the ground shook as though there were an earthquake.

"The monster is coming out. Flee, flee, or it will eat thee also," Maruda cried.

But the Prince seized her in his arms and carried her to a height some way off, and then came back to wrestle with the Lamia. And the Lamia was a great marvellous monster with crooked claws and a pair of wings, each of them reaching from here down to yonder plain. She issued from the well and clutched the earth with her claws, ready to pounce. And when she saw the Prince she said:

"Ah, well did my old Lamia-mother tell me: 'Many a man wilt thou eat, but one day there will come such a one, and of him thou must be afraid.' "

Then the Prince rushed upon the Lamia, club in hand, and belaboured her, and he cut off with his sword first one head and then another, till he slew her utterly, and there was not even a nostril left, as the saying goes.

The people, great and small, every one of them, and the King with his Council of Twelve, were on the walls of the city watching the fight. And when the monster was slain, the water began to issue forth with a loud roar, and all cisterns and fountains were filled, and the cauldrons which the people held ready.

Then the Prince took Maruda by the hand in order to lead her back to her mother, and she gave him her ring and said:

"I am thine now."

And when they came to the cottage, and the old woman saw them, she would not yet believe that the monster had really perished, but in the end she believed. Then said the Prince:

"I have achieved this feat thanks to the morsel which thou gavest me; the morsel which thou hadst kneaded with thy tears. It was that which gave me strength, and I overcame the monster. Now thou wilt give me thy daughter for wife, and I shall be for ever thy son."

So they embraced each other, and Maruda gave him her ring, and he gave her his, and the betrothal was concluded.

But the King and his council were displeased that a stranger should have succeeded in accomplishing so great a feat, while they had fought for so many years and failed. And they wished to destroy him. They came forth with bows and swords, a great army, and they marched towards the cottage in order to seize him. When the old woman heard of this, she said:

"You two must now flee and escape. I am an old woman, leave me here, I do not care if I die."

"How shall we flee, my dear mother?" answered the Prince. "Can I become an eagle and fly? I am but a man. Let them come, and God's will be done."

Then the old woman said:

"This eagle which my husband left me, and which I have nourished for so many years, 'tis he who will carry you out."

They asked the eagle and said:

"It is thy turn now to help us, who have nourished thee for so many years."

"This is the very hour for which I have been waiting," answered the eagle. "You two mount on my neck, and take with you many provisions. Take three hundred okes of meat and three hundred okes of water, and let us fly."

"Where shall we find the meat, and where shall we find a bottle big enough to hold so much water?" they asked.

"Slay the she-buffalo which also you have nourished for so many years. Flay her and on her flesh we shall feed, and of her skin make a bottle and fill it with water."

They slew the she-buffalo and loaded the eagle with the meat on one side and the skin on the other, and the Prince with the maiden mounted on his neck, and the eagle spread his wings and by little and little soared up.

"God be with you," cried the old woman, and fell down and died.

The eagle soared and soared for twelve long years, and by little and little the provisions began to fail.

"*Kra, kra,*" cried the eagle.

"What dost thou want?"

"I am hungry."

Then the Prince cut off the muscle from his left arm and put it into the eagle's beak.

"*Kra, kra,*" cried the eagle again.

"What dost thou want?"

"I am thirsty."

Then the Prince set his mouth close to the eagle's beak and gave him saliva to drink.

So day by day they drew nearer to the Upper World. But once more the eagle grew hungry and the Prince cut off the muscle from his right arm and gave it to him to eat. Then he cut off the muscle from his left leg, and next from his right leg. And he watered him from his own mouth, till they reached the Upper World, and saw the light of the sun, and they alighted on a mountain close to the city of his father.

Then the eagle said:

"I will remain on the top of this mountain. You go into the city, and if perchance you ever be in need, think of me. Take this feather, burn it, and I shall understand from the smell and come at once." And he pulled a golden little feather from his brow and handed it to them.

When they reached the city, the Prince asked:

"Where is the road which leads to the palace?" and the people showed it to him.

Twenty-five or thirty years had gone by since he had left, and his father and mother had grown old, and he himself had grown taller and looked even more heroic than before. Yet his mother, as soon as she saw him, knew him at once. Eh, does a mother ever forget her child? Let ever so many years go by, when she sees it, she will still know it, even as a ewe, when she has lost her young one, seeks for it here and there and everywhere, and finds it by the smell.

Even so the Prince's mother, as soon as she saw him, rose from the throne on which she was sitting with the king, opened her arms and cried out:

"Our son! our son whom we deemed lost. Dost thou not know him, husband?"

The King on hearing this, rose too; but the others—the Council of Twelve—said to him:

"Thou must first examine him, lest he be an impostor; for we know that thy youngest son has been dead ever so many years."

Then the King set about examining him, and the Prince related everything as it had happened; but they would not believe him.

"How can that be?" says the King. "These things thou speakest of: a Nether World and Lamias are things we have never heard of."

Then said the Queen:

"My husband, thou art not right. This is our own child. I know him: my heart tells me that."

Then the King ordered his secretaries to find in their books the time when the Prince disappeared, and other secretaries to write down everything as he narrated it now. Afterwards he turned to the Prince and said:

"Well, suppose we credit what thou sayest about going down below, how hast thou come back?"

Then the Prince related how the eagle had brought them to the Upper World, and they wondered even more, and refused to believe him.

"This thing must be attested by witnesses," said the King. "Where is this eagle? What has become of the bird?"

"Look at my limbs which I have cut in order to feed him, if you will not believe otherwise," answered the Prince, and he showed his arms and his legs, from which he had cut off the flesh. But still they found it hard to believe.

Then Maruda bethought herself of the feather, and said:

"What hast thou done, my husband, with the feather which the eagle gave us? Now is the time to burn it, and he will come to bear witness for us."

"Thou speakest well," said the Prince. "I had forgotten it." And he took the feather from his pocket. And when the others saw it, they wondered, for they had never in their lives seen such a beautiful golden feather.

Then the Prince put it close to the fire in the charcoal-pan, which stood in the middle of the room, and ignited it, and the palace was filled with a fine odour.

It became known outside in the city that such a bird would come, and all the people went out to see it. As they were awaiting the eagle's coming, they suddenly saw a great cloud, and by little and little the eagle came down with a loud whirr and sat upon the terrace of the palace.

Then said the Prince:

"My King, let us all go up to the terrace, and the eagle will come there."

And they all went up to the terrace, and saw the eagle, and the eagle did homage to the King, and the King asked him:

"Tell us, O eagle, how didst thou ascend from the Nether World?" And the eagle spoke and related everything.

And when he finished, he cried *glu, glu* and vomited forth one piece of flesh.

"This is," he said, "from thy left arm, which thou cutst off in order to feed me," and he set it in its place, spat, and stuck it. Next he brought out another piece and stuck it to the right arm, and likewise to the legs.

Then they all believed, and the king embraced his son and Maruda, and seated them near him, and said:

"So thy brothers sought to destroy thee?" and he ordered them to be seized and slain; but the Prince fell to his feet and kissed the hem of his robe, and begged him to forgive them.

"They sought to do me ill," he said, "but it has turned out well; for had they not flung me into the well, I should not have seen that world, nor should I have performed so many feats and deeds of valour, and become famous."

After a deal of trouble he prevailed on the king to forgive them. Then they embraced all round, and lived happy ever after. May we be happier still![400]

Balaur

When it dries up, one knows the worth of the fountain.

Balaur, **Bul'ar** (singular); **Balauri** (plural)

Related names: Zmeu

Romania is a land known for its vampires, especially the infamous Count Dracula. The tales also make room for dragons, such as the male creature called Balaur. In fact, it's been mentioned how Bram Stoker's character Dracula, unwittingly perhaps, takes on the characteristics of four of the personalities found in Romanian folklore:

> Dracula incorporates from this folklore the "undeadness" of Strigoi, the supermanly strength and wickedness of Zmeu, the mystery of Balaur and the power of attraction of Făt Fromes. No one can imagine that Bram Stoker studied the folklore and mythology of that "horseshoe of the Carpathians" to obtain this picture of his Dracula. It is pure chance that the folkloric background conveys to the reader who is acquainted with that folklore this picture of Dracula.[401]

Strigoli belong to the world of the undead, wizards, in fact. Balauri represent dragons, while Zmei (plural), often called dragons, are more like giants or ogres, and Făt-Frumos is the hero who slays both creatures. Balaur and Zmeu are often interchanged within stories, and they share characteristics with what you've learned about dragons from the Balkans. However, they also have traits that make them their own unique creatures.

Origins

Like other variations of dragons, Balaur originates from a snake that a human hasn't seen for long periods of time—seven, nine, or more years, during which time no sunlight touches the creature. Or he may even result from a snake that hasn't bitten a human for that duration. For each year the snake remains in isolation, he may grow an additional head. If the snake is living under your threshold and goes unseen by you for seven years, he will, upon maturity, fly toward the sky, where he transforms into a dragon or storm cloud.[402]

Other folktales tell how every seven years in the springtime, these snakes gather at a special place: a ravine, an abandoned, crumbling building, or in wetlands where fallen leaves have decomposed into fertile soil, producing rich vegetation. The creatures put their heads together and blow hard until thick foam drools from their mouths. Due to all their blowing, the foam solidifies into a beautiful diamond, brighter than the sun. The precious gem is the size of a hazelnut, walnut, or hen's egg.

Each snake fights to lick the diamond, because it quenches his hunger and thirst. One of them becomes so greedy in licking the gem that he swallows it. This snake is destined to become a dragon. After consuming the stone, the snake darts into the forest and conceals himself in an underground nest. His body thickens and stretches, he grows wings, and depending on the size of the gem, he grows multiple heads. If he's successful at hiding from humans for seven years, he'll develop further and achieve his goal of becoming a fearsome Balaur. If he's unfortunate and someone sees him, he'll shrink and lose his marvelous head and wings, reverting to a common snake.[403]

Etymology

Although the actual origins of the name Balaur are unknown, it possibly comes from the Thracian root *bell-* or *ber-* for "beast," "dragon," or "monster-serpent" (Nandris, 124). Additionally, it has a connection to the Indo-European roots *bhel-* (meaning "to shine") (Nandris, 124), *bhleu-* ("swell, overflow, roar"), and *bel-* ("strong") (Anarchelariu).

The snakes themselves have another interesting mythological story told about their origin: "[T]he wolf was originally created from clay by the Devil, but that God resculpted it better, and gave it life. In the process, a fragment of clay fell off and became the snake."[404]

This wolf-serpent/dragon connection ties in nicely with the battle standard used by the Dacians, a branch of the Thracians.

> When the wind blew through the open mouth into a long bag forming the body of a serpent, it became inflated, as it appears on Trajan's Column. This animal has been identified as a wolf, but it seems rather to be a serpent, a dragon.[405]

Appearance

Unlike other dragons, Balaur doesn't appear as a human. His body and head are like a serpent's, but he's more massive than a snake. This monstrously sized creature has a jaw that reaches both heaven and earth when it's open. And he "plants his footsteps on the mountain and touches the violet skies with his lofty crest."[406]

Although he has wings on his back, two horns on his head, and breathes fire the way other dragons do, he usually lacks legs in stories. They're hidden beneath his skin, so you see them only if someone cuts off his head.[407]

His scales radiate a golden hue, giving him the apt name of a "golden serpent."[408] This many-headed dragon, sports three, seven, nine, or twelve heads, if not more, depending on the years he's spent in isolation. Some stories also describe Balaur with only one head, while others feature a creature with a head at both ends of its serpentine body. The beast can also have fins, feet, and bat-like wings. Not least of all, he's a being that has the ability to speak and reason like a human, even though he doesn't look human.

Getting to Know Balaur

Once Balaur has surfaced from his underground isolation, he'll slither along the ground, burning the grass so badly it'll never grow again. He spends his time in uninhabited places at the edge of the human world: rocky forests; niches in wet, mountainous locations; within the depths of lakes, seas, wells, and springs; abandoned churches and other buildings; or sometimes closer to humanity under bridges. Unlike other dragons, he remains a solitary creature, neither wedding nor producing a family, nor forming any kind of dragon community.[409]

Three variations of this dragon exist: one type lives in the sky, another on land, and a third in water. Like Hala, the cloud-dwelling dragon personifies rain storms. He spews out fire (lightning) from his mouth and creates thunder as he roars in fights with other dragons. At other times, he travels along the rainbow and drinks water from the seas and lakes, storing it in the clouds. Only his tail is visible; when he lowers it, he creates driving rain that batters the ground.[410]

Balaur, Three-headed dragon.
Illustration by fotokostic. Stock illustration via Depositphotos.

In some locations, people perceive the dragon as being the clouds themselves. These cloud-dragons guzzle massive amounts of water. A wizard rides in his chariot throughout the sky, whipping these creatures until they burst, thus spewing water across the land.[411]

The land-dwelling Balaur is much sought after, because he guards treasure. It's not the stolen treasure hoard you'll find other types of dragons keeping watch over. The precious gems Balaur protects are ones he's produced with his own saliva. In some cases, he'll go to great extents to retrieve these gems, as you'll discover in this story about the Moon that follows:

> God created the Sun as a golden man with wings of fire. The Sun lived alone and sad for seven years, so God, aided by the Devil, decided to create the Moon as a silver girl, with wings made of precious stones, in order to light the night. God built for her a silver way, so she could walk after the Sun, but never catch up with him. Now, when the Sun walks the sky, the Moon reposes in the solar house. The Moon is a woman who periodically becomes a child, then a young, mature and finally an old, woman, before undergoing her monthly rebirth. She is raised by seven imps (servants of the Devil). Sometimes her wings are eaten by balauri, because they are the creators of the precious stones which make up her wings.[412]

The third kind of Balaur is similar to Lamia and is popular in stories. This evil creature lives in village wells, fountains, or other water sources. He has great strength and vitality and is constantly at war with heroes, such as Făt-Frumos and Saint George, whom you'll learn more about in the "Dragon Slayers" chapter.

If you come in contact with this Balaur, he may be whistling. This is a certain sign he's summoning a demon. It's best not to let the dragon catch sight of you. A hungry Balaur consumes any creature that crosses his path—animal or human. You'll be fortunate if you're armed when the beast begins munching on you. Your weapon will become lodged in the dragon's throat, and he won't be able to swallow you. If the odds are even more in your favor, a hero will saunter along that path. He'll kill the dragon and free you.

This doesn't always mean you'll survive. Balaur's teeth are poisonous, and you're likely to die if he chews on you while trying to swallow you. Besides that, the dragon's breath is toxic. So, even if you escape being eaten by him, you may soon die from a disease you've contacted by breathing in the air he's exhaled.

If the dragon has tried to eat a deer, however, its antlers will prop open the beast's mouth. He'll be stuck that way until a hero assists him. Since Balaur wasn't eating a person, the hero will cut off the deer's antlers, so the dragon can swallow his food. In circumstances like this, Balaur shows a generous side. He'll grant the hero any wish he asks for. Well, within reason. There are always actions in fairy tales that magical creatures cannot perform. Most often, this means Balaur will help the hero whenever he's in danger or when he can't reach his destination in the land beyond the human realm.

Balaur's favorite snack, though, is a tender young girl. He demands one as his annual due. The community will pay it, because if they don't, they won't be able to draw water from any source. Once he's eaten all of the tasty females, he'll leave that community to look for another place to live.

Giving a girl to Balaur wasn't initially an evil deed. People once presented her to him as a bride in an attempt to "calm" him or keep him happy.

> Numerous images depict the girl holding the balaur tied with a cord, a chain, or all sorts of other ties…. The act involves eroticism and we also subscribe to the hypothesis that, initially, the balaur's hunger referred to sexual hunger. From a community, he was always offered girls (often dressed in bridal robes), by a waterfront or at the mouth of a cave. The girl calmed him down and "tied" him. In a later epoch, the girl was denied the quality of heroine; she was transformed into a poor victim, being required to have a boy save her (including St. George).[413]

Other than eating people, Balaur prefers to limit his contact with humans. People, after all, try to kill him (with reason), or like the Solomonari, control him for their own benefit.

Solomonari

Solomonari (singular, Solomonar) are wizards, sometimes called wandering scholars,[414] who can bend the will of dragons. The Romanian saying "I have the needle for your coat" (*Am eu ac de cojocul tau*) would make a good motto for these men. It means taking revenge, knowing exactly what to do to get back at someone. Because that is what these men are good at—revenge. Fanciful tales of their activities occur mostly in oral accounts rather than in dragon fairy tales.

The wizards display characteristics similar to Balauri. While in training, the Solomonari live underground, in isolation. Even when they've "matured" to their final stage of being a wizard, the men separate themselves from the rest of the community.

Not everyone can become a Solomonar. It takes seven years of intensive training in a school called Solomonăriă, which is located underground, with no chance of the men seeing sunlight. The devil himself selects ten students to learn the mysteries of nature, all manner of superstitions and magic, incantations, and every conceivable language spoken by both human and animals. At the end of this term, only one student will become a Solomonar, the devil's apprentice.[415]

Not only does the chosen student become powerful like his master, but his appearance transforms so he looks the spitting image of the devil—or at least how popular belief portrays the devil. These features include red hair (which in many cultures indicates a person who works with the devil), bulging eyes, a hairy body, and, of course, a tail. The wizard's long, white robe covers the bulk of these deformities, however.[416]

Even after the devil awards the man this position, the wizard's instruction continues. Mysterious beings visit him, teaching him how to oversee the celestial wars. In addition, they give him gifts, like *un frâu de aur*, a golden bridle he'll use to capture and harness a dragon.

> ## Did you know?
>
> You'll be lucky throughout the year if you kill a balaur on June 29, St. Peter's Day (Murray, 137).

Whenever the wizard desires to cause a hail storm, he'll call up Balaur from the bottom of a lake. The Solomonar walks around the lake once or twice, chanting secret words from his book of wisdom. In some instances, he'll start a fire around the lake. Instead of evaporating the water, it freezes the lake. The higher the flames reach, the thicker the layer of ice on the lake grows. When it's sturdy enough, the wizard walks toward the middle and cuts a hole into the ice. Above the opening, he shakes the golden bridle and performs another incantation to summon a dragon to the surface. If it's not large enough to carry him, the Solomonar hits the creature on the head, sending it back.

When a suitable Balaur rises out of the water, he says, "What do you want, my master?"

The Solomonar throws the bridle over the dragon's head, jumps onto the beast's back, and replies, "See this ice on the lake? Break it into pieces, then we'll go this way or that way."

The dragon stomps on the ice, shattering it into millions of shards. The wizard yanks on the reins, and the dragon soars into the sky. A trail of crushed ice follows in their wake.[417]

You can tell when the duo approaches. Dragon and rider hide within those small clouds that appear right before stormy, gray clouds start to form.[418] From this hideaway, the Balaur-riding Solomonar hurls the hailstones he created from the lake ice. He does this sometimes simply because he's bored. This innocent pastime doesn't harm anyone, because, in this case, the wizard creates hail storms over wastelands, snowy hills, large water bodies, and any other place where no one will normally be. Most often, however, he hurls hail on someone's property, because the wizard is taking revenge on a person who's hurt or neglected him.

You may wonder how he can be neglected when he chooses to live apart from the community. If you see a blind or lame person wearing ragged clothing and begging for alms around the village, it's likely the wizard in disguise. Be sure to give him gifts to appease him, or else he'll target your farm the next time he's throwing down hail.

> ## Did you know?
>
> Clouds are the sun's bulls, pulling a cart filled with water; if the animals get lazy, water pours over the edges, deluging the earth (Anarchelariu).

The wizard may decide to put aside the beggary and instead appear in the village as a magician, storyteller, or singer. Even so, he makes sure he's in disguise so people don't recognize him. This is how he earns an income so he can maintain his way of life. He also makes money by hiring himself out to those who have a grudge against a neighbor. You can make arrangements for the wizard to ride a dragon to bring hail to your enemy's fields.

When the wizard is done having his "fun," he'll descend from the dark clouds, which almost touch the ground, so it's unlikely you'll catch a glimpse of him. He jumps off the dragon, removes the bridle, and murmurs more secret words. The lake fills up, and the dragon returns to the murky bottom, ready to await the Solomonar's next call.

Despite their evil intent, these wizards had a noble beginning. In the same way that the Church distorted dragons from primordial cosmological creatures into demons, Solomonari were transformed from pious priests of the old religion into sorcerers who performed magic and the work of the devil.[419]

Even their name has a lofty origin. Sources say the word "Solomonari" comes from the biblical King Solomon. He was not only wise, but also an extraordinary, mysterious person in Romanian tradition. The Solomonari's high ideals represent the king's wisdom, and those people who don't abide by these ideals are worthy of punishment in their opinion.[420]

Solomon had another ability according to these accounts. He could dominate evil spirits.

Some of these spirits were trapped by him in bottles, whose corks he sealed, and then the bottles were thrown into the sea. The evil spirits saw Solomon's seal on their bottles, and did not dare to emerge. He cast other spirits into the Earth's depths in a similar way, leaving only a few spirits free to cause much trouble on Earth and in the sky.[421]

However, an early twentieth-century account of these men is not so favorable.

Another meteorological event still worse than thunder is hail, which comes down in the heat of summer to beat down whole fields, just ready for harvest, reducing thus to naught in one hour the hopes of the whole season, and, haply, the food of the whole next year. In connection with this dreadful evil, charlatanism has found its way among the credulous people, namely, the warding off of hail by incantations and witcheries, dealt in by some cunning charlatans called Solomonari, who manage to get hold of people's fancy and of people's pence, in many a quiet village, which they pretend to preserve from hail.

As chance will often have it, their incantations seem to have really kept away a hail that has been raging a few miles off; if they do not, well, then, it is because of the sins of the people, who surely have not faithfully kept some feast or fast! Many a peasant is ready to doubt the power of the Solomonari, "but after all, who knows, it is better not to draw their anger upon oneself," for they are said by some to be able to bring down hail on unbelievers; and then their demand upon the peasant's purse is not so great, about fivepence, at most one franc for the season from each head of a family, is ample supply for the charlatan.

And then there are such clever Solomonari who can drive rats away from barns, and make them run away in flocks by mere incantation, and cure animals of various complaints, and so on. And, to conclude this subject, there is no end of supernatural means of making and unmaking things otherwise beyond human power, means based on direct suggestion or employed at a distance, apt to puzzle others besides simple credulous children.[422]

Granted, this interpretation is from a non-native source, so it demonstrates an outside world view of the people and their culture. For who truly knows what powers humans can possess?

How to Appease

The best way to appease Balaur is to avoid him. Complimenting him and giving him gifts doesn't help. He wants to eat your flesh, or that of your daughters. And, be mindful of the needs of the Solomonari, for, as you've learned, they're the ones who control the beasts.

RAINBOW CONNECTION

Storm demons, cloud dragons, or by whatever other name people call these beings, these creatures have fascinating connections to the rainbow. That arc in the sky can be a long, colorful waist-belt dropped by a heavenly being (Saint Elijah or Granny Zunka). This imagery exists in wedding songs, in which people say "the bride, beautiful as the sun wears the rainbow as her belt" (Konstantinova).

The rainbow can also be a road that dragons travel along to reach their home in the "other world," or it can be a dragon itself. The creature curves its body as it dips its tail into a lake while it sucks up the water with its mouth.

People also use the rainbow to make forecasts about the harvest. The dominant color has special meanings: red for abundant grapes, yellow for wheat, and green for grass (Konstantinova).

But, wait. There's more. Some other intriguing "facts" about dragons and rainbows may surprise you.

Many people are aware of the legend that says you'll find a pot of gold at the end of the rainbow. However, did you know that the rainbow drinks from a magical, silver cup hidden near a spring? Luck awaits anyone who finds it: he'll gain knowledge of his future, and all his dreams will come true (Konstantinova).

In Romania, the rainbow is a two-headed Balaur, and it can change more than your fortune. If you're so inclined, you can travel on your knees from one end of the rainbow to the other where the dragon drinks water. Do this with caution. It's not a pot of gold at the end you'll discover. Instead, you'll change your sex: male to female, or female to male (McBeath). In Bulgarian stories, you can achieve this goal if you drink from the silver cup at the end of the rainbow, or even if you walk under a rainbow (Konstantinova).

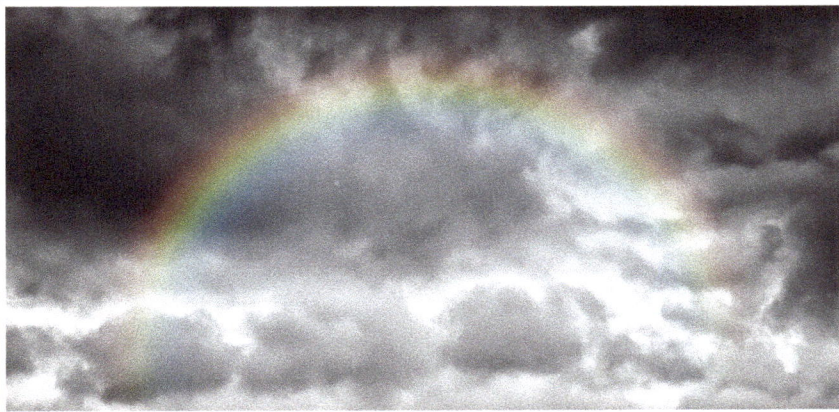

The Ends of the Rainbow.
Photo by magann. Stock Image via Depositphotos.

How to Defeat

Heroes defeat Balaur, in the same way they do many other dragons: with weapons and cleverness. However, the Balaur-riding Solomonar presents an additional problem. If you suspect your enemy has hired a Solomonar to destroy your crops with hail, you do have a recourse to fight him. You can hire a Contra-Solomonar. This person is as well-versed as a Solomonar in casting spells—only these spells are for protection rather than destruction. Before he starts any incantation, though, he'll try to reason with the Solomonar. The Contra-Solomonar will seek his opponent out where he's hiding in the clouds, requesting that the Solomonar spare the property.

Did you know?

A Solomonar, like a vampire and other evil creatures, detests the smell of garlic (Moldován, 181).

If the Solomonar agrees, then the problem's averted. Everyone's happy, except, perhaps, your enemy who didn't get his way. However, if hail batters your property, watch out. Your hired Contra-Solomonar is going to use all his powers to drive the Solomonar away. He'll recite his magic spells to force the winds to drive to a desolate location the clouds the Solomonar is hiding within. With a scythe, the good wizard will slash the clouds—and the Solomonar. You'll know the Contra-Solomonar has succeeded when a barrel filled with ice falls to the ground, along with the dragon and evil wizard. The heavy, hail-filled clouds press down until they crush their fallen victims. All that remains is a great pile of ice over their bodies.[423]

Balaur Tales

Fàt Logofàt

In the notes section of the story of "Fàt Logofàt," the author says: "It is one of the prettiest stories of the series. Some of the epithets which pass between the lovers are charming."

✱6 h stay! Fàt Logofàt! of the fair wavy locks, for yonder upon the hill top a black Balaur is awaiting thee."

"Fair maiden with the laughing mien and with the silken sash, I fear not the Balaur, for I am armed."

"Rash youth, with thy glance of fire and handsome with all beauty, the Balaur is strong and wicked; oh stay!"

"Angel of the stars, with the dove-eyes and lily cheeks, the Zméui all tremble at my name."

"Great warrior, with thy gilded arms and with thy gentle voice, the Balaur plants his footsteps on the mountain and touches the violet skies with his lofty crest."

"Bird of the mountains with thy flower-dyed wings, when I bestride my murgo he can spring with me from sea to sea, and his feet spurn the clouds."

"O Fàt Logofàt, with the wavy hair and gentle voice, with the bright smile and fearless heart, do not leave these halls; for I love thee. Oh stay!"

"Sweet maid, with every beauty, if thou lovest me then will I try to be worthy of thy love."

So, deaf to the pleading of the maiden, he kills the Balaur and returns to make her his bride.[424]

Balaur the Serpent

In this story, a hero saves a man from being devoured by Balaur.

I have seen the pride of the fields; it was by the road side, near the town of Paromb. But it was not a flower; it was the green eye of the Balaur, which should be neither seen nor dreamed of.

He had devoured the half of a young man well armed, and the youth cried, "Help me, brave traveller, or the serpent will swallow me."

A beautiful youth on a black courser, who is seen coming along the road, prepares to rescue him. But the serpent addresses him thus: "Begone, thou rogue of a horseman, if thou wilt not share the same fate as thy countryman!"

"Serpent," replied the cavalier, "if you swallow up my poor brother I will cut off your head."

"Cut it off or not," answered the Balaur, "I will not give up this man; his mother gave him to me when she rocked him as an infant in his cradle, and said that the serpent should take him if he did not sleep quietly."

But the cavalier drew his sword and killed the serpent. He saved the youth and carried him to a cottage. There he bathed him in milk. So the youth and the cavalier dwelt together for ever afterwards, and passed their lives in killing serpents.[425]

The Emperor of the Fish

In this tale, you'll discover two representations of Balaur: one a gem-producing creature (which has a unique way of producing gems that doesn't involve his saliva) and the other a monster that consumes youths.

nce upon a time, if it hadn't happened, it wouldn't have been talked about, and the story would've ended here.

There once was a man, who fished for a living; and this man had a son and he taught him his craft, because he didn't know anything else.

One day, while using his net, he caught a great, beautiful fish; his scales shone bright like diamonds. After he caught it, he took it to the shore and gave it to his son to hold. The son brought the fish to the pond, to try to catch it once again.

As soon as the fisherman went away, the son heard the fish talking with a soft voice, as though crying, "You, little boy, little boy, throw me back into the water, because I'm the Emperor of the fish. If you do me good, I'll do you good, as well."

The boy was in awe when he heard the fish talking, and because he felt sorry for him, for his begging that could soften a heart made of coal, he threw him into the pond.

The fish, seeing himself in his environment, dived deep once and returned to the surface, then he dived deep into the water for good.

A while had passed and the fisherman returned, swearing like a mad man, because he hadn't caught any other fish. "At least we have the other fish," he said.

"I threw it into the water, dad, because he spoke and begged me to let him go. He said he was the Emperor of the fish," responded the boy.

The fisherman didn't wait to try to catch anything else. Since he was sad, he started beating the boy. The fisherman hit the boy and kept hitting him until the fisherman got tired and let the boy go.

They went home, and that evening they really fasted. They fasted even more than they did on Easter's Eve, because they had literally nothing to eat.

The second day, the fisherman started to beat the boy again, today, tomorrow, and so on, until at one point, the boy couldn't stand the beatings anymore, and he left.

He went straight ahead for a long time and reached a city. As soon as he entered it, a dwarf appeared near a wall and greeted him. Being alone, the boy gladly made friends with the dwarf and became blood brothers, swearing never to part and whatever they had to share in half. They swore to share, but what could they share? Both being broke, they decided to become servants.

They found a place with the same master; they got hired, and it was done. One day, while lying near the gate, because his errands were finished, the dwarf saw a man mounted on a horse, and this man was leading five other horses and had a servant, too. The next day, at around the same time, the man with the horses passed again with another servant, the third day again, and every single day he passed by with different servants.

The dwarf, seeing that he was always changing his servants thought, "I wonder what he's doing with the old servants." But he couldn't figure it out. One day, he decided to follow the man, to see where he went and what he did.

So, he left for the market; there he waited for the rich man to pass by. The rich man saw a guy doing nothing, so he hired him, mounted him on his horse, and left together. The dwarf followed them. They passed through a beautiful garden, full of flowers; then they entered a forest and walked for a while, until they stopped at the roots of a great tree. When they stopped, they got off the horse, and the rich man took a rope out of his bag, hung it in a hook, hammered it onto the tree, and the servant climbed up.

The man climbed up to the top of the tree, and guess what he saw?

Believe it or not, it was a huge basket full of gemstones.

"Oh my God, my lord, they almost blinded me, all these gems!" said the servant from the tree.

"Come on and bring it down," said the rich man, "and stop yelling from there."

The servant took the basket down. The rich man emptied it into bags and then gave the servant the basket to put back in the tree.

The servant climbed back up, put the basket back, and when he wanted to come down, there was no rope anymore!

"Hang the rope back, my lord, so I can get down. I can't jump from here. I'll break a bone and become a cripple."

The rich man placed his bags on the horses without answering.

"Hey, can't you hear me? Stop fooling around," said the servant.

He kept talking, but the rich man ignored him and mounted on his horse, leaving.

"Hey, lord, hey, wait, wait. Hey, come back and help me get down. We didn't agree to leave me here."

The lord kept running, like running for his life.

The poor servant, seeing that it wasn't a joke anymore and the lord had gone, started crying in the most lamentable way.

The dwarf stayed hidden, because he wanted to see what happened next.

While the servant kept yelling, suddenly, a balaur, with a frightening mouth, appeared from a burrow of the tree and started climbing upward. When he reached the top, where the poor man was sitting, it opened its great mouth, with its teeth the size of a shovel and swallowed the man whole. After it swallowed him, it spit gemstones back into the basket—some were red, green, others were white—until the basket was full, then it climbed down and went back to its burrow.

The poor dwarf was petrified with fear, and he felt sorry for the poor Romanian, but when he saw the balaur going back into its burrow, he turned around and went back home.

The second day, when the rich man passed with his wagon through the market, guess who offered to help him in the woods? The poor dwarf, him indeed! Who knew what he had in mind?

The two bartered, and off he went. He passed with the rich man through the town, through the garden, and through the forest until they reached the said tree. As soon as they arrived, the rich man hung the rope, and the dwarf climbed up, took the basket as he was told, and then climbed back down.

After the rich man emptied the gemstones into his bags, he gave the dwarf back the basket and told him to put it back. The dwarf refused, claiming to be dizzy.

How could he climb up? If he climbed, he would have to climb down, because he wasn't crazy to stay there, and if he climbed down, and nobody was left in the tree, the balaur wouldn't leave other gemstones.

"Climb up, man! I'll even give you a handful of those gemstones."

The dwarf turned him down.

"Climb up. That was our deal."

"Aww! My good lord, everything is spinning around me," shouted the dwarf, while rolling on the ground and ignoring the lord's words.

Seeing there was no other way, the lord took the basket and climbed up to put it back.

That's what the dwarf expected. As soon as he saw the man up in the tree, nothing was spinning around him anymore. He took the rope out of the hook and left the rich man hanging in the tree.

"Don't touch the rope! What are you doing? Let me climb down!"

"I think you're exactly where you need to be," said the dwarf.

"Hey, dwarf, I'll give you bags full of gemstones! You only have to hang the rope back, so I can climb down."

The dwarf kept refusing. After he finished his work, he mounted the horse and left while saying, "Farewell, my perched cousin," and went back into the town.

The poor rich lord tried to go up, tried to move down, nothing worked! If he jumped, he would split his head open, and that would be it for him. So, he started crying and crying, until the balaur heard him! The great serpent climbed up, ate the lord—and this is how the rich man met his end.

Now what the dwarf wanted was to find the lord's house, but he didn't know where to start looking for it. He let the horses go wherever they wanted, and they led him straight to the lord's home. There the dwarf found the gates locked, but located the keys in the lord's bags, opened the gates, and went inside. He'd never seen more wealth in his entire life, but he came back to his senses, emptied the bags, and left to find his friend.

The poor fisherman boy was sad—he didn't know where the dwarf was. The moment he saw the dwarf, his eyes lit up with joy.

"What have you done? Where have you been?" he kept asking.

"Don't worry. I'll tell you everything eventually," said the dwarf. "Now take your bag and come with me."

The boy listened, went to his master, told him he was leaving and needed what he had earned.

"Are you crazy, man, or what? How come you're suddenly leaving me?"

"You have to give me what's mine," said the boy. "I'm not staying here anymore."

"He's a mad one," thought the master. "I'd better give him what he wants and get him off my mind; you never know what he could do next."

"Here, now. God's speed, boy," he said, giving the boy what he had earned.

The boy left, and the dwarf took him to the rich man's house. Upon entering the house, the boy froze in awe, when the dwarf told him that all that wealth was theirs.

"My friend, have pity on my soul!"

"I swear to God!"

"All this wealth is ours?"

"Yes, indeed."

"You did great, my friend!" he finally said, after he heard the dwarf's story.

Because the fisherman's son and the dwarf got royally rich overnight, everybody heard about them. At that time, the Emperor had a daughter he wanted to marry and told the entire world that whoever managed to stay for a whole night in the same room with her would be her husband. This girl was married ninety-nine times before, but every single groom died and only their bones were found the following day. Nobody knew who ate them.

Hearing that, the dwarf wasted no more time and went to the Emperor's palace to tell him that he had a sworn brother, who would try to marry the girl.

The Emperor accepted gladly and told him to come as soon as possible. If he stayed alive until the next day, the girl would be his bride.

The dwarf went running home, took his friend, and they both went together to the palace.

At night, when the fisherman's boy entered the room with the Emperor's daughter, the dwarf went in with them and sat on the floor.

Overnight, the dwarf woke up, took his friend off the bed, removed his sword and started his watch. It wasn't long before a great balaur came out of the girl. As soon as the dwarf saw it, *snap!* He cut off the head of the beast with the sword.

Afterwards, he woke his sworn brother and said, "Do you remember our deal, brother? Whatever we have, we'll share in half."

"Indeed," answered the boy.

And the dwarf went toward the girl, with the sword in his hand, threatening her that he would cut her in two, so he could have his half.

The girl gasped from fright and spit out an egg. The dwarf threatened her twice more, and two more eggs were out.

"Now," he said, "take your wife and be well. Before I killed the balaur, it made three more eggs, for three more balauri."

And then he told the boy that he was the fish his father had caught. Because the boy had set him free, he promised to do him well, so he gave the boy wealth and made him an Emperor's son-in-law.

"And now," he added, "take care of your bride and wealth and stay well."

As soon as he said that, he disappeared.

When the day came, so did the Emperor and saw them safe and unharmed. He was so happy; everybody was so happy! They celebrated in laughter and songs for seven days and seven nights.

I was also there, and the sun shone over me.
I ate
I got bloated
And remained fat,
Like a pregnant cricket.[426]

Zmeu

Choose a wife to please yourself, not others.

Zmeu (singular); **Zmei** (plural)

Feminine: Zmeoaică (singular); Zmeoaice (plural)

Related names: Balaur

Slang: Like Zmey and Zmaj, Zmeu is a word used to refer to a child's kite.
Brave, bold people are compared to a Zmeu, with the saying "He fights like a zmeu."[427]

Zmeu and Balaur are often interchanged in folklore. It's sometimes Zmeu, and not Balaur, that the Solomonari ride into the clouds. And Zmeu may be the name of that multi-headed dragon the hero battles. However, Zmeu, according to popular belief, is not even a dragon; he's a giant or ogre.

Romania has been called an "oasis of Latinity in a sea of Slavs,"[428] so it's possible that Zmeu's dragon connection stems from the relationship of his name to that of the Slavic Zmey. Or the fact that Zmeu can fly and breathe fire. Or even his proclivity for kidnapping beautiful women and bringing them to his palace. It's likely people call him a dragon due to a combination of all the above—because those are activities some Slavic dragons perform.

Origins

Zmeu has various incarnations: dragon, giant/ogre, demon/evil spirit. The dragon origin mirrors that of Balaur. The source of the other embodiments, however, is less certain. It's possible they're meant to be a distortion of the devil, who was mostly called "drac." Little else is written about this demonic origin.[429]

Appearance

As mentioned, the multi-headed dragon appearing in stories may be called Zmeu, instead of Balaur. However, unlike Balaur, who always maintains a dragon form, Zmeu's physical appearance is not well defined, because, as the people say, "the devil can take any form he wants."[430]

He lacks the tiny wings beneath his arms that Zmey possesses, yet he still manages to glide along the wind on his own merits. In some accounts he does possess wings, while in others, he rides a magnificent horse. He's gigantic, being able to plant his feet on mountaintops, while his head hides among the clouds. He mostly has human features. Sometimes he's described as being a huge, ugly man, while other times, he's a tall, dark-haired stranger with a black moustache, or even a golden-haired youth who creeps into a girl's dreams.

Some stories describe him as more demonic, having a human face and arms, but a furry body, a long, scaly tail, goat legs, and eyes that glow.[431] On his head, a magical precious stone shines as bright as the sun.

Alternately, as an evil spirit, he can appear as a round flame, with a long, fiery tail, a shooting star like the Slavic Zmey.[432]

Getting to Know Zmeu

Possibly the most popular of the three types of Zmeu is the giant. He builds his magnificent palace or fortress high on mountains or deep within dense forests, well away from the people's village. He has

Etymology

The word "Zmeu" is believed to be of Slavonic origin, derived from the name "Zmey." Both names come from the word *zmijĭ*, which when translated from Old Church Slavonic means "serpent" and is related to *zemlja* for "earth," signifying the idea of how snakes crawl on the earth (Nandris, 119).

However, for the most part, the creature Zmeu is not conceived of as a serpentine being, and so the Slavonic origin of the word has been challenged. Some etymologists say the word comes from the Dacian language, and others that it's related to the Romanian word *zmeură* for "raspberry," due to the being's red color. Although scholars think the latter is possible, most also considered it unlikely (Silverfox57).

Another unsubstantiated theory is that "Zmeu" is actually "Z-meu," a shortened form of *Zeul Meu*, which means "My God." In this case, the god in question is the Greek Zeus (Quroa.com), god of the sky, lightning, and thunder.

"limitless physical strength,"[433] which aids him both in his wrestling activities and during battles, as the warrior hurls his heavy mace at his enemy, a hero called Făt-Frumos. It's a battle between the destructive forces of greed and selfishness (exemplified by Zmeu) and selfless bravery (exhibited by Făt-Frumos).

You may recall from the Dracula reference in the Balaur chapter that the Count had characteristics of various Romanian folklore personalities, one of them being Zmeu, where the Count incorporates "the supermanly strength and wickedness of Zmeu."[434] This creature is the "embodiment of audacity and courage," and Romanians have used the name of Zmei (plural of Zmeu) to identify those they considered "illustrious warriors."[435] Add to that a magical mace that returns to him after he's hurled it at enemies,[436] and you have a formidable foe.

Another aspect of Zmeu relates to his family life. He has a wife, mother, child, siblings, and other relatives. His wicked mother, the Mother of the Forest (a figure like Baba Yaga), helps Zmeu in his evil pursuits.[437]

He's gregarious, loving to pursue hedonistic activities, especially gluttony, with his buddies. Each Zmeu can drink twelve barrels of wine and eat twelve loaves of bread in one sitting, as well as consume a vast number of cooked animals. He'll even eat people who dare to venture into his palace, and like the giant in *Jack and the Beanstalk*, he can smell his prey from great distances—or hidden anywhere within his home.

His breath is as powerful as his sense of smell. Each time he inhales, he can suck in the person next to him, and with each exhale, the person soars away like a bird in flight.

His main pursuit in life is stealing treasures, whether it's golden apples, the sun and moon, or the lovely, fair-haired princess Ileana Cosânzeana. Zmeu loves beautiful, hard-working human females, especially those of royal blood or from a family of good fortune. Unlike the Slavic Zmey, whose intentions are mainly good, Zmeu is considered evil. He's not the "loving husband" type.

> Keeping the discussion in the marital context, in Romanian folklore the *zmeu* appears as the one who kidnaps an unmarried girl, takes her to his shelter/cave/land and *lives together* with her (frequent euphemism for sexual embrace) until she is saved … by her future husband. As a sexual premarital initiator of virgins, this *zmeu* has anthropomorphic conformation, with features of wild virility (very tall and hairy), which might be decoded as an alter ego of the domestic husband.[438]

Zmeu.
Illustration by Dmitry Yakhovsky. © Bendideia Publishing.

He has a chauvinistic attitude toward his love interest once he's secured her in his home. He'll keep the girl he abducts locked away, constantly under supervision. She's often more of a personal servant than a lover. He expects his meal ready on the table—served neither too hot nor too cold—when he returns from trolling the human realm, where he's caused mayhem and destruction. To give her advance warning of his arrival, he'll throw his mace toward the castle three times from a great distance. Sometimes, it'll fall by the door; other times, it may land on the table. However, each time it returns to him like a boomerang.

Families take extra precautions to safeguard their daughters from such a fate, even hiding them from the rest of the world to prevent Zmeu from discovering the girls. Zmeu won't rest until he's made her his own, though. He'll steal a girl from a village dance, but he doesn't arrive hidden in clouds or a whirlwind. Instead, he's mounted on a horse, which flies him and his captured beauty away. Such an event occurred, villagers say, in the days when "happened all sorts of wonders ... bad wonders, the *zmei* walked, here on the earth."[439] The kidnapping in the account below happened on the day of a dance, when beautiful girls had come to the village from over the mountain.

> And there came the *zmei* and took a girl from the fair, he took her from the dance. And he flew away with her. And nobody knew anything about her anymore. And since then everybody got scared, and no one went there, to the fair. From that year on (…) they moved the fair down, at Titeşti. Haven't you seen during night time some star that lightens? That is said to be the *zmeu*. Some say that they [the *zmei*] were straddling … dressed like human beings and mounted…. And they took her and put her on the horses and flew together with the horses. They passed over the mountains, who could know?[440]

Human maidens aren't the only females Zmeu abducts. He's been known to carry off fairies who shirk their duties, while dallying with a human lover. Such is the case for Mariora Floriora, a beautiful mountain *zina* (fairy), called the Sister of the Flowers. Each time Mariora strolls in the fields, the flowers laugh joyously and pour forth their perfume for her. She covers them with kisses and places them in her hair. The mountain itself grows young at the sound of her approaching footstep; he clothes himself in a green and crystal robe to greet her. The birds sing their praises to her and seek to provide all she desires.

All this she neglects when one day she meets a handsome stranger, mounted on a black horse with a white star on its forehead. She has dreamed of finding love, and now he has come. "Intoxicated with love," she forgets every being she has taken care of. She sees not the moon nor stars shining with splendor. She travels with her lover over the meadows and mountain, but sees not her friends. The mountain sheds his verdant robe, and the tree leaves turn yellow and wither. The flowers droop their heads and fade. Mariora has eyes only for her lover. That's when her troubles begin.

> The coursers, flying upon wings swift as those of desire, arrive in a single bound at the borders of a stream. Mariora descends to bathe; and the water cradles and caresses her, as if she were a lily and grew there. The enamoured waves play with her hair, and leave upon every tress some bright drops to sparkle in it. But the sun dries up the bright drops, and transforms them into a cloud, which rises slowly towards the heavens.
>
> "Mariora," says the Sun, "thou art fair and lovely; thou art happy, but hast thou no thought that fortune is fickle, and that the sweetest dreams end bitterly? Dost thou know, that the flowers of the field have faded away since thou hast left them uncared for, and, returning to the skies, have complained that thou hadst forgotten them. Mariora," adds the Sun, "my beloved, the Lord will chastise thee, and thou must not murmur; still know that in this fleeting life and perishable world a sweet day of love is worth an age of vulgar happiness."
>
> "When fortune changes," exclaims the poet, "more griefs are crowded into one sad hour than are enough to darken years."
>
> Upon the third day Mariora felt her spirits saddened. She was pensive, and wept in silence on her lover's bosom. No one knew why she wept, for she wept as weep the flowers for the morning.
>
> The day was lovely, the mountains were bathed in light, and the valleys in silence. The birds kept within the pleasant shadows, and neither flew nor sang. The shadows were the only moving things: they struggled against the light, and when vanquished fled far into the forest.
>
> Mariora sighs, and embracing her lover, she says: "Sing, my beloved, that thy soul may pass into mine."

Hero Protecting Golden Apple.
Illustration by Nelinda. © Bendideia Publishing.

"Sweet have my days grown since I met thee, O my soul," sings the youth; "forget for me thy skies, fair angel sister to the golden stars, for I have forgotten my world for thee."

Suddenly there is a plaintive sound in the air, as of a mother's voice mingled with mournful bells. The earth trembles; Mariora looks round fearfully: she sees a black cloud hovering over her, dark and menacing as a Zméu spreading its sombre and awful wings over the horizon. It is the same cloud which rose from the bright drops in her hair, which the waves gave her. Mariora grows pale, and bending over her lover, she says, with anguished looks:—

"Farewell, O my love, foretold to me by the star! God has sent a Zméu from the mountain to tear me from thine arms; for since I have loved thee I have forgotten His flowers. They have faded, and complained to Heaven that I abandoned them."

She weeps as she speaks, and the cloud rises and overspreads the skies. The thunder rolls, and the valleys and mountains re-echo it; the lightning flashes, the rain falls, the winds moan, and poor Mariora hides her face in despair!

But fate is not to be pacified; the Zméu arrives and seizing her in his arms flies away with her over the mountain; after which the clouds vanish and the heavens become serene.

Where is Zina, the Flower Nymph? The beautiful Mariora Floriora, into what far country is she gone? Is she wandering over nine lands and nine seas, or is she seeking for the garden of Paradise, where dwell the Nymphs and the stars?

None ever told, none ever knew; but, when the full moon is shining on a serene night, her plaintive murmurs are sometimes heard in the caverns of the mountain.[441]

The One Who Flies

Another way Zmeu abducts women resembles the method the Slavic Zmey uses. Concealed within a shooting star, Zmeu enters a girl's room through a window. People describe him as a flame, whose power resides within his fiery tail. With it, he hits everything around him, and the place where he abducts the girl remains forever burnt.[442]

This aspect also makes him similar to the Romanian *zburător*, whose name means "the one who flies." As a handsome, golden-haired youth, he visits impressionable young girls, those who are prone to falling in love,[443] or he may appear as a longed-for lover for maidens who lack a loving relationship. In both cases, he invades the chosen girl's dreams, because sleep is believed to be a state of consciousness that enables communication with the supernatural. It's in this in-between world that he tortures his victim while she sleeps.[444]

> This is a spirit with igneous consistence (flame, fire roll, star) and fluid appearance, however of an undetermined shape, which usually (but not exclusively) visits women in the state of a long sexual absence/abstinence (spinsters, maidens who were not allowed to marry the ones they loved, lonely widows).[445]

He arouses her sexual desires, bringing her to a point of agony.

> His "dreaming-erotic activity" marks both the body and the soul of the victim with the signs of sexual excess. The visited humans fall ill. The *zburător* does not enter the body of a human, but causes in it, from outside, uncontrolled reactions, as if she/he is possessed (in terms of altered state of consciousness) by an alien entity. The victim is "psycho-physic impassioned, fallen under the obsession of pathological hyper-sexuality, of fidgeting combustion of the senses, of illusory orgasm."[446]

A popular song from a village relates one such encounter.

In a Wallachian village, on a night when

> "...the stars began to shine one after another,
> ...
> Followed by the late Moon,
> And, sometimes, a star fell like a bad omen..."

a young maiden called Florica had erotic dreams, which tormented her even after she awoke. She thought this might be because a handsome flying magician came at night to eat her dreams, vanishing before morning. However,

"In the height of the night, from the sky's midst,
The black attire sown by stars
Covers a world which dreams
Unknown incidents..."

the old women from the village asked themselves:

"What light was that like a lightning strike
Sending out sparks in the mid-night?
Is it a star that falls? Is it an emperor who dies?
Or a damned Zmeu?
Probably, it was a Zmeu
Who came down to Florica
Through her house's stove-pipe,
...
A Balaur of light with a fiery tail...."[447]

Many consider this type of attack demonic in nature, not by a devil with horns and a pitchfork, but by an angry spirit of the dead, likely a former lover. While this may be true among other cultures, as in Slavic lore, the case may not be accurate for Romanian traditional legends.

The *zburător* is not a medium at the disposal of two lovers, but a self-contained entity, with own spirit and identity, who is shown as acting independently; in fact, he is the one who generates the specific sexual behaviour of the victim. However, he may also represent the materialization and external projection of the internal and unsatisfied erotic desires of the dreamer.[448]

Likewise, in the form of this "fiery dragon," Zmeu also enters the girl's bedroom. He removes his scaly skin and appears as a dashing young man,[449] in order to seduce her and carry her away.

On a more malicious note, Zmeu may also enter houses to search for boys and girls he can torture—just for fun. His cruelty doesn't end with his misadventures in the home; as a flaming ball, he'll land on anyone walking alone at night and kill or disfigure the individual.[450]

Protection Methods

The best way to protect the lovely ladies in your community is to keep them out of Zmeu's sight. If he doesn't know they exist, he can't carry them off to his palace.

How to Appease

It's best to stay away. Zmeu wants what he wants and sets out to get it. No amount of flattery or good intentions will deter him once he's made up his mind.

How to Defeat

Făt-Frumos or another hero is the only one who can defeat Zmeu. Although Zmeu is clever, the hero is always smarter and faster and defeats Zmeu in the end.

Zmeu Tale

In this story, Zmeu captures a princess when she's not locked away. Romanian fairy tales like the one below often start off with a nonsensical quip that has nothing to do with the story.

There once was a mosquito with ninety-nine iron kilos at one leg. As light as he was, to the glory of heaven he flew. It was just like a fairy-tale.

He was an emperor, from youth to old age, but he bore no sons. At old age, he bore a daughter. A zmeu came at her birth and bragged that she would be his wife. After hearing that, the emperor thought and thought, what to do to get out of this conundrum. It seemed like there was nothing to be done.

"Let's make her a glass house and lock her inside. This way we can guard her and it's the only way to keep her safe."

They made the house and locked her in; they kept her there until she was fourteen. When the girl saw how merry the rest of the world was, how the rest of the world celebrated, she cursed her mother and father, for not birthing her dead, for birthing her alive, for hurting that much without a single fault. The emperor heard her, so did the Empress. They kept thinking and thinking, and the Empress said, "Oh Lord, your Lightness, gather your strength, your whole army. Let's go to the public garden and surround her with armed hefty young men, instead of a fence."

He spread the order in the whole country and gathered all the hefty men to surround the garden. And:
The girl they took,
Through the garden she wandered,
Among flowers,
And among beauty.
Then an equerry to His Majesty said: "Your Highness, let us go. You never know what time can bring."

The Emperor listened to him and took the girl outside. Before they could step through the gate, a great beast from the heaven's grace came and snatched the girl from his hands. They fired their rifles in vain, nothing could save her—the Emperor with His Empress fainted and fell as dead, pitying their daughter. Three days and three nights were they as dead. Upon waking up, the first thing they asked was about their daughter's whereabouts. And they were told: "Your Highness, a hag took her in the glory of the sky; there was nothing we could've done."

The Emperor sent word into the country, asking for the girl: *maybe somebody knows if she's alive, if she's dead.* Nobody knew anything except for a hefty lad, who served in the Emperor's army for three years, finished his campaign and went home. Walking on the road, he reached a fountain and rested there. He was so tired and said: "Oh, my mother, I'll rest here for a bit. I'll eat and sleep." While resting, all of a sudden, he saw the beast above him, and it had the girl in its claws. The lad saw it then and said: "They did not rule the empire right, leaving a lad on his way, without a single weapon. If only I had a weapon to save that Christian girl from that beast."

He could do nothing, but he knew the letters and described the girl: she was covered in gold and had golden earrings. The boy left—far away—and reached an inn. There he heard people talking about the girl. He had nothing else to say, only what he saw with his own eyes. Everywhere he listened he heard about the girl. Then he went to the inn keeper and told him: "Let me leave my bag with you and I'll go see His Royal Highness."

He went there. When he saw the Emperor's face, he lost himself and forgot it all, except that he had a letter in his pocket, so he threw it into the Emperor's lap. The Emperor, while looking over the letter said: "Boy, you bring me that girl, or I shall put your head where your feet are."

"Your Highness," he said, "let me go outside for three hours to think about how to get her back to you."

He went outside and took him two hours to make a plan. Then he went back inside.

"Have you thought about it?"

"I have. But you have to give me what I ask."

"I'll make her your wife."

"I have no need for that. I'm a ploughboy and she's an Emperor's daughter. Give me three hundred sturdy lads, the wisest of them all."

The Emperor gathered all the most upstanding men in the country and the boy chose three hundred of them. He chose some and let the others go. And the lad kept saying: "Your Highness, make them swear three times, that now I'm their Emperor instead of you."

That was exactly what the Emperor did. He gave them money to spend, clothes to wear, horses to ride and off they went. They kept going for three years and arrived in a great wilderness. They finished their food and had money, but there was no one to buy anything from, because there was no one around. So, the lad said:

"Because we reached the middle of nowhere, because we have money but nothing to buy, instead of eating grass with our horses, I say we each take a log in the night, climb on it and listen. Maybe we'll hear a bell ring, or a dog's bark, or a rooster's song."

They listened and listened in vain, but suddenly the lad heard a rooster singing and a bell ringing at the Black Citadel, from the north side. He climbed down and went toward the sound. Upon arrival he saw a block of stone. There was no gate to get inside. The lad told the other boys: "Charge your weapons and fire three times over this wall, maybe someone will come out."

The third time firing, a man came out with a sword and a red hat and asked:

"What are you doing here in the middle of nowhere? No bird flies over here, but here you are, walking."

"Let us inside, my lords, and we'll tell you all about our issue. We're dying of hunger, right next to our horses!"

Then another one came out, the biggest of them and asked them again, what they were doing in the wilderness. After he was convinced, he ordered his men to open the two gates.

When they got inside,

They sat at the table,

And ate for three days in a row.

Then the biggest one of them asked:

"Where are you coming from, where are you heading to and what are you looking for?"

"Oh, God, we don't even know anymore where we are coming from, nor where we're heading to. We left in search for the Emperor's daughter, who was kidnapped by a zmeu."

"Well, well... did you say you've travelled for three years?"

"Yes, three years."

"You have three more to go until you reach the zmeu's house."

Then he fed the lads bread and gave them moonshine. Afterwards, he showed them their way.

"Well," he said, "look eastward. Do you see anything there?"

"Yes, my lord," they answered.

"What do you see?"

"A white cloud."

"That's the zmeu's palace. You have to travel three more years to get there."

Three years more they travelled and reached a stone castle, shaped like a cloud. But they couldn't go upwards, nor did they find a gate. The hero told the other lads: "Hear me out. Take my horse, kill it and skin it."

While the lads were doing as they were told, the hero took his weapon and hid under the skin of the dead horse. From there he told them:

"You, there, go away from me for three days straight. After three days have passed, come back. If you still find me here, untie me and we'll all go wherever God sends us. If I'm not here anymore, wait for me for six weeks."

They came back and did not find him. The beast came from the sky, grabbed him in his claws and took him up. While he was tearing the horse's skin apart, the hero fired his rifle and killed the zmeu right there, from under the skin. He cut the zmeu's claws off and placed them into his bag, to have proof. He found the emperor's daughter in the zmeu's house.

"Oh," she said, "what was in your head to come here? If the zmeu returns, he'll eat the both of us."

"Don't worry. I took care of him."

"I cannot believe it, not until I see it."

Then, the hero grabbed his bag, took out the claws, and the girl believed the zmeu was defeated. Afterwards, they celebrated for three days and three nights.

"Well, boy," she said, "we should get going, because the zmeu has a brother and if the other beast comes, we'll both be its food." And they started their way back, in the world underneath. When they reached the wall, to climb down, the girl said: "You should climb down first, boy."

"I barely got myself up. You go down first," he said.

She went down in the valley and was surrounded by three hundred men. And he climbed down after her. But his men started shooting at him, missed him, but did not miss his ropes and he was left there hanging. No way down, no way up. The men took the girl and left. The hero was left there, whining. After a while, a zmeu came howling, the brother of the one killed, and took the hero in his claws.

"Oh," he said, "I should eat you, just like you've eaten my brother."

"Eh," the hero said, "take me up, because there's nothing good waiting for either of us downwards."

And up they went

Three times was he teased.

"Calm down. I won't eat you," the zmeu said. "You did good to me, and I shall return the favor. But you'll have to swear on your life," he said, "that whatever you won't have, you'll give me."

"How can I give you something I don't have?"

"Swear it!"

And he swore.

"My brother's wife will be your wife. Don't worry, even if she left. And you'll have a golden child. When he's born, as soon as he's born, we'll cut him along the spine and share him. That's what you did not have, but will."

They celebrated afterwards and the zmeu said: "Do you want to go back where you came from? You'll be there in a blink of an eye. Eh," he said, "climb on my back. How do you want to go, with the speed of the wind or of a thought?"

"Yes," he said, "with the speed of a thought."

Quick as a thought, he arrived at the Emperor's gate, ahead of the men, who still had six years to walk. In the Empire, he made a small house for the zmeu to lie in and he became a foreman. But the zmeu also gave him a golden hen and a golden tray. He spent all his days breaking nuts, eating and drinking wine. In the morning he would sell the golden eggs that the hen made. He was seen by the Empress and she called the Emperor to buy the golden eggs. He (the boy) asked for something that didn't cost a thing and he couldn't break. And the Emperor said: "Foreman, why do you sit over there? Aren't you worried that some foe might come and steal your treasures?"

"Very well, Your Highness, I'll come—with your blessing."

With the Emperor's blessing he went into the Emperor's courtyard. He counted in his head how many years it would take for the men to return. At some point, those years would arrive. And he dreamed about when she would come.

"Well, your Royal Highness, I had such a wonderful dream, that you'll receive news."

The Emperor responded: "I'll believe it when I see it."

He told him once again, but the Emperor still didn't believe him. The third time: "Prepare yourself because the news I've dreamed shall come true." It wasn't long after that the Emperor received the news to go greet his daughter. It happened and she came.

When everybody saw the Emperor's daughter, the foreman didn't go. That's why he said: "Oh, God, your Royal Highness, all the shepherds have seen her already, but I haven't."

"Go and see her with your own eyes."

The Emperor asked his daughter who saved her from the beast. She said that a guy, who was left behind. "I have to go after him."

"You shall be his!"

They had a wedding and celebrated afterwards. And when the time came for the newlyweds to go to bed, he took his son-in-law and went outside and he (her father) went inside and asked her: "Is this the one who saved you from the dragon?"

"Well," she said, "I guess so."

"Should I say it was me?"

"Well," she said, "you do look alike, but I don't think so. Where were you?"

He reached for the claws in his bag and showed them to her.

"Oh, Father," she said, "this is the man who saved me."

And it was as he said it. He grabbed his rifle and shot all the remaining men and they had a second wedding. And after one year, they made a golden baby. Upon the child's birth, the zmeu was at the door. The father asked: "Who are you?"

"Do you really have to ask?"

When the zmeu stepped inside he said: "Take him away from his mother. Grab his right leg, I'll grab his left one and let's cut him along his spine. Don't go sideways, neither for me, nor for you."

He took the child, and the father grabbed the knife, moved his hand to cut the child. At that moment, the devil stopped the father's hand.

"Oh! I shall make my side your gift, for you stood by your word."

And he gifted the child.

And health there was, only health from then on.[451]

Dragon Slayers

"A hero is no hero who is not able to defend his own."

Dragon slayers appear in both fairy tales and folk tales. Fairy tales are those stories that are entirely fiction, although they may have an underlying message about a certain time period—whether it's political, religious, or otherwise. Folk tales are based off of a real person or event, but they can also contain many fictional elements, making the hero larger than life.

One of the main reasons heroes fight a dragon, as you've already learned, is to force the dragon to release the water to restore fertility and natural order to the land. This theme has long been present in dragon myths.

> One of the oldest versions of the dragon slaying myth is found in a Hittite text, considered an ancient prayer song asking gods for rain and abundance of crops: the story recounts the Storm-god's fight against the dragon Illuyankas; at first the god appears weak and is defeated, however, with help from a mortal human, who uses tricks instead of force, the dragon is defeated and dies together with the human.[452]

When the hero isn't conquering a beast to restore fertility and order, he's saving a maiden, often a princess, whom the dragon has abducted. Rescuing a maiden is a variation of the fertility myth.

> [B]y threatening the life of a girl/princess, the dragon obstructs the function of a woman and/or goddess of fertility, threatening the community in which she marries and procreates; thus it is the duty of the hero to fight and restore order.[453]

You've already learned that dragons exude potency and sexuality. In contrast to this, a maiden locked away in a palace is seen as sexual repression.

> The zmey is nothing else but sexual power. The castle is the human body. In the castle, the princess sighs, i.e., the soul that the poorly managed sexual power holds captive. The knight-prince is the human ego or the spirit. The weapons with which he can defeat the zmey are the means at the disposal of the spirit, and these are the will, self-control, and the ability to control and use this power.[454]

A dragon-slaying hero is often a brave man (and occasionally a woman) who has tremendous strength and endurance. These traits by themselves aren't always enough to make the hero successful; his fate, frequently determined at birth, guides him.

> She [*Nature*] heralds his birth with terrific demonstrations, flashes lightning, hurls thunderbolts, causes the earth to rock from side to side, and on the whole behaves in such a startling fashion that the people, and above all the troubled parents, regard the child with very mingled feelings, and are uncertain whether to cherish or to expose him.[455]

Nature continues to assist the hero throughout his lifetime, and even at his death.

Seldom can the epic hero be said to be alone, for, though leagues of plains and mountains may separate him from his comrades, he has the fellowship of the trees of the forest, the mountain peaks, the winds, the clouds, stars, moon, and sun—all of which in articulate human words cheer him and give him timely warning and advice.[456]

Nature isn't the only assistance a hero receives. A dog may be a man's best friend, but for heroes, his marvelous horse is his closest companion and most faithful of all creatures, always ready to guide him in the right direction and provide advice when asked—and even when not requested.

The life of the epic horse, then, resembles that of the epic hero. He is often of supernatural origin. Sometimes he is glorious when he first appears, often enough he is the ugly duckling of the fairy story. Frequently he has to pass some ordeals before he is recognized as worthy to become an epic actor. He is not only a great fighter, but a far-sighted, devoted friend, with all the virtues and seldom with any of the vices of his master. His vision pierces the future and the veil that hides gods and fairies from men. Usually his career ends with that of the hero he has served. Sometimes the latter, feeling that his own death is inevitable, kills his old friend to prevent his falling into the hands of a stranger.[457]

The horse may have been a gift, spoils of war, purchased from a dealer, or a hereditary possession. Often, in the stories, the horse is destined to belong to a certain hero. These heroic horses are at times related to each other. Frequently, especially in fairy tales, these horses can speak.

Thus aided and ready for battle, the hero sets forth on his quest. These dragon slayers come in many varieties: fairy-tale heroes, saints, and legendary heroes.

Fairy-Tale Heroes

Fairy tales or wonder tales are called *skazki* in Russian and tell the story of a hero who undertakes a personal quest. The goal of these hero stories is "to transport the listener into a fabulous fairy-tale world."[458] Although the tales don't start with "once upon a time," many have a common beginning: they take place "in a certain kingdom."

The dragon slayer of fairy-tale ilk centers around either a nameless hero, a person with a common name like Ivan or John, or a character with a fanciful name like Rolling Pea. The Eastern European hero, whether prince or peasant, is always handsome, noble, and pure of heart.

From an early age, the hero is special. For example, Ivan, the Tsar's son, is a precocious child. At the age of nine days old, he can speak. He informs his father he is going to his wedding with Peerless Beauty, whom his father has promised him for a bride. The infant proceeds to instantly become a full-grown youth the moment he steps out of his cradle.

The hero's survival is a result of his strength and wisdom, as well as his readiness to assist those in need. This includes not only humans, but also an assortment of creatures—whether mammal, bird, fish, or insect: wolf, bear, fox, dog, lion, hawk, raven, crow, crane, chicken, pike, lobster, frog, bee, and more. Those he helps, in return, aid him with tasks that would have otherwise been impossible for him to achieve by himself.

The hero in fairy tales often accomplishes little on his own: people tell him how to find the monster he seeks, and creatures help him destroy the beast. But in the end, it's the hero who claims the victory.

His horse is especially critical to his success, and choosing one is an important task. In one tale, Ivan meets an old man, whom Ivan is at first rude to but then regrets his actions and becomes courteous. The old man then tells Ivan how to choose a horse that will get him where he wants to go.

"What shall I do?" asked the Tsarevich, thrusting his hands into his belt and standing with feet wide apart. "I have no horse of mettle or whip of silk for such a ride."

"Why, your father has thirty horses of the best," said the old man, "and the trouble with you will be to make a wise choice. Go to the stables and tell the grooms to take the thirty to bathe in the deep blue sea. When they come to the shore you will see one of them push forward into the water up to its neck and drink. When this happens watch with care to see if the waves rise high and break in foam upon the beach. If so, take that horse, for it will bear you safely to the edge of the white world and to the place where the sun peeps up, which is called the Golden Kingdom of the East."[459]

THE OTHER WORLD

The fairy-tale hero's quest takes him to a distant land, the "other world." This is in another dimension, a wilderness on "the edges of the civilised world," located "at the fringes of human experience and control" (Pluskowski, 117). It bears various names, including:

- The beyond
- End of the world (*kraisvet* in Bulgarian) (Georgieva, 29)
- End of the earth (*kraizemya* in Bulgarian) (Georgieva, 29)
- Other space or other realm (*taramul celalalt* in Romanian) (McBeath)
- Dark world (compared to the land of the living, which is called the "white world") (Douglas, 5)

These are all euphemisms for the land of the dead.

When a person dies in the real world, he is seen as taking a long journey (often forty days) to the other world, revisiting places that held meaning in his life. The dead person's relatives perform rituals to ensure that the deceased's journey is a successful one.

The other world in folklore, however, is not "a world of dead souls but rather one of spirit-beings who hold in thrall the still living humans" (Warner, 54). Maidens captured by dragons are secured deep within caves in this land, either to be wives or servants of the beast, with no means to escape on their own.

To reach this mysterious destination where the dragon lives, the hero must travel "beyond thrice-nine lands" or to "the thrice-ten-kingdom" (Warner, 54). This location may be "high up, on top of a glass or crystal mountain, underground, with its entrance hidden by a rock or a metal slab; 'at the edge of the world, far far away'; across the ocean; or on the other side of a fiery river or in a deep pit" (Warner, 55).

In Romanian stories, the dragon's palace is said to exist "over there, where the Devil weans his children" (Ispirescu, xii). Among these stories, it's believed that the land of the living and that of the dead are connected through "Saturday's water" (*Apa Sâmbetei*), an ocean encompassing the world. Souls of the deceased travel on rivers to this water source, which transports them to the afterlife (Atlantic Religion).

In Bulgarian folk belief, the other world is called *Zmeykovo*, Dragon Village. It houses the palace of the Sun (whom the dragon symbolizes). Other mythological creatures besides dragons also live there: enchanting woodland nymphs or fairies called *Samodivi*; mermaids

continues

(Moral: Remember to always be polite, especially to your elders, or you may miss out on golden opportunities.)

Once the hero has his faithful horse, he's ready to set off to find his opponent. Getting there is never easy, since the dragon's abode exists in the "other world." To reach this land, he travels vast distances "through deserted places or where no human has been before."[460]

But first, he has to find his destination. To do that, he needs assistance. Magical beings such as the witch Baba Yaga, "a silver bird with a golden crest," "a frog carried in a jar of water," and others provide him with special knowledge or magical gifts so he can achieve this goal.[461]

THE OTHER WORLD *continued*

called *Rusalki*; the *Oristnizi*, or Fates, three sisters who determine a child's destiny on the third day after his birth; and diseases, personified as invisible female beings.

The other world is located at the point where the sky, or the heavens, touch the earth.

> [You go] there, afar,
> At deserted places,
> At the margin of the world,
> Where the Earth finishes,
> In the thick forests,
> The cocks don't sing,
> And the dogs don't bark (Douglas, 8).

The quietness of the roosters and dogs in the above indicates that spirits are nearby.

The other world has also been described as being "the most distant place along a horizontal line" (Georgieva, 81) or "at the edge of the white world at the place where the sun peeps up" (Wilson, 294). This place where the heavens touch the land has two edges, steep banks, between which the sun rises and sets. Beyond these banks lies water, which the sky covers like a lid (Georgieva, 29).

In ancient times, the heavens were considered a solid crust made up of seven layers. This "lid" covered the entire earth. Various stories said it was "made of glass, soil or metal or was a tight-stretched ox-hide, a copper threshing-floor or a shirt of unwoven fabric." The lowest level, which people could see, contained the sun, moon, and stars (Georgieva, 21).

> In popular beliefs, the sun was below the heavens and walked under the heavenly lid. It lived at the point of contact between heaven and earth. Its palace was beyond a tall mountain and a sea at world's end. From there, along a special route under the earth and yet by sea, it went to the exit, that is the east (Georgieva, 22).

The land, however, was originally flat, and the sky could not cover it. To solve the problem, stories explain how God sought counsel with the devil, who told God to beat the earth. In this way, the edges, or mountains, were formed (Georgieva, 29).

The journey takes the hero a long time, often three years. When he reaches the border of the other world, he can enter in various ways. One means is by crossing a river. Another is by descending into a hole or well and traveling along an underground passage, which is believed to terminate "at the root of the heavens."[462] This may take him an additional three years to reach the bottom. He can also arrive at the other world (or return from there) by riding on the back of a gigantic bird, or because his horse can perform far-reaching leaps.

Now that the hero is finally in the dragon's realm, he must find the dragon and discover how to defeat the creature. On the way to the dragon's palace, the hero meets and helps various animals. In return, they offer him assistance. Sometimes, their aid will help him get a horse he needs in order to escape from the dragon (if he doesn't already have such a creature); other times, the animals help him destroy the dragon itself. (Moral: be kind to those you think are weaker than yourself.)

The hero's weapon of choice to defeat a dragon is often a sword, mace, or bow and arrow. With his sword, he'll chop off the dragon's head. Here again, he may require assistance from companions to defeat the dragon, but only after he's battled multiple dragons, and the final one has one more head than the hero can manage by himself.

In the excerpt from the story that follows, Ivan single-handedly defeats dragons on three successive nights: first a three-headed one, then a six-headed one, and finally a nine-headed one. On the fourth night, when a twelve-headed dragon appears, Ivan tells his six companions (who have gotten drunk on the previous nights when they were supposed to keep watch) to keep their eyes on a bowl. When it fills with blood, they have to assist him in the battle. Then he goes out to battle the beast—alone.

> He returned and stood against the serpent; they rushed and struck each other. Ivan at the first blow cut four heads off the serpent, but went himself to his knees in the earth; when they met the second time, Ivan cut three heads off and sank to his waist in the earth; the third time they met he cut off three more heads, and sank to his breast in the earth; at last he cut off one head, and sank to his neck in the earth. Then only did his comrades think of him; they looked, and saw that the blood was running over the edge of the bowl. They hastened out, cut off the last head of the serpent, and pulled Ivan out of the earth.[463]

However, in Romanian stories, cutting off the dragon's head may not kill the beast. The creature's head can still attack and breathe fire. Even if the hero cuts the beast into a million pieces, those bits wiggle and squirm until they reconnect, making the dragon whole again.[464] A decapitated dragon can also "regenerate his heads by touching the stumps with a fiery finger."[465] The hero has to keep slicing away at the dragon until sunset, when the fragments cease moving, and the dragon dies.[466]

Defeating a dragon in battle may be only one step in the hero's victory. If the dragon has a wife, daughters, or brothers, these family members will seek revenge. The females have been known to be clever in their endeavors, as you'll see in the fairy-tale excerpt that follows.

> After this the wives of the three dragons met together and took counsel together. 'Whence did those men come who slew our husbands? Well, we *shall* be women if we don't get rid of them out of the world.'
>
> The youngest said: 'Now then, sisters! let us go by the highroad, where they will go. I will make myself into a very beautiful wayside seat, and if, when wearied, they sit down upon it, it will be death to them all.'
>
> The second said to her: 'If you do nothing to them, I will make myself into an apple-tree beside the high-road, and when they begin to come up to me, the agreeable odour will attract them; and if they taste the apples, it will be death to them all.'

Fät-Frumos.
Illustration by Nadia Bulighin, 1927. Public domain via Wikimedia Commons.

Well, the heroes came up to the beautiful wayside seat. Little Rolling-pea thrust his sword into it up to the hilt—blood poured forth! They went on to the apple-tree.

'Brother Little Rolling-pea,' said the heroes, 'let us each eat an apple.'

But he said: 'If it is possible, let us eat; if it is not possible, let us go on further.' He drew his sword and thrust it into the apple-tree up to the hilt, and blood poured forth immediately.

The third she-dragon hastened after them, and extended her jaws from the earth to the sky. Little Rolling-pea saw that there was not room for them to pass by. How were they to save themselves? He looked about and saw that she specially aimed at him, and threw the three horses into her mouth. The she-dragon flew off to the blue sea to drink water, and they proceeded further.[467]

The tale doesn't end there. The third dragon pursues them again and again. Each time, Little Rolling-pea throws different beings into her mouth: falcons, hounds, and even his two companions!

At other times, the hero merely seizes the captured maiden and rides away on his horse. He then has to escape from the dragon that will certainly pursue him. This is where he uses the magical gifts he's received, such as mirrors, handkerchiefs, and more. He throws behind him one item after the other to hinder the progress of his pursuer. The objects turn into a forest, lake, fire, mountain, or some other obstacle.

Parting with items is seen as a self-sacrifice or a "partial death of self."[468] It was the belief that by giving away a possession, the hero would receive assistance in another form.

Făt-Frumos

Făt-Frumos from Romanian folklore is a fairy-tale hero. His name means "Beautiful Boy" (or "Handsome Son") and is the equivalent to "Prince Charming." Făt-Frumos comes from the Latin *fetu-* for "boy" and *formosu-* for "handsome."[469]

Făt-Frumos is less of a specific character and more of "a generic title for an almost archetypal heroic inspiration that may reside in almost any human suddenly thrust into a potentially deadly situation."[470] In some stories, he may be called by a given name, such as Petru, but is called Făt-Frumos as well.

From birth, and even before, Făt-Frumos is no ordinary person. His conception is miraculous and his growth wondrous.

In ancient times there lived a dark and thoughtful emperor that had such a young and joyful empress that she appeared like the brightest core of the day.

Fifty years had passed since the war between the emperor and his neighbor started. His neighbor's death left behind the same hate and enmity as an inheritance to his sons and nephews. Fifty years had passed and the emperor was living in complete solitude, similar to an old lion weakened by struggles and sadness. An emperor who had never laughed in his life, who could not offer a smile to his innocent child's song, to his wife's loving smile or to the joyful and ancient stories of the soldiers aged in battles. Feeling weak and closer to death, he had no one to accept his hatred as inheritance. He was overwhelmed by sadness each time he got up from his imperial bed, from beside his young empress. Their golden bed was desolated and cursed. He was going to war with an untamed heart, leaving his wife crying alone in her solitude. Her beautiful golden hair was falling on her white and round breasts and her big blue eyes were crying rivers of soft watery pearls. They were touching her pale face and her blue tiny veins that were visible like a living marble on her white skin.

Straight from her bed, she was resting on the stone stairs of an arch made in the wall, where a silver icon of the Mother of Sorrows was watching over a smoking candle. Touched by the prayers of the empress, the cold icon's eyelids got wet and a tear visibly fell from the darkest eye of the Mother of God. The woman got up and pressed her dry lips to the cold tear, trying to breathe it into the depths of her soul. She left while feeling her aching heart.

A month had passed, then two months, then nine, and the empress gave birth to a child, his skin white like the milk froth and golden hair as the moon. The emperor smiled, the sun smiled too and his fiery kingdom stayed still, for three days there was no night, but only clear sky and happiness. The wine was flowing from the barrels and the shouts of joy were splitting the sky above.

His mother called him Făt-Frumos din lacrimă [*Handsome Boy of the tears*].

The boy grew up and grew tall as the forest firs. He was growing in one day as others in a year.[471]

Făt-Frumos.
Romanian Postage stamp, 25 June 1965. Mi:RO 2421, Public domain, via Wikimedia Commons.

Besides being charming, Făt-Frumos is brave, cunning, fearless, and adventurous, "impelled toward adventure and a mission of mystic significance."[472] He's chivalrous, saving maidens from the evil Zmeu (or sometimes Balaur). This damsel-in-distress is often the emperor's beautiful daughter, Ileana Cosânzeana, described as the "ideal of feminine beauty and grace," who's "so dazzling that she appears to be a daughter of the sun."[473]

Făt-Frumos' strength is such that he has a special mace made for himself, because an ordinary one will be like a pinhead to him.

> When he was old enough, he had an iron mace forged for him that he threw up into the sky, caught it back with one finger and the mace broke in two. Then he had a heavier mace forged for him that he threw up close to the moon's cloud castle; after falling from the sky, it did not break on the boy's finger.[474]

Similar to other heroes, he requires a special horse to carry him to his destination and be his companion. In one story, the hero seeks out water from the well of Zâna Zorilor (the Fairy of the Dawn) in order to cure his father, the emperor, of his "weeping eye." In this story, he is called Petru, and he has two older brothers, who attempt the mission before him, but fail. The eldest son chooses the best and most beautiful horse. But that doesn't help him when he encounters a three-headed Balaur; the jaw of one head reaches to the sky, while another touches the ground. This son "didn't even wait for the dragon to bathe him in fire, but he spurred his horse and went as if he hadn't been here."[475] The middle son, too, runs away when he faces a dragon.

Now all hope for success is left to the young Petru. He chooses a horse and sets off to reach the well. On his way he meets a seven-headed Balaur. Petru shouts at the beast three times to get out of his way, but instead it breathes fire at him from all its heads. The sky darkens from the smoke, and flames race around on his right, on his left, in front of him, and behind him. The horse whinnies and rears onto two legs. Unable to defeat the dragon, Petru, instead of running far away as his brothers did, returns home to find a better horse. With the help of an old woman and her magic, he obtains his marvelous horse.

> "You see, my beloved Petru," the old woman began to lecture him, "you will not be able to go to the fountain of Zâna Zorilor unless you will be carried by the horse that your father, the emperor, rode in his youth. Go ahead, look for where that horse is, then ride away and leave."
>
> Petru showed gratitude for her advice and then he went to seek out the horse.
>
> "What a leap in the dark!" the emperor snapped. "Who is the one that taught you to ask me this? Of course, it sure was that witch from Bîrşa. Can you imagine this? Fifty years have passed since my youth! Who knows where my horse's rotten bones lay now? It seems to me the only thing I have left from it is a bridle belt forsaken in the attic of the stable. That's it and nothing else."
>
> Petru stormed out and went to confess the story to the old woman.
>
> "Just wait," she said loudly and laughing with joy. "In this case, we've got it made. Go and get me the piece of belt, I know precisely how to make use of it."
>
> The stable's attic was packed with horse belts and saddles. Petru carefully chose the most consumed, rotten and grubby pieces, as already agreed. The old woman grabbed them, passed them through incense smoke and after a soft uttered saying she turned to Petru, "Take them all and hit them on your house's beam."
>
> Petru did exactly what he was asked to. The old woman's sorcery was successful. He barely touched the house when all of the sudden something left him speechless. A horse of unseen beauty was standing in front of his eyes. He was not able to take his eyes off the

splendor of its harness and its golden saddle filled with precious stones. It was a stunning horse with a beautiful saddle and reins specially made for Făt-Frumos.

"Go ahead and hop on his back," the old woman said, while making the sign of the cross in the air and murmuring another short saying.

After following her instructions, Petru found himself three times stronger in both his arms and heart.[476]

This horse, of course, can speak, since it's a magical creature. It's quick to give Petru exactly the advice he needs in order to defeat the dragon at the bridge.

"Hold on tight, my master, because there is a long way to go and we have to speed up," said the horse. And away they went. They went and they flew like no other horse and young man did before.

When reaching the bridge, they were suddenly faced with a fierce dragon as never seen before, a dragon that had twelve enormous heads surrounded by flames. Not even a bit frightened, Petru rolled up his sleeves and got ready to fight the beast. "Out of my way!" he shouted while the dragon started to furiously spit fire. Without any other word, Petru pulled out his sword and rushed toward the animal.

"Hold on, master, and do as I say!" said the horse at once. "Firmly grasp your feet around my girdle, take out your sword and be ready to jump over the bridge and the dragon. When you see yourself on top of the beast, cut off its largest head, clean the blood from your sword, place it back in its position and be all set when coming back on the ground."

Petru precisely followed the commands—he pulled out his sword, cut the dragon's head, cleaned the blood using his cloth and he immediately felt the land underneath them.

And that is how they crossed the bridge.[477]

From there, Petru encounters additional dangers and receives assistance from other people, to aid him in defeating his foe and retrieving the water for his father.

Hero vs. Koschei the Deathless

In some stories, the creature the hero must battle is unnamed, but often he's the well-known antagonist called Koschei the Deathless (or Koschei the Immortal). The beast doesn't always appear as a dragon or snake; he's likely to be a skeletal man, and his name may, in fact, mean "skeletal."[478] Within the same story, the villain can appear as both Koschei and a dragon or snake.[479] However, he's as much a "ravisher of beauty" as the dragon.

The hero encounters Koschei hidden in a locked room of a castle. Although the hero has been forbidden to enter, of course, you know that's exactly what he does. Koschei is bound by various means, such as twelve chains or three iron barrel hoops, or he may be seated on a horse that's chained to a cauldron. Koschei pleads with the hero to give him a drink of water or wine, or unchain his horse. Each of the three times the hero gives in to the request, one of Koschei's bounds snaps or Koschei becomes stronger, getting closer to being set free. Koschei then captures the hero's wife, beloved, mother, or sister, and carries her far away.

From here, the story has a couple of variants. In return for the hero's assistance, Koschei may immediately promise to deliver the hero from three deaths. Later on, Koschei will let the hero go after he's been captured, but with a warning.

'Now,' says he, 'this time I will forgive you, in return for your kindness in giving me water to drink. And a second time I will forgive you; but the third time beware! I will cut you to bits.'[480]

"The Death of Koschei the Deathless."
Illustration in *The Red Fairy Book*, 1890. Public domain via Wikimedia Commons.

The third time he catches the hero, Koschei delivers on his promise and murders the man.

> Koshchei galloped off, caught Prince Ivan, chopped him into little pieces, put them into a barrel, smeared it with pitch and bound it with iron hoops, and flung it into the blue sea.[481]

All is not lost! Another character or characters bring the hero back to life. First, someone sprinkles the water of death onto the hero, so all his body parts are joined; then, the person applies the water of life, to restore the hero's breath.

> Then the Eagle hurried to the blue sea, caught hold of the barrel, and dragged it ashore; the Falcon flew away for the Water of Life, and the Raven for the Water of Death.
> Afterwards they all three met, broke open the barrel, took out the remains of Prince Ivan, washed them, and put them together in fitting order. The Raven sprinkled them with the Water of Death—the pieces joined together, the body became whole. The Falcon sprinkled it with the Water of Life—Prince Ivan shuddered, stood up, and said:
> 'Ah! what a time I've been sleeping!'[482]

The hero now has to figure out a better way to steal back the woman Koschei stole. He encourages her to ask Koschei where he got his marvelous horse that overtook them each time they tried to escape. Often, it's from the evil Baba Yaga or an unnamed witch. Koschei is quick to share his knowledge, thinking no one can get another horse like his.

> 'Beyond thrice nine lands, in the thirtieth kingdom, on the other side of the fiery river, there lives a Baba Yaga. She has so good a mare that she flies right round the world on it every day. And she has many other splendid mares. I watched her herds for three days without losing a single mare, and in return for that the Baba Yaga gave me a foal.'
> 'But how did you get across the fiery river?'
> 'Why, I've a handkerchief of this kind—when I wave it thrice on the right hand, there springs up a very lofty bridge, and the fire cannot reach it.'[483]

Needless to say, the hero acquires the horse and is finally able to escape with the captured woman.

In other variations of the story, Koschei, or an unnamed dragon, is more difficult to defeat, because he has a soul that doesn't reside within his physical body. This "external" or "separable" soul,[484] called his "strength" or his "death," is hidden far away. It resides within multiple layers of animals or objects like Russian nesting dolls, each having to be peeled away and destroyed. The final location frequently resides within an egg, which is associated with the renewal of life in many cultures.

Some of these hiding places include:

- Within an egg, inside a duck, inside a stump, floating on the sea.
- Within a sparrow, inside a pigeon, inside a hare, inside a boar, inside a dragon, within a lake, near a royal city.
- Within three pigeons, inside a hare, inside a silver tusk of a wild boar, on a mountain.
- Within a needle's point, inside a hare, within a chest, high upon an oak.
- Within an egg, inside a duck, inside a hare, inside a coffer, buried under an oak, on an island, in the ocean.

Before the hero can destroy the soul, he must find it. When he finally reaches the captured woman, he gets her to try to find out from Koschei where he hides his soul. She attempts to trick Koschei into telling her, but he doesn't give up that information right away. Either to entertain himself or out of mistrust, the dragon first fabricates a hiding place. The woman then performs some sort of homage to the object, at which Koschei laughs or scorns her. In some stories, she tries to destroy the object, without success, because his soul isn't really there.

For example, he says his strength is:

- *In a broom under the threshold*. She gilds it, decks it with ribbons, and sets it on the table. When he asks why she did it, the woman says, "How could your death lie under the threshold? The table is a better place for it."[485]
- *In a goat*. She adorns it with ribbons and bells and gilds its horns.[486]
- *Tied up in a birch broom*. She gilds it with pure beaten gold, covering each twig. When he returns and asks what the gilded broom means, she replies, "See how I honor you, for I gild even Death for you."[487]
- *Concealed within an oak fence*. She again gilds the fence to honor him.[488]
- *In the hearth*. She kisses and caresses it, saying, "O beautiful hearth, where my master's strength is hidden! How happy are the ashes that cover your stones!"[489]
- *In a certain tree*. She throws her arms around it, saying, "O tree! Most beautiful tree in the world, guard carefully our master's strength and let no harm come to it!"[490]

Koschei the Immortal.
Painting by Viktor Mikhailovich Vasnetsov, 1917–1928. Public domain via Wikimedia Commons.

After giving her false information a couple of times (like Sampson with Delilah), Koschei finally relents. He either gets tired of her asking (this option gets my vote), or he decides the woman is sincere about her love for him, and so he tells her the truth. She proceeds to relay that information to the hero. Off the hero goes to retrieve and destroy the beast's soul.

Along the way in both variations of the story, the hero encounters creatures that he either assists or doesn't kill even though he's hungry. In gratitude, they help him either perform the task Baba Yaga sets out for him (in the first variation) or destroy the nested creatures the soul hides within (in the second variation).

In the first scenario, the hero overcomes Koschei with the help of the horse he acquired. The dragon chases the hero again, but luck is not on his side this time.

> After a time he came up with Prince Ivan, lighted on the ground, and was going to chop him up with his sharp sword. But at that moment Prince Ivan's horse smote Koshchei the Deathless full swing with its hoof, and cracked his skull, and the Prince made an end of him with a club.[491]

In the second scenario, having retrieved the soul, the hero has control over the beast. He may kill him right there by destroying the soul, or he may take the soul back and torment Koschei before killing him.

> Ivan Tsarevich, took the egg from his bosom, and showed it to Koshchei. 'What is this?'
>
> The light grew dim in the eyes of Koshchei; then he became mild and obedient. Ivan Tsarevich threw the egg from one hand to the other. Koshchei Without-Death staggered from corner to corner. This seemed pleasant to the Tsarevich. He threw the egg more quickly from hand to hand, and broke it; then Koshchei fell and died.[492]

The captured woman may also be the one who destroys Koschei.

> The young man placed the egg in the warm napkin within his pouch and ran forward, ever forward, until he came to Peerless Beauty, who was stooping over the stove in the kitchen. Ivan put his arms about the cake-baker, who grasped his hands and pressed them; and when she stood upright the egg was in her left palm.
>
> Ivan turned and saw Koschei sitting on the window ledge and scowling at him, because he expected that the cakes and baked meats that Peerless Beauty was cooking were all for him. But as the two rushed to the grip, Peerless Beauty dropped the egg upon the stove. It broke, and as the shell cracked, Koschei's heart broke also, and he fell down dead.[493]

In other versions, Koschei (or an unnamed dragon or snake) dies when the hero hits him on the head with the egg or with a small stone within the egg yolk.

Saints

Saints are patrons of many things, including natural elements and places both in the cosmos and on land. Folklore takes this concept further, maintaining that saints are *rulers* of, and have power over, these spaces and elements. When the land became Christianized, saints took this role over from ancient gods. In this way, saints bridge the gap between characters from nature myths and historical heroes, as they are a little of both.

The saints' holidays mark the seasons. Their presence guarantees fertility, prosperity, stability, and harmony. At times, when the weather turns bad, people believe the saint has become incapacitated. His removal from the role of overseer violates the natural order of the cosmos. And so, the only way to restore both social order and the balance of nature is to free the saint from whatever affliction prevents him from carrying out his duty.

In addition to agricultural aspects, saints also have warlike characteristics. Foul weather indicates an outside force (the dragon by whatever name it's called) has enchanted the land and taken away its fertility. People call upon the saint to remove the obstacle that's preventing the natural order.

St. George.
Photo and art © Valentin Yokov. Used with permission of the artist.

St. George

St. George (Georgi, Egorii), one of the greatest Christian martyrs, is likely the most universally well-known dragon slayer, with both art and literature portraying him as a knight on a white horse, his spear thrust into a dragon. The name of the dragon he slays varies among the Eastern European nations: Zmey/Zmaj (in Russia and others), Lamia or Hala (in Bulgaria), Balaur (in Romania).

Little is known about the historical George. The "De Libris recipiendis" of Pope Gelasius in the year 495 includes the saint among those "whose names are justly reverenced amongst men, but whose actions are only known to God."[494] Nonetheless, it's believed he came from Cappadocia (in modern-day Turkey). He was a Greek soldier, who served as a Roman officer under the reign of Diocletian (emperor of the Roman empire from 284 to 305). Refusing to recant his Christian faith, St. George was possibly martyred on April 23, 303, during the emperor's persecution of Christians. That April date in the Julian calendar (May 6 in the newer, Gregorian calendar), then, became one of the saint's most celebrated holy days, and it marks the beginning of summer and the agricultural season.

For Bulgarians and other Eastern Europeans, though, George has a more traditional role as the patron of shepherds and their livestock, and he's the protector of wild animals (wolves, in particular) and nature. His victory over the dragon symbolizes nature's triumph over a harsh winter that's brought death and destruction, while the return of spring brings forth growth and renewal of life. Even George's name, *Geōrgios*, has a connection with these springtime activities: *geos* ('earth') and *orge* ('cultivate'),[495] making the name George in Greek mean "farmer."[496]

Some sources say George may be based on Gerovit (Yarovit), the Slavic god of agriculture and fertility, whose main feast likely occurred in the second half of April. A pagan priest, speaking the words of the god to the people, once said:

> I am your god, I, who clothe the plains with grass and the woods with foliage, the produce of the fields and the trees, the offspring of the flocks and everything that is of use to man are in my power.[497]

Not only that, but Gerovit was a god of war, whom the ancient Romans called Mars. This military aspect relates to George's dragon-slaying activities.

Likewise, George displays similarities to the Thracian Horseman or Heros, who may have been a human hero who acted as a mediator between people and gods. Other legends say he was a god or lesser deity himself, the son or lover of the goddess Bendis. He ruled the underworld, was a god of nature, vegetation, and animals, and also a protector of flocks and horses. Horses, in particular, had great prominence in Thracian culture, being symbolic of Thracian kingship and the Sun,[498] and the Horseman was always seen riding one. He hunted wild boars, which destroyed crops and were considered the enemies of fertility.[499]

Like Gerovit, the Thracian Horseman, and possibly other gods, this duality between "hero" and "farmer" exists with St. George. As George replaced whatever god he supplanted, "the newly converted peoples still kept their ancient mythological ideas of the dual unity between the patron deities of agriculture, and war."[500] It's this warlike trait that prevails in the dragon-slaying stories, while the agricultural aspect remains largely forgotten.

The origin of the dragon story remains as obscure as much as that of St. George himself. It traces back to around the eleventh century. (Some sources claim it's as late as the thirteenth century, while other say as early as the tenth.) The dragon story is speculated to be "a response to the warlike spirit of the crusade period."[501]

However, six centuries before St. George battled a fire-breathing dragon, stories circulated about his conquest of a different sort of dragon—a human one, Persian King Dadianus, who persecuted the saint and

www.dinkovwoodcarving.com

St. George.
Photo and art © Plamen Dinkov. Used with permission of the artist.

other Christians. This king was called the "dragon of the abyss." In the legend, the princess St. George rescued was the king's wife, Queen or Empress Alexandra.

> At one point in the tedious and detailed narrative of the saint's tortures and sufferings, Dadianus decided to take a different tack and use a more gentle kind of persuasion. Taking George to Alexandra's chambers, he left him there in her company, that she might lead him back to the worship of the pagan gods. But very soon George had converted her to Christianity, and after that she took George's part against Dadianus.[502]

The concept of George killing the dragon was symbolic, "evidence of the power of faith in Christ over faith in many gods (paganism)."[503]

> [O]n the way back from a war, he [St. George] saw a crying girl by a lake near a city of pagans. From her he learned that the inhabitants of the city worshiped as a god a huge zmey that lived in the lake, so every year they sacrificed a girl to him, and this year it was the turn of the king's daughter herself. In vain the warrior-saint was trying to persuade her father to renounce his god and bloody sacrifices in honor of the monster, and to accept the Christian faith, which requires humble kindness and mercy above all. In the end, the king agreed to be baptized with all his people only if the young warrior proved the power of his God and defeated the zmey. Georgi sat by the lake and, bowing his head in the lap of the beautiful girl, fell asleep. Suddenly the waters of the lake started raging and a huge zmey appeared from them, which rushed towards his doomed victim. The girl started crying, a tear fell on the young man's face and woke him up; jumping to his feet, he grabbed his weapon, said a prayer to his God, and headed to the zmey—with a single blow he cut off his malodorous head, and then tore him apart. All the girls who had been swallowed up earlier, came out of his torso and enjoyed their freedom and hugged their weeping parents. The king kept his word and accepted Christianity together with all his people, and St. George returned to the lands where he was born, where they had already heard of his glorious feat.[504]

Oral stories handed down by villagers tell a similar tale, but are less grand and may be about Hala or Lamia instead of Zmey. Their purpose is to demonstrate why the saint must be honored on his day, as shown in the story that follows.

> There was a poor man working for a large-land owner, and the owner had an unmarried daughter. And on our water fountain, whichever girl was coming for water, the hala was swallowing her—some kind of a big zmey. She swallowed all the maidens and only one left—the daughter of the large land owner. And George said: "I will save your girl."
>
> He took a horse and brought a big spear, and the girl was carrying the jug behind the horse. Saint George on the horse stabbed the hala in the water, and the blood was running into the water for three days and three nights. Then he returned to the village. The father and the mother of the girl were waiting for him and started crying when they approached.
>
> Then the large-land owner asked: "George, what do you want as a reward for saving my daughter?"
>
> And he answered: "I don't want anything but a lamb from the shepherd and a bread from the plowman."
>
> The best of the production dies, if you don't make a sacrifice on the day of St. George.[505]

The blood that ran from the three heads of the slain beast was said to produce rivers of yellow wheat, sparkling wine, and honey,[506] the latter being the food of the gods, which symbolizes immortality. In other songs, such as the one below that's sung on St. George's Day, the rivers of blood produce grain, milk, and wine.

St. George has sallied forth,
Early in the morning of St. George's day,
That he may cross the country while
    the corn is green.
To meet him, lo! A fallow Lamia comes,
A fallow Lamia with three heads.
Thus begins St. George to speak:
"Take thou heed, thou fallow Lamia,
I shall wield my golden mace
And shall smite off thy three heads;
Thence three torrents will rush forth,
Torrents of the blackest blood."
But the fallow Lamia turned not,
So the saint brought forth his mace,

And struck off the heads all three;
Then three streams came rushing out,
Torrents of the blackest blood.
For the labourers was the first,
    Yielding finest corn;
For the shepherds was the second,
    Yielding freshest milk;
For the vine-dressers the third,
    Yielding noble wine.
Master of this house, arise,
'Tis to thee we sing,
Pray to God for thy good health,
And all sorts of happiness.[507]

St. George.
Photos and art © Plamen Dinkov. Used with permission of the artist.

St. Elijah

Another well-known saint comes from the Bible: St. Elijah (Iliya, Ilya, Elias, Elie). You're likely to know him as the prophet who ascended into heaven in his fiery chariot. Like George, Elijah has a connection to nature; he's a rain-bringer and thunder-wielder. A folk song relates how the saints cast lots to divide the world among themselves. St. Nicholas got control of the sea, St. Peter received the keys to paradise, and St. Elijah became lord of summer clouds, thunderstorms, and lightening:

> A share fell to St Iliya
> To be the master of summer lightning and thunder,
> To fly under the clear skies
> And to vanish into the dark clouds.[508]

Like Zmey and the eagle, in the summer, St. Elijah leads clouds to the sea to drink until they are full. He collects moisture from the clouds, which he locks for safe keeping in barrels in the Black Sea. When the soil is thirsty for dew and summer showers, he'll lead the clouds back home, so they can scatter rain across the land.

Villagers rejoice and pay homage to the saint when bright, clear clouds appear in the sky. They are a promise of light rains that will irrigate the land and bring fertility. But, when the clouds turn dark, fear overwhelms the people, because Hala or Lamia is near. Villagers cower in fear, huddled within their homes, and pray to the saint for mercy in the hopes he'll battle the evil dragon.

Sometimes, however, while fighting the beast, the saint is defeated and imprisoned. That's when drought strikes. One story tells how St. Elijah was held against his will for three years. The other saints gathered, reading books, trying to discover how to rescue St. Elijah. They finally crushed the stone wall holding him captive. As soon as he was freed, nourishing rain fell to the land, producing wheat, millet, pears, and nuts. The fertility brought to the land was said to nourish powerful new heroes who could fight the black cloud.[509]

Did you know?

You can prevent disastrous effects of a thunderstorm by sticking an axe in the middle of your yard and pouring a handful of salt over it (Stratilesco, 187).

Illness may also prevent St. Elijah from performing his duties. Unable to rise from bed, he can't "unlock" the clouds. A folk song tells of a time when:

> Thunder-wielder St Iliya fell ill lying in bed for nine years. No cooling wind blew for nine years, nor did fresh dew fall. When he had a drink of doe's milk, he got well. He unlocked the Black Sea. A cool breeze began to blow and drizzle set in.[510]

As he races across the sky, you'll hear the rumble of the wheels of his chariot. That thunder-like sound may also be the pounding of his horses' hooves. Sometimes, he creates even more noise as he busily rolls barrels among the clouds. When he pours nourishing rain from these barrels to the earth below, he may struggle with his load. If that happens, his colorful belt loosens and falls off, stretching in an arc across the sky. People seeing this rainbow are bound to say, "St. Elijah dropped his belt."[511]

In some stories, the saint and Zmeĭove join forces to fight evil dragons. Zmeĭove may ride within St. Elijah's chariot or harnessed to it. Fighting alongside each other, they prevent Lamia from stealing grain and Hala from devastating crops with hail and floods. Sparks fly from the hoofs and nostrils of St. Elijah's horses, and lightning splits the sky as the saint and Zmeĭove shoot their fiery arrows—lightning—at their dragon foes.

Prophet to Dragon Slayer

How did Elijah progress from a prophet to a dragon slayer?

It hasn't always been dragons he's fought. Stories tell about him battling devils, which any good saint will do. Devils, however, are often represented as dragons in religious writings. The saint destroys these devils with his fiery arrows or with stone hammers, much like Thor, another well-known thunder-wielder.

> According to folk legend, at the first rumble of thunder heralding Ilya's approach demons scattered in terror and tried to hide: under the caps of toadstools, in trees or stones, in buildings, inside a cow or even a human being. Ilya was immovable in his righteous anger and sent down his lightning shafts against animals and humans alike in his effort to destroy Satan.[512]

Thunder for St. Elijah is "an instrument of divine retribution," and he wields lightning "in a cosmic battle against the Devil."[513] But it's a never-ending battle as you'll learn in the story below.

> God had given St. Elie special power to kill all the devils, ever since the day He thrust them out of heaven Himself, but later on He thought better of it—according to other legends the advice came from the devil himself—and made up His mind to spare some devils, as otherwise men would possibly feel no more need to worship Him, as there would be no more devils to tempt them to sin. St. Elie being rather displeased with the limitation put

St. Elijah.
Illustration by Morphart. Stock illustration via Depositphotos.

upon his killing power, God, to cheer him up, promised him, that on his name's day he would be allowed to kill all devils. But then God never tells St. Elie when his name's day is, and that is why there are still devils alive.[514]

Before the saint took on the role of fighting dragons, it belonged to Zmey. In fact, folklorists say that "[t]he study of the extensive Indo-European heritage shows that the earliest hypostasis of the dragon-slayer and thunder wielder was the dragon itself."[515]

Did you know?

A quick flash of lightning is really Perun winking (Poor, 370).

Others have held this role as well, among them Perun, the supreme god of the ancient Slavs. He has been described as being "the only deity who has a distinct form; the traditions describe him as tall and well shaped, with a long golden beard."[516] He is the god of thunder and lightning. Today, the word *perun* retains the meaning of "thunder" or "lightning bolt" in some Slavic languages.

Did Elijah replace Perun as the Slavic people embraced Christianity? Many sources say yes, but not everyone agrees. Some say Elijah's role was confined to that which was told of him in the Old Testament.

However, although the link between Ilya and thunderstorms is clear, any direct connection between Ilya and Perun remains speculative. The profile of Ilya the Thunderer, as he was known, probably owes more to the Old Testament account of the ascent to heaven of Elijah in a chariot of fire and to early Christian moralistic writings in which fiery bolts of lightning are presented as God's weapons against Satan and his minions, than to some atavistic memory of a pagan deity.[517]

Similarities between Perun and Elijah do exist, though, so it's easy to see why the comparison has been made.

He [*Perun*] rides in a flaming car, and grasps in his left hand a quiver full of arrows; in his right, a fiery bow. In the spring he goes forth in this fiery car, and crushes with his arrows the demons whose blood streams forth.[518]

Did you know?

During a storm, you should avoid being near plane trees, in narrow glens, around windows and doors, and even near goats and cats, because devils hide there to escape from St. Elijah's thunderbolts (Stratilesco, 186-187).

Perun restores order to the world by hurling his weapons of thunder and lightning against the god Veles, who symbolizes a serpent or dragon living deep in the tree's roots. Thunderstorms are a sign of the supreme god's wrath, not only to defeat opponents who shut off the water and cause droughts, but also "to dispel the demons of darkness and renew the power of the sun."[519] Other scholars call this a "somewhat fanciful theory."[520]

Before Christianity arrived, Slavic people prayed to Perun during times of drought. Among the Bulgarians, it was said:

Young men and women got together, elected one of them and covered him with a fishing net making a wreath of weeds for him. They then made the round of the houses dancing and singing and "often mentioning the fury". They would also pour water over themselves and over the elected Perun and people would give them alms, this they spent on a feast in honour of Perun.[521]

Perun has also been connected to war and warriors, as well as fertility, although it has been said that such myths about him were reconstructed on "the flimsiest of evidence."[522]

Legendary Heroes

Throughout the ages, Eastern Europe has been a hotspot for domination. One ethnic group after another has vied to control the land and the people—from the Romans to the Turkish Ottoman empire, along with Thracian, Greek, Slavic, and other nationalities. Each has left behind traces of its culture and beliefs.

The people needed leaders to vanquish these formidable foes, and so, in stories, the struggle with foreign oppressors took the form of heroes slaying a mighty beast, the dragon. These types of epic tales (called *byliny,* "tales of old time,"[523] in Russian) were told in a fanciful way. The heroes were historical figures, defenders of their homeland. They were completely dedicated to protecting their country and their faith. Fact blended with fable within their stories to create the mighty hero.

While fairy-tale heroes undertake a personal quest to vanquish beasts, legendary heroes often pursue a godly quest. Stories of the Russian *bogatyrs*, for example, arose during "the period of dual faith when Christianity was still struggling against the monsters of paganism."[524] Dragons were, and still are, symbols of sin, evil, Satan, and paganism, and defeating them is a means for salvation, a way to banish evil from the world.

Dragons also represent the power and oppression of human conquerors. For example, in the Smok chapter, you learned about the Wawel Dragon.

> In addition to attempts to explain the legend of the Wawel Dragon simply as a symbol of evil, there might be some echoes of historical events. According to some historians, the dragon is a symbol of the presence of the Avars on Wawel Hill in the second half of the sixth century, and the victims devoured by the beast symbolise the tribute pulled by them.[525]

Whether the beasts are represented as Satan and paganism or as human conquerors, dragons are no longer seen as protectors of the people within these types of tales.

King Marko

King Marko (or Prince Marko, Kraljevich Marko) was a ruler from Prilep (in Macedonia). Little is known about the historical figure. He was born around 1335, became ruler in 1371 when his father was killed while fighting, and died May 17, 1395. He reluctantly fought for the Ottomans, to whom he was a vassal. It's said that he spoke these words before his final battle: "I pray to God to grant the victory to the Christians, even if I have to pay for it with my own blood!"[526]

Tales of the folkloric Marko, however, abound and are popular in Serbia (Kralj Marko), Macedonia (Krale Marko), Bulgaria (Krali Marko), Croatia, and Romania.

In some stories, he's the son of King Vukashin, and his mother is Yevrosima. Other tales say his mother is a Vila (nymph or fairy) and his father is a Zmey (dragon).

> One day, some time before Marko was born, Yevrosima and her attendants were walking along the bank of the Vardar River when they saw a gypsy child fall into the stream. The queen at once leaped into the water and saved the child. The gypsy was grateful and thanked Yevrosima. Then she suddenly asked her:
> "Do you wish your child to be a king or a hero?"
> The queen was surprised and replied, "Of course he will be a king like his father."

King Marko Kills the Zmey (Крали Марко убива змея).
Illustration © Keazim Issinov. Used with permission of the artist.

"I know that," replied the gypsy. "A king rules and everyone hates him, and when he dies he is at once forgotten. But everyone loves a hero, and his fame is never forgotten. If you wish a hero for a son, found a church in honor of the Mother of God, and cultivate nine vineyards for the poor and the orphans. Mark also nine springs in nine different places, and bathe three times a day in the waters of the River Boyana. Besides this, drink a skin of sheep's milk from Mount Shar every day."

Yevrosima desired her child to be a hero rather than merely a king, so she did as the gypsy told her. The wonder-child that was born to the Queen in due season was Marko. Yevrosima was overjoyed, and sought everywhere for the gypsy to reward her properly, but the gypsy was nowhere to be found. So Yevrosima knew that the gypsy was a saint or a vila who had appeared to her to foretell Marko's birth.[527]

Marko is a "knight without fear, without reproach—the lover of justice, the hater of all oppression."[528] This Marko has no qualms about defying the Tsar's requests, because he fears only God. He has been called the "Great Liberator," rescuing maidens from dragons and tyrants, freeing roads from monsters, redeeming Christians from Turks, and freeing slaves.

He's a heavy drinker, always imbibing wine, but doesn't get drunk. Stories tell how "[h]e hardly ever starts on an expedition without taking with him a skin filled with red wine, which he places on one side of Sharats [*his horse*] as counterweight to his heavy mace on the other side."[529]

The hero is "kind and dutiful, the protector of the poor and abused," including animals.[530] He is tender and dutiful to his mother, and most often, he strives to be courteous to and help maidens in need.

When offended or humiliated, however, he can be cruel and brutal, not only to enemies, but also to women such as the beautiful maiden Rosanda (Rosa). She makes the fatal mistake of spurning his courting with "shameful words":

> Liever had I remain unwed,
> In this our realm of Prizren
> Than go to Prilep castle,
> And be called Marko's wife.
> For Marko holds of the Sultan,
> He fights and smites for the Turks,
> Never will he have grave nor burial,
> Nor o'er his grave will burial service be read.
> Wherefore with all my beauty should I be wife to a Turkish minion?[531]

Her insults toward her other suitors are worse: she says a gray Arab mare gave birth to Miloš, and calls Relja a bastard found in the street. Marko's "anger blazed like living fire" and he would have murdered Rosa's brother if Miloš hadn't stopped him. Instead, Marko waits and requests that Rosa send her maidens away, on the pretense he wants to look upon her lovely face. Then he has his revenge.

> Marko raged and was wroth out of wit,
> One step he made and a mighty spring,
> And by the hand he seized the damsel,
> He drew the sharp dagger from his girdle,
> And cut off her right arm;
> He cut off her arm at the shoulder,
> And gave the right arm into her left hand,
> And with the dagger he put out her eyes,
> And wrapped them in a silken kerchief,
> And thrust them into her bosom.
> Then spake Marko in this wise:
> "Choose now, thou maid Rosanda,
> Choose now which thou wilt,
> Whether the Turkish minion,
> Or Miloš the mare's son,
> Or Relja the bastard!"[532]

Marko has supernatural powers and can't be killed "By means of might or by sharp sword, / By war-spear or by battle-mace."[533] This is a result of a blessing he received from the Tsar: "May thy sword always be sharp in battle! May no hero be found anywhere superior to thee!"[534]

Marko, Miloš, and Vila Ravijojla.
Painting by Paja Jovanović, 1906. Public domain.

He is also known for his extraordinary strength. He carries a club that weighs one hundred pounds and is made of sixty pounds of steel, thirty pounds of silver, and ten pounds of gold. With this, he can behead an enemy with one blow, and one stroke of his saber will rip open a foe. Also, using only his little finger, Marko is able to knock out seventy teeth from a woman he strikes.

In his youth, he receives his strength from a Vila (also called a Samovila or Samodiva), a woodland or mountain nymph or fairy.

> As a child he was physically the weakest among his companions. While he was tending his father's horses one day, he found a little girl crying and comforted her. This little girl was the daughter of a samovila, who rewarded Marko by allowing him to suck her milk. In this manner, Marko became the strongest man alive, and the little girl—Giorga Samodiva—helped him with advice.[535]

In some stories, he fights with a Vila, while at other times she is his *posestrima*, "sworn sister," who comes to his aid and shares the secrets of the future with him. She is also the one who gifts him his marvelous horse, Sharatz (Sharats, Šarko, or Šarac), meaning "piebald."

Variations of the tale from one country to the next explain different means by which he obtains his horse.

- He buys a foal suffering from leprosy and cares for the animal until it heals.[536]
- He captures a sick horse that roams on a mountain. When he cures the animal, its crusted spots grow white hair, making it a piebald.[537]
- A Vila tells him how to capture a horse with wounds. When the creature scratches itself on a tree, Marko, who is hiding, jumps on the horse's back. The horse is unable to throw him off and speaks, saying Marko is more of a hero than it is, and it allows Marko to become its master.[538]
- After serving a master for three years, Marko is allowed to choose a horse from among those grazing in a certain field. He needs one that will hold his great weight. Whichever one he fails to lift by the tail and swing around is the one he chooses.[539]
- Marko leaps onto a three-year-old colt, which is the offspring of the mare his father rode. The colt, however, doesn't know this at the time. It runs about furiously and dashes into the water, nearly drowning Marko. The colt cannot unseat the hero, so it eventually bows down to Marko, asking his name. The horse, Sharatz, is overjoyed when it learns who Marko is and accepts the hero as its master.[540]

When seated on this horse, Marko is described as "a dragon mounted on a dragon."[541]

Sharatz can speak and fly. He is the strongest and fastest horse in the world, able to overtake a flying Vila. When the horse runs, sparks of fire explode from his hoofs, and the earth cracks beneath his weight. When he breathes, blue flames burst forth from his nostrils.

Marko shares his victories with Sharatz, and also feeds his horse with food from his own plate and wine from his own cup. Both man and beast can drink more wine than anyone else.

Sharatz is intelligent and uses his abilities to protect Marko.

> He knew just when to kneel down and save his master from the adversary's lance. He knew how to rear and strike the enemy's charger with his forefeet. When roused he would spring up three lance lengths forward. … He has been known to bite off the ears of the enemy's horse; sometimes he trampled Turkish soldiers to death.[542]

Dragon Fights

Although Marko mostly fights against human oppressors, he also has battles with dragons, such as a three-headed one that attempts to steal a bride at her wedding. When all the wedding guests flee, Marko stands his ground and cuts off the beast's heads.[543]

In another story, he fights with a three-headed dragon that blocks a main roadway.

> Marko gathers thirty heroes, they drink wine, and he proposes that they set out to kill the three-headed dragon that has blocked the highways and passes. When they meet the dragon, the heroes are amazed because it has one head in the clouds, another on the ground, and a third in between—a truly cosmic dragon. All flee except Marko and his horse Šarko. Marko tells Šarko that they will certainly perish in the jaws of such an adversary, but Šarko says that with his teeth he will off the uppermost head, with his hooves he will trample the nethermost, and Marko can dispatch the middle head. And so they do.[544]

Worse yet, stories tell about how he rescues animals and humans who have been swallowed by a dragon. One day, Marko brings his infant son with him while he goes hunting. What happens next is a horror story when Lamia devours the boy. Marko, however, defeats the beast with the help of his animals.

> And Marko said to the hounds and the hunting dogs:
> "Run to the Thessaloniki field,
> To catch that damn lamia,
> To catch her, to eat her feet,
> To eat, to take her eyes out:
> Go fast now, or you will get into trouble!"[545]

You can read the full song at the end of this chapter.

Death of Marko

For 150 years, Sharatz remains Marko's closest friend and companion. At the end, the horse, aware of Marko's pending death, stumbles and sheds tears, something the animal has never done before. A Vila explains that Sharatz saw Marko's death approaching, not one from his enemies, but a natural death (for Marko has lived 300 years): "You will die, my dear Marko, / From God, the old murderer."[546] Thus, a curse Marko's father put on him earlier in his life comes true: "My son Marko, may God kill thee! Mayest thou have no children and no grave, and may thy soul not leave thy body before thou hast served the Tsar of the Turks as his vassal!"[547]

> Early one Sunday morning Marko was riding up Mount Urvina. As he climbed it, Sharatz began to stumble, and shed tears.
> Marko was greatly troubled. "What does this mean, Sharatz?" he said. "One hundred and fifty years we have been together. Never before have you stumbled, and now you stumble and weep. God knows, nothing good will come of this. Some one will lose his head, either you or I."
> This time Sharatz is dumb. A Vila maiden, calling to Marko, tells him that his last hour has come and that Sharatz weeps at the thought of parting from his old friend.
> "Part from me!" cries Marko. "Shall I give up my faithful steed that has borne me over many a long road and through many a dark place? Never while my head is upon my shoulders!"

"No one will take Sharatz from you," says the Vila, "but the enemy who spares no living being will come for you, Marko. Look at your face in the spring, and you will see the face of a dead man."

Marko looked and saw that he must surely die.[548]

Not only does Marko die that day, but so does his horse, because Marko loved him more than he had loved his own brother.

 Warned that the day was at hand, Marko killed his beloved Sharatz, that he should never be mounted by a Turk. He broke in pieces his trusty saber and his lance, lest they be a Moslem's triumph. Taking his great mace, so terror-striking, in his strong right hand, he flung it far into the sapphire ocean, saying, "When my club returns from the sea shall a hero come to equal Marko." Attended by the spirits of the mountains, he lay down under the pines and died.[549]

While the historical Marko died in a battle, legends claim "the circumstances of his death are enveloped in mystery." He's believed to have been hidden in a cave, where his wounds healed. Like King

Death of Marko.
Painting by Novak Radonjic, 1848. Public domain via Wikimedia Commons.

Arthur, "he lies hidden, destined to appear on some future occasion to rescue his people from their oppressors."[550]

The concept of a hero retiring to a cave until he's once again needed is symbolic of immortality. The withdrawal and re-emergence have "remnants of the image of an ancient deity bearing the characteristics of the agrarian cyclic deities that periodically disappear and appear again."[551]

In other stories, all heroes disappear with the arrival of guns. One day, Marko and the Devil compete with each other in throwing their maces. Marko easily catches the Devil's 300-pound mace, but when Marko throws his mace, which weighs three times as much, it knocks the Devil to the ground. The Devil, humiliated, seeks his revenge.

> He forged an iron tube in his smithy, loaded it with a little dust and a leaden bullet, and made a hasty return to the human realm to challenge Marko.
>
> "Since you so easily beat me the other day," the Devil said, "let's try again. Surely you can catch this little ball, which weighs hardly anything."
>
> Marko laughed. "Throw your little ball, and we'll see if I can catch it."
>
> Then the Devil took his tube, lit the powder (perhaps with a spark from his tail), and the bullet struck Marko in his palm, going all the way through.
>
> Marko looked sadly at the wound and sighed. "Now that guns are invented, this earth is no place for heroes any longer!"
>
> A dragon happened to be flying by, so Marko motioned for him to come down. He got on the dragon's back and flew away forever. The same day all the heroes followed his example, and that is the reason that there are now neither dragons nor heroes in the country.[552]

Dobrynya Nikitich

Bogatyrs appear in Russian epic poems; stories of these warrior heroes date from the tenth to fourteen centuries.[553] Many of the bogatyrs, like the saints, are based on historical persons. The tales about the bogatyrs also contain fantasy aspects, such as having extreme strength and being exceptionally brave and courageous.

The goal of their exploits is not to acquire fame or wealth, obtain a bride, or even seek revenge or conquer new lands. Their one true aim is to be "the defender of the native soil,"[554] to rid their country or community of evil enemies—whether they are human or beast.

> All through the Russian epics the heroes are the guardians of the people's independence, but by no means the oppressors of the people. Whenever the numerous Mongol tribes in ancient times would assail Russia, the princes of the various Russian States would call the *bogatyrs* (knights, lords, heroes), who always personified the people, to defend the Russian soil. They would leave their plows, their peaceful tilling of the land, gather to their princes, drive away the enemy, take no rewards, nor acquire any privileges by their defense, and afterward would not form a military caste around the prince, but would return immediately to their soil.[555]

Three of the most famous bogatyrs are Dobrynya Nikitich, Ilya Muromets, and Alyosha Popovich, with Dobrynya Nikitich being called the dragon killer. Two historical figures are believed to make up the mythical Dobrynya. One was Dobrynya, the maternal uncle of Vladimir I, also called Vladimir the Great, who reigned over Kievan Rus from 980 – 1015. In the *byliny*, Dobrynya becomes the nephew of Vladimir, rather than his uncle.

The other was a merchant's son, Dobrynya Nikitich of Ryazan, called "Golden Belt." He was one of many bogatyrs who died in battle in 1224, of which it was said: "Of the warriors so many fell, that hardly one man in ten could escape; and seventy great and valiant knights were all killed."[556]

The hero's birth has been described as follows:

> The day of the birth of Nikitich had been a day of trouble for wide distances across the open steppe. For upon that wonderful day a great storm seemed to arise, and yet not a great storm but a strange commotion, unseen, unheard, but keenly felt. From far across the open plain came a herd of beasts, wild beasts and fearsome dragons large and small, and sought the shallow valley of the Dnieper river. At their head ran the Skiper-beast, with woolly fleece, twisted horn, and hoofs which struck sparks from the pebbles of flint. Then the waters of the Dnieper were strangely troubled, the banks of the river quaked and fell, and trees which once had waved upright now spanned the stream. Such had been the day of the birth of Nikitich.[557]

He is called young or very young. His hair is yellow, and he has a distinguishing birthmark on one of his legs.[558] He is "melancholy and reflective." His life consists of "ungrateful toil," the prince sending Dobrynya to perform dangerous tasks for which he receives no appreciation. Despite the violence Dobrynya must inflict on his enemies, the hero is "eminently compassionate: he deplores the wanton shedding of blood, spares even the young of the Loathly Worm of the Mountains, and his devotion to his mother has an epic note of grandeur perhaps unparalleled."[559]

Like most heroes, Dobrynya is incredibly strong. He thinks his strength is waning, however, when his blows cause no harm to a warrior maiden he attacks.

> [H]e rode after the warrior-maiden, and smote her upon her turbulent head with his mace of damascened steel. But the warlike virgin sat her good steed firmly, wavering not nor glancing back. Dobrynya sat his good steed in terror, and departed from that bold polyanitza: "Plainly," quoth he, "Dobrynya's valour is as of yore, but his strength is not the strength of other days."
>
> Now there stood, near by in the plain, a damp oak, six fathoms in girth. This Dobrynya smote with his mace, and shivered into atoms; and he marvelled greatly.
>
> "Of a truth," he said, "Dobrynya's might is as of old, but his courage is not the courage of earlier days!"
>
> Then he again rode in pursuit of the bold warrior-maid, and smote her honourably upon her tempestuous head.—She wavered not, glanced not behind. But Dobrynya was sore amazed, and tested his might upon a damp oak of twelve fathoms, and shivered it in splinters. Thereupon, Dobrynya waxed wroth, as he sat his good steed, and rode after the bold virgin-warrior a third time, and smote her with his mace.
>
> Threat she turned and spoke: "Methought the Russian gnats were biting, but lo! 'tis the Russian hero tapping!"[560]

His strength and boasting also have no effect on Death when she comes to take his life.

> Death the Terrible comes up to Dobrynya in the open field and informs him that he has been about long enough in the white world, shedding guiltless blood. He asks her who she is; is she a Tsar or a Tsar's son, or a King or a King's son or a mighty bogatyr, and she informs him that she is Death the Terrible. He then threatens to take his sharp sabre and to

Dobrynya Nikitich Rescues Zabava from the Gorynych.
Illustration by Ivan Bilibin, 1941. Public domain via Wikimedia Commons.

cut off her foolish head, but she bids him say farewell to the white world, and will take out her sharp sword, which is unseen, and will cut through his bones, and he will fall from his good horse. Then Dobrynya prayed her for two years in order to obtain forgiveness for his sins, but she would not give him one hour nor one minute, and then she drew out her iron sword, cut through his sinews and so he fell down dead.[561]

Early thought about these types of dragon-slaying stories was that the heroes were a personification of nature. According to some, Dobrynya represents the "active, warlike principles" of the sun, and he "wages incessant war with darkness, triumphing over it every morning, and with winter, whose fetters he strikes asunder every spring with the sword of his rays."[562] Other scholars claim the tales have been borrowed from the Orient, with Dobrynya being the Krishna of Indian folk-lore. And still others say these heroes are insignificant men from the fourteenth and fifteenth centuries to whom the exploits of Oriental heroes have been attributed.[563]

Among the dragons Dobrynya battles is one named Zmey Gorynych (Змей Горыныч), whose name means "son of the mountain." The dragon may be green and winged, with three to twelve heads. The creature stands on his back legs only, due to the fact his front ones are stunted claws. He also appears as a giant serpent with a human head or as a human. Unlike Zmey from the Balkans, Zmey Gorynych represents evil and never protects villages. He does love the ladies, though—sometimes to kidnap for a companion and other times to eat.

In one story, Dobrynya threatens Zmey Gorynych, whom the hero finds in the embrace of the dragon's witch lover, Marinka.

> When Marinka refuses to let Dobrynya in, the *bogatyr'* in his fury seizes a huge log of wood to use as a battering-ram and knocks the door off its hinges. The dragon swears at him, calling him a good-for-nothing peasant, but flees with his tail between his legs when Dobrynya draws his sharp sabre and threatens to chop him into tiny pieces, like meat for a pie, and to scatter them over the open steppe.[564]

Besides battling Zmey Gorynych, Dobrynya also fights with nameless dragons. The tale of "Dobrynya and the Dragon" (which you can read at the end of this chapter), is one of dual faith. The dragon may be symbolic of paganism, which Christianity (specifically in this case, Dobrynya) must conquer.

> Some scholars have suggested that the River Puchai is a distortion of the Pochaina, a river near Kiev, in which, according to legend, the citizens of Kiev were forcibly baptized in 988. In such a context the enigmatic 'hat from the Greek land' with which Dobrynya strikes his enemy has been interpreted as a symbol of Christianity. This is no ordinary hat, then, but the characteristic headgear inherited from the 'Greek land', that is Byzantium, worn by priests of the Orthodox Church and sometimes by pilgrims who had visited the Holy Land.[565]

The dragon may also symbolize enemies of Kievan Rus:

> …such as the nomadic Polovtsians who swept across the southern steppe-lands in the eleventh to twelfth centuries or the Tartar-Mongol hordes who ravaged Rus in the thirteenth century, sacking Kiev and destroying its glory…. Much in the behaviour of the dragon might be a reflection of the pagan Polovtsians and other steppe nomads: the unexpected raids, the rustling of cattle and the seizure of prisoners as slaves and concubines. The chronicles refer to the Polovtsians as oath-breakers and 'serpents'. The description of the

dragon's lair deep in the mountain is reminiscent of a medieval dungeon or torture chamber.[566]

Dobrynya has an encounter with a dragon in which he must rescue a royal maiden named Zabava from the beast's clutches. This adventure follows the themes common in other rescue missions: the hero receives magic objects to assist him in his quest. But, the story also has elements that demonstrate the peasants' veneration of the earth (*zemlya*). It was thought of as "a living entity whose good will must be earned and whose feelings must be respected."[567] The land had to be convinced to accept the dragon's vile blood—all of it. Dobrynya could not leave a single drop in the beast, in order to prevent the creature from coming back to life.[568]

> According to popular belief, the earth would not accept the bodies of unrepentant sinners. For the same reason, the earth does not at first absorb the blood of the infernal dragon killed by the knight Dobrynya in the *bylina* 'Dobrynya and the dragon'. There are some versions of the *bylina* in which the dragon's evil continues to work even after its death: 'When Dobrynya killed the accursed dragon, she unleased her dragon's blood. From the East the blood flowed down towards the West, but Mother Moist-Earth would not consume it.' The resulting flood, which threatens to drown Rus, is only averted when a voice from the heavens instructs the knight to strike his spear against Mother Moist-Earth and commands her to 'open wide, in all four directions'.[569]

Like other heroes, Dobrynya has a magic horse. His has been handed down from several generations. The creature is the brother of the horses of other famous Russian heroes, such as Ilya Muromets and Churilo, and so can accomplish amazing feats.

Death of Dobrynya

Although a fairy-tale hero lives happily ever after, the same is not true of a folk epic hero. He is based on a real person, and so his life must come to an end, despite his supernatural powers. Not every tale of the epic hero tells of his death, though, but he never dies on the battlefield. Instead, he dies from suicide, is turned to stone by a supernatural force, or dies hidden away in a monastery.

Arrogance and boasting are common causes of the hero's demise. He is a mighty man fighting for God, and so, in the eyes of the Church, he should demonstrate Christian humility. To do otherwise is a sin worthy of punishment. As the King James Bible version of Proverbs 16:18 says, "Pride goeth before destruction, and an haughty spirit before a fall."

History may have recorded that Dobrynya Nikitich died in a battle in 1224 that occurred on the Kalka river, along with ten thousand other men, but in an epic-tale about the battle, the bogatyrs survive. But the day does not end well for Dobrynya. During the battle other bogatyrs brag about their valor in achieving the victory, and they further boast that they will be able to defeat heavenly powers if only there is a staircase to heaven. Those heavenly powers cause the slain enemy to return to life and fight the battle once more. The bogatyrs who boasted so boldly now flee in despair and kill themselves with their own swords.

Although Dobrynya is not among the braggers, he also later dies from suicide, due to "guilt by association."[570] In Russian folk epic tradition, it's believed he shares in the guilt of the other warriors who do boast of their mighty powers, and therefore, he is destined to suffer the same fate.

> On his way back from the battlefield Dobrynya Nikitich is challenged to combat by an 'old hag' (*baba*) named Latyngorka. The old hag overpowers the epic hero in a hand-to-hand

fight. Fortunately, Il'ya Muromets arrives in time to save Dobrynya and free him from Latyngorka, who then flees. But Dobrynya cannot bear his humiliation and kills himself:

And he drove the sharp spear into the damp earth,/And he fell on the spear with his ardent heart./Thus death came to Dobrynya.[571]

Dragon Slayers Tales

The Dragon's Strength: The Story of the Youngest Prince Who Killed the Sparrow

There was once a King who had three sons. One day the oldest son went hunting and when night fell his huntsmen came riding home without him.

"Where is the prince?" the King asked.

"Isn't he here?" the huntsmen said. "He left us in midafternoon chasing a hare near the Old Mill up the river. We haven't seen him since and we supposed he must have come home alone."

When he hadn't returned the following day his brother, the second prince, went out to search for him.

"I'll go to the Old Mill," he said to the King, "and see what's become of him."

So he mounted his horse and rode up the river. As he neared the Old Mill a hare crossed his path and the second prince being a hunter like his brother at once gave chase. His attendant waited for his return but waited in vain. Night fell and still there was no sign of the second prince.

The attendant returned to the palace and told the King what had happened. The King was surprised but not unduly alarmed and the following day when the Youngest Prince asked to go hunting alone the King suggested that he go in the direction of the Old Mill to find out if he could see what was keeping his brothers.

The Youngest Prince who had listened carefully to what his brothers' attendants had reported decided to act cautiously. So when a hare crossed his path as he approached the Old Mill, instead of giving it chase, he rode off as though he were hunting other game. Later he returned to the Old Mill from another direction.

He found an old woman sitting in front of it.

"Good evening, granny," he said in a friendly tone, pulling up his horse for a moment's chat. "Do you live here? You know I thought the Old Mill was deserted."

The old woman looked at him and shook her head gloomily.

"Deserted indeed! My boy, take an old woman's advice and don't have anything to do with this old mill! It's an evil place!"

"Why, granny," the Prince said, "what's the matter with it?"

The old woman peered cautiously around and when she saw they were alone she beckoned the Prince to come near. Then she whispered:

"A dragon lives here! A horrible monster! He takes the form of a hare and lures people into the mill. Then he captures them. Some of them he kills and eats and others he holds as prisoners in an underground dungeon. I'm one of his prisoners and he keeps me here to work for him."

"Granny," the Youngest Prince said, "would you like me to rescue you?"

"My boy, you couldn't do it! You have no idea what a strong evil monster the dragon is."

"If you found out something for me, granny, I think I might be able to overcome the dragon and rescue you."

The old woman was doubtful but she promised to do anything the Youngest Prince asked.

"Well then, granny, find out from the dragon where his strength is, whether in his own body or somewhere else. Find out to-night and I'll come back to-morrow at this same hour to see you."

So that night when the dragon came home, after he had supped and when she was scratching his head to make him drowsy for bed, the old woman said to him:

"Master, I think you're the strongest dragon in the world! Tell me now, where does your strength lie—in your own beautiful body or somewhere else?"

"You're right, old woman," the dragon grunted: "I am pretty strong as dragons go. But I don't keep my strength in my own body. No, indeed! That would be too dangerous. I keep it in the hearth yonder."

At that the old woman ran over to the hearth and, stooping down, she kissed it and caressed it.

"O beautiful hearth!" she said, "where my master's strength is hidden! How happy are the ashes that cover your stones!"

The dragon laughed with amusement.

"That's the time I fooled you, old woman! My strength isn't in the hearth at all! It's in the tree in front of the mill."

The old woman at once ran out of the mill and threw her arms about the tree.

"O tree!" she cried, "most beautiful tree in the world, guard carefully our master's strength and let no harm come to it!"

Again the dragon laughed.

"I've fooled you another time, old woman! Come here and scratch my head some more and this time I'll tell you the truth for I see you really love your master."

So the old woman went back and scratched the dragon's head and the dragon told her the truth about his strength.

"I keep it far away," he said. "In the third kingdom from here near the Tsar's own city there is a deep lake. A dragon lives at the bottom of the lake. In the dragon there is a wild boar; in the boar a hare; in the hare a pigeon; in the pigeon a sparrow. My strength is in the sparrow. Let any one kill the sparrow and I should die that instant. But I am safe. No one but shepherds ever come to the lake and even they don't come any more for the dragon has eaten up so many of them that the lake has got a bad name. Indeed, nowadays even the Tsar himself is hard put to it to find a shepherd. Oh, I tell you, old woman, your master is a clever one!"

So now the old woman had the dragon's secret and the next day she told it to the Youngest Prince. He at once devised a plan whereby he hoped to overcome the dragon. He dressed himself as a shepherd and with crook in hand started off on foot for the third kingdom. He traveled through villages and towns, across rivers and over mountains, and reached at last the third kingdom and the Tsar's own city. He presented himself at the palace and asked employment as a shepherd.

The guards looked at him in surprise and said:

"A shepherd! Are you sure you want to be a shepherd?"

Then they called to their companions: "Here's a youth who wants to be a shepherd!" And the word went through the palace and even the Tsar heard it.

"Send the youth to me," he ordered.

"Do you really want to be my shepherd?" he asked the Youngest Prince.

The Youngest Prince said yes, he did.

"If I put you in charge of the sheep, where would you pasture them?"

"Isn't there a lake beyond the city," the Prince asked, "where the grazing is good?"

"H'm!" said the Tsar. "So you know about that lake, too! What else do you know?"

"I've heard the shepherds disappear."

"And still you want to try your luck?" the Tsar exclaimed.

Just then the Tsar's only daughter, a lovely Princess, who had been looking at the young stranger, slipped over to her father and whispered:

"But, father, you can't let such a handsome young man as that go off with the sheep! It would be dreadful if he never returned!"

The Tsar whispered back:

"Hush, child! Your concern for the young man's safety does credit to your noble feelings. But this is not the time or the place for sentiment. We must consider first the welfare of the royal sheep."

He turned to the Youngest Prince:

"Very well, young man, you may consider yourself engaged as shepherd. Provide yourself with whatever you need and assume your duties at once."

"There is one thing," the Youngest Prince said; "when I start out to-morrow morning with the sheep I should like to take with me two strong boarhounds, a falcon, and a set of bagpipes."

"You shall have them all," the Tsar promised.

Early the next morning when the Princess peeped out of her bedroom window she saw the new shepherd driving the royal flocks to pasture. A falcon was perched on his shoulder; he had a set of bagpipes under his arm; and he was leading two powerful boarhounds on a leash.

"It's a shame!" the Princess said to herself. "He'll probably never return and he's such a handsome young man, too!" And she was so unhappy at the thought of never again seeing the new shepherd that she couldn't go back to sleep.

Well, the Youngest Prince reached the lake and turned out his sheep to graze. He perched the falcon on a log, tied the dogs beside it, and laid his bagpipes on the ground. Then he took off his smock, rolled up his hose, and wading boldly into the lake called out in a loud voice:

"Ho, dragon, come out and we'll try a wrestling match! That is, if you're not afraid!"

"Afraid?" bellowed an awful voice. "Who's afraid?"

The water of the lake churned this way and that and a horrible scaly monster came to the surface. He crawled out on shore and clutched the Prince around the waist. And the Prince clutched him in a grip just as strong and there they swayed back and forth, and rolled over, and wrestled together on the shore of the lake without either getting the better of the other. By midafternoon when the sun was hot, the dragon grew faint and cried out:

"Oh, if I could but dip my burning head in the cool water, then I could toss you as high as the sky!"

"Don't talk nonsense!" the Prince said. "If the Tsar's daughter would kiss my forehead, then I could toss you twice as high!"

After that the dragon slipped out of the Prince's grasp, plunged into the water, and disappeared. The Prince waited for him but he didn't show his scaly head again that day.

When evening came, the Prince washed off the grime of the fight, dressed himself carefully, and then looking as fresh and handsome as ever drove home his sheep. With the falcon on his shoulder and the two hounds at his heels he came playing a merry tune on his bagpipes.

The townspeople hearing the bagpipes ran out of their houses and cried to each other:

"The shepherd's come back!"

The Princess ran to her window and, when she saw the shepherd alive and well, she put her hand to her heart and said:

"Oh!"

Even the Tsar was pleased.

"I'm not a bit surprised that he's back!" he said. "There's something about this youth that I like!"

The next day the Tsar sent two of his trusted servants to the lake to see what was happening there. They hid themselves behind some bushes on a little hill that commanded the lake. They were there when the shepherd arrived and they watched him as he waded out into the water and challenged the dragon as on the day before.

They heard the shepherd call out in a loud voice:

"Ho, dragon, come out and we'll try a wrestling match! That is, if you're not afraid!"

And from the water they heard an awful voice bellow back:

"Afraid? Who's afraid?"

Then they saw the water of the lake churn this way and that and a horrible scaly monster come to the surface. They saw him crawl out on shore and clutch the shepherd around the waist. And they saw the shepherd clutch him in a grip just as strong. And they watched the two as they swayed back and forth and rolled over and wrestled together without either getting the better of the other. By midafternoon when the sun grew hot they saw the dragon grow faint and they heard him cry out:

"Oh, if I could only dip my burning head in the cool water, then I could toss you as high as the sky!"

And they heard the shepherd reply:

"Don't talk nonsense! If the Tsar's daughter would kiss my forehead, then I could toss you twice as high!"

Then they saw the dragon slip out of the shepherd's grasp, plunge into the water, and disappear. They waited but he didn't show his scaly head again that day.

So the Tsar's servants hurried home before the shepherd and told the Tsar all they had seen and heard. The Tsar was mightily impressed with the bravery of the shepherd and he declared that if he killed that horrid dragon he should have the Princess herself for wife!

He sent for his daughter and told her all that his servants had reported and he said to her:

"My daughter, you, too, can help rid your country of this monster if you go out with the shepherd tomorrow and when the time comes kiss him on the forehead. You will do this, will you not, for your country's sake?"

The Princess blushed and trembled and the Tsar, looking at her in surprise, said:

"What! Shall a humble shepherd face a dragon unafraid and the daughter of the Tsar tremble!"

"Father," the Princess cried, "it isn't the dragon that I'm afraid of!"

"What then?" the Tsar asked.

But what it was she was afraid of the Princess would not confess. Instead she said:

"If the welfare of my country require that I kiss the shepherd on the forehead, I shall do so."

So the next morning when the shepherd started out with his sheep, the falcon on his shoulder, the dogs at his heels, the bagpipes under his arm, the Princess walked beside him. Her eyes were downcast and he saw that she was trembling.

"Do not be afraid, dear Princess," he said to her. "Nothing shall harm you—I promise that!"

"I'm not afraid," the Princess murmured. But she continued to blush and tremble and, although the shepherd tried to look into her eyes to reassure her, she kept her head averted.

This time the Tsar himself and many of his courtiers had gone on before and taken their stand on the hill that overlooked the lake to see the final combat of the shepherd and the dragon.

When the shepherd and the Princess reached the lake, the shepherd put his falcon on the log as before and tied the dogs beside it and laid his bagpipes on the ground. Then he threw off his smock, rolled up his hose, and wading boldly into the lake called out in a loud voice:

"Ho, dragon, come out and we'll try a wrestling match! That is, if you're not afraid!"

"Afraid?" bellowed an awful voice. "Who's afraid?"

The water of the lake churned this way and that and the horrible scaly monster came to the surface. He crawled to shore and clutched the shepherd around the waist. The shepherd clutched him in a grip just as strong and there they swayed back and forth and rolled over and wrestled together on the shore of the lake without either getting the better of the other. The Princess without the least show of fear stood nearby calling out encouragement to the shepherd and waiting for the moment when the shepherd should need her help.

By midafternoon when the sun was hot, the dragon grew faint and cried out:

"Oh, if I could but dip my burning head in the cool water, then I could toss you as high as the sky!"

"Don't talk nonsense!" the shepherd said. "If the Tsar's daughter would kiss my forehead then I could toss you twice as high!"

Instantly the Princess ran forward and kissed the shepherd three times. The first kiss fell on his forehead, the second on his nose, the third on his mouth. With each kiss his strength increased an hundredfold and taking the dragon in a mighty grip he tossed him up so high that for a moment the Tsar and all the courtiers lost sight of him in the sky. Then he fell to earth with such a thud that he burst.

Out of his body sprang a wild boar. The shepherd was ready for this and on the moment he unleashed the two hounds and they fell on the boar and tore him to pieces.

Out of the boar jumped a rabbit. It went leaping across the meadow but the dogs caught it and killed it.

Out of the rabbit flew a pigeon. Instantly the shepherd unloosed the falcon. It rose high in the air, then swooped down upon the pigeon, clutched it in its talons, and delivered it into the shepherd's hands.

He cut open the pigeon and found the sparrow.

"Spare me! Spare me!" squawked the sparrow.

"Tell me where my brothers are," the shepherd demanded with his fingers about the sparrow's throat.

"Your brothers? They are alive and in the deep dungeon that lies below the Old Mill. Behind the mill there are three willow saplings growing from one old root. Cut the saplings and strike the root. A heavy iron door leading down into the dungeon will open. In the dungeon you will find many captives old and young, your brothers among them. Now that I have told you this are you going to spare my life?"

But the shepherd wrung the sparrow's neck for he knew that only in that way could the monster who had captured his brothers be killed.

Well, now that the dragon was dead the Tsar and all his courtiers came down from the hill and embraced the shepherd and told him what a brave youth he was.

"You have delivered us all from a horrid monster," the Tsar said, "and to show you my gratitude and the country's gratitude I offer you my daughter for wife."

"Thank you," said the shepherd, "but I couldn't think of marrying the Princess unless she is willing to marry me."

The Princess blushed and trembled just as she had blushed and trembled the night before and that morning, too, on the way to the lake. She tried to speak but could not at first. Then in a very little voice she said:

"As a Princess I think it is my duty to marry this brave shepherd who has delivered my country from this terrible dragon, and—and I think I should want to marry him anyway."

She said the last part of her speech in such a very low voice that only the shepherd himself heard it. But that was right enough because after all it was intended only for him. So then and there beside the lake before even the shepherd had time to wash his face and hands and put on his smock the Tsar put the Princess's hand in his hand and pronounced them betrothed.

After that the shepherd bathed in the lake and then refreshed and clean he sounded his bagpipes and he and the Princess and the Tsar and all the courtiers returned to the city driving the sheep before them.

All the townspeople came out to meet them and they danced to the music of the bagpipes and there was great rejoicing both over the death of the dragon and over the betrothal of the Princess and the brave shepherd.

The wedding took place at once and the wedding festivities lasted a week. Such feasting as the townspeople had! Such music and dancing!

When the wedding festivities were ended, the shepherd told the Tsar who he really was.

"You say you're a Prince!" the Tsar cried, perfectly delighted at this news. Then he declared he wasn't in the least surprised. In fact, he said, he had suspected as much from the first!

"Do you think it likely," he asked somewhat pompously, "that any daughter of mine would fall in love with a man who wasn't a prince?"

"I think I'd have fallen in love with you whatever you were!" whispered the Princess to her young husband. But she didn't let her father hear her!

The Prince told the Tsar about his brothers' captivity and how he must go home to release them, and the Tsar at once said that he and his bride might go provided they returned as soon as possible.

They agreed to this and the Tsar fitted out a splendid escort for them and sent them away with his blessing.

So the Prince now traveled back through the towns and villages of three kingdoms, across rivers and over mountains, no longer a humble shepherd on foot, but a rich and mighty personage riding in a manner that befitted his rank.

When he reached the deserted mill, his friend the old woman was waiting for him.

"I know, my Prince, you have succeeded for the monster has disappeared."

"Yes, granny, you are right: I have succeeded. I found the dragon in the lake, and the boar in the dragon, and the rabbit in the boar, and the pigeon in the rabbit, and the sparrow in the pigeon. I took the sparrow and killed it. So you are free now, granny, to return to your home. And soon all those other poor captives will be free."

He went behind the mill and found the three willow saplings. He cut them off and struck the old root. Sure enough a heavy iron door opened. This led down into a deep dungeon which was crowded with unfortunate prisoners. The Prince led them all out and sent them their various ways. He found his own two brothers among them and led them home to his father.

There was great rejoicing in the King's house, and in the King's heart, too, for he had given up hope of ever seeing any of his sons again.

The King was so charmed with the Princess that he said it was a pity that she couldn't marry his oldest son so that she might one day be Queen.

"The Youngest Prince is a capable young man," the King said, "and there's no denying that he managed this business of killing the dragon very neatly. But he is after all only the Youngest Prince with very little hope of succeeding to the kingdom. If you hadn't married him in such haste one of his older brothers might easily have fallen in love with you."

"I don't regret my haste," the Princess said. "Besides he is now my father's heir. But that doesn't matter for I should be happy with the Youngest Prince if he were only a shepherd."[572]

A Sea Lamia Swallows Marko's Child

The damn lamia went out,
Went out from the deep sea,
To the wide Thessaloniki field
To go to Marko's towers,
To swallow Marko's male child!
Erina Samovila heard her,
Samovila, Marko's close friend,
And she went to Marko, and told him.
Marko said to young Markoitsa [*Marko's wife*]:
"Bathe my male child,
Wrap him in silk diapers,
Put him in a silver cradle
And in a golden fabric
I will take him for a walk.
And go to the long stable,
Take out my saddle,
Tighten it with nine belts."
Then young Markoitsa went,
She went to the long stable,
And took out his saddle,

And she made it, she armed it well
And she put in a white tent,
A white tent and a sharp sword,
A sharp sword and a golden mace.
In his lap, she put her male child
With a silver cradle, wrapped in golden fabric.
And Marko went to the green forest,
To the green forest, to the dark gorge
And he unfolded the white tent,
And he put there his male child.
He led hounds and hunting dogs,
He led eagles,
He went to the green forest,
To hunt wild animals.
He caught the prey, but he forgot his child,
And the windy lamia went out
From the deep sea to the Thessaloniki field,
And she swallowed his child from the tent.
Then Marko remembered about the child.
But when he went to see the child,
He found only an empty basket,
And the child couldn't be found anywhere!
And Marko said to the hounds and the hunting dogs:
"Run to the Thessaloniki field,
To catch that damn lamia,
To catch her, to eat her feet,
To eat, to take her eyes out:
Go fast now, or you will get into trouble!"
And they caught her in the Thessaloniki field,
The hounds ate her feet,
The eagles took out her eyes;
And Krali Marko caught her,
He caught that damn lamia;
And he took out his sharp knife,
Then he tore her miserable heart,
And he took out his male child.[573]

Deli Marko Defeats the Fierce Zmeyna

The following song about Marko is sung at Christmas. The dragon in this story is a zmeyna, a female. The name "deli" refers to a brave young man, a crazy head. It's a common name in songs for a boy and a hero.

Three brave young men are drinking wine,
Three brave young man on a rug.
Their tables are full, even [*flat, like a wheat field*],
Their glasses are overflowing.

The first one was Novachko the young,
The second one was Boydan the soldier,
And the third one was deli Marko.
One by one they bragged,
Novachko the young was bragging:
"Eat, and drink, my comrades,
I'm going to look over
What the fierce zmeyna is like,
Whether it's a zmeyna for catching,
Or it's a zmeyna one should run away from."
And he got up and went,
She felt him from afar
The head was shaking—breaking trees,
Smashing all the stones around
He turned around,
And he came back to his comrades:
"Eat, and drink, my comrades,
It's not a zmeyna for catching,
It's a *zmeyna* one should run away from."
One by one they bragged,
Boydan the soldier was bragging:
"Eat, and drink, my comrades,
I am going to look over
What the fierce zmeyna is like,
Whether it's a zmeyna for catching,
Or it's a zmeyna one should run away from."
And he got up and went,
She felt him from afar
The head was shaking—breaking trees,
Smashing all the stones around
And he came back to his comrades:
"Eat, and drink, my comrades,
It's not a zmeyna for catching,
It's a zmeyna one should run away from."
One by one they bragged,
Deli Marko was bragging:
"Eat, and drink, my comrades,
I am going to look over
What the fierce zmeyna is like,
Whether it's a zmeyna for catching,
Or it's a zmeyna one should run away from."
And he got up and went,
She felt him from afar
The head was shaking—breaking trees,
Smashing all the stones around
Deli Marko didn't care,
He spun around
His golden mace

He hit her, dazed her,
Chained her, bound her,
And he tied her in front of the horse:
He was riding his horse; he was spinning his sword,
The fierce zmeyna was begging him:
"Let me go, let me go, deli Marko,
Or I will breathe hot fire,
I will burn forests and fields,
And deli Marko in his flat yard."
Deli Marko answered:
"Breathe, breathe fire, you angry zmeyna,
As much as you want!
I have near at hand
Near at hand—a blue and white copper kettle,
A blue and white copper kettle full of sparkling wine:
It will extinguish forests and fields,
And deli Marko in his flat yard."[574]

Dobrynya and the Dragon

Young Dobrynya took his stout, death-dealing bow, his fiery little arrows, and went a-hunting, and came to the Blue Sea.

At the first bay he found no geese, swans, nor small gray ducks; neither did he find them at the second bay, nor at the third. Then Dobrynya's restive heart grew hot within him; he turned about quickly and went to his home, to his mother, sat down upon the square hewn bench, and dropped his eyes upon the oaken floor. Therewith came his mother to him, and said:

"Aï, young Dobrynushka Nikitich! Thou art returned in no merry mood."

"Aï, my mother!" quoth Dobrynya; "give me thy leave and blessing to go to the Puchai river."

"Young Dobrynya," his mother made answer, "I will give neither leave nor blessing. None who hath gone to the Puchai stream hath ever returned thence."

"Aï, little mother," said Dobrynya, "if thou give thy leave I will go; and if thou give it not, I will go."

So his mother consented. He threw off his flowered raiment, and put on garments meet for a journey, and on his head a wide-brimmed hat from the Grecian land. Then he saddled and bridled a good steed which no man had ever ridden, took his stout bow, his fiery arrows, his sharp sword and far-reaching spear, and his battle-mace.

And as he rode forth, accompanied by his little page, his mother laid her commands upon him.

"If thou wilt go to the Puchai river, young Dobrynya, immeasurable heats shall overcome thee: yet bathe thou not in Mother Puchai flood; for she is fierce and angry. From her first stream fire flasheth; from her second, sparks shower; from her third, smoke poureth in a pillar."

They saw the good youth mounting, they saw him not as he rode. There seemed but a wreath of mist far out on the open plain.

When he was come to Mother Puchai river, intolerable heat overpowered him, and he heeded not his mother's behest. He took from his head his cap from the Grecian land, put off his travelling garb, his shirt, his foot-gear of the seven silks, and began to bathe in the Puchai.

"My mother said this was a wild and angry stream," quoth he; "but 'tis gentle—peaceful as a pool of rain-water." He dived like a duck beneath the first stream, and through the second likewise.—And lo! there was no wind, but the clouds sailed on; there were no clouds, yet the rain dropped down; no rain was there, yet the lightning flashed; no lightning, yet sparks showered fast. No thick darkness was it that obscured the sky, nor gloomy clouds descending, but a fierce Dragon flying down upon Dobrynya, the savage Dragon of the Cavern, with her twelve tails.

"Aha! young Dobrynya Nikitich!" quoth the Dragon. "Now will I devour Dobrynushka whole! I will take dear little Dobrynya in my tail, and bear him into captivity."

"Ho, thou accursed Dragon!" said Dobrynya. "When thou shalt have captured Dobrynya, then will be the fitting time to boast; but thou hast not yet Dobrynya in thy claws!" Then he dived swiftly beneath the first stream, and out through the second. But his young page had been overhasty, and had driven away Dobrynya's good steed; he had carried off the stout bow, the sharp sword, far-reaching spear, and war-mace. The cap alone was left, the wide-brimmed cap from the Grecian land.

Dobrynya seized his cap, filled it with sand from the river-bank, and with it smote the cursed worm, and hewed off three of her tails—the best of all. Then the Dragon of the Cavern besought Dobrynya:

"Aï, thou young Dobrynya Nikitich! Give me not over to fruitless death, shed not my innocent blood! I will not fly in Holy Russia, I will imprison no more heroes, nor strangle young maidens, nor orphan little children. I will be to thee a submissive Dragon; and thou, Dobrynya, shalt be my elder brother, and I will be thy younger sister."

Dobrynya was taken with her wiles, and loosed her at will, and returned to his home, to his mother, to the banquet hall, where he sat himself down upon the four-square bench.

But the wily Dragon raised herself upon her wings over royal Kief town, caught up Beauty, niece to Prince Vladimir, and bore her off to a cavern in the hills.

At that time Royal Vladimir made an honourable feast for many princes, nobles, bold warrior-maidens, mighty heroes, and wandering good youths. And Dobrynya prayed his mother's leave and blessing to go to that honourable feast.

"Nay," she made answer: "abide thou in thine own dwelling, Dobrynya, with thy mother; drink green wine until thou art full drunken, and lavish golden treasure at thy will. But go not to this feast." But when her son would have gone in any case, she gave both leave and blessing, and Dobrynya arrayed himself as was meet.

On his little feet he put shoes of green morocco, with lofty heels and pointed toes. About their sharp peaks an egg might roll, under the heels might sparrows fly. His garments were of flowered stuffs, his mantle of black sables from beyond the sea.

He saddled his good steed, and rode forth to the spacious court. When he was come thither he bound his steed in the centre, to the ring of gold in the carven pillar, and entered the banquet hall. There he crossed his eyes as it is written, he did reverence as prescribed, to two, to three, to four sides, and to the Prince and Princess in particular. Then they led him to the great place of honour at the oaken board, with its savoury viands and honeyed drinks, and poured him a cup of green wine, a second of beer, a third of sweet mead:— the measure of that cup was a bucket and a half, and the weight thereof, a pood and a half. This Dobrynya took in one hand, and drained at one draught.

Royal Vladimir, as he paced the banquet hall, stroking his curls, looked on the heroes, and spoke this word: "Aï, ye stout and mighty heroes I will lay upon you a great service. Ye must go to the Tugy mountains, to the fierce Dragon that hath carried off our royal niece, Beauty the Fair."

Then the great hid behind the lesser, and they, in turn, behind the small, and from the least in rank, no answer came. From the middle table spoke Semyon, lord of Karamychetzka: "Little father Vladimir of royal Kief! But yesterday in the open plain, I beheld Dobrynya beside the Puchai river in conflict with that Dragon. And the Dragon beguiled him, calling him her elder brother, herself his younger sister. Send Dobrynya, therefore, to the Tugy mountains, for the Princess Beauty."

So Vladimir laid his commands on Dobrynya, and Dobrynya mourned and was sad. He sprang to his nimble feet, in his place within the granite palace, and stamped upon the oaken floor. The tables rocked, the liquor quivered in the glasses, and the heroes were thrown from their seats with the shock. Dobrynya rushed forth into the courtyard, loosed his good steed from the golden ring, mounted and rode to his own dwelling. When he had spread fine Turkish wheat before the horse, in the midst of his own courtyard, he entered his mother's dwelling, sat on the wall-bench, and hung his turbulent head.

"Why art thou sad, Dobrynya?" his mother inquired of him. "Was thy seat at meat not to thy liking, or unbefitting thy rank? Did the cup pass thee by? Did some drunken boor spit in thine eye, or did the fair damsels scoff at thee?"

"Mine was the place of honour at meat," Dobrynya answered, "the greatest place, not the least; no fool offended, no damsel scoffed. But Prince Vladimir hath laid upon me a great service. I must go to the Tugy mountains, and free his niece from the fierce Dragon of the Cave."

"Grieve not, Dobrynya," spoke his mother, the honourable widow, Afimya Alexandrevna. "Lie down to sleep early this evening; to-morrow will be wise, for the morning is wiser than the evening." Her son heeded her; and the next morning, rising early, he washed himself very white, and arrayed himself for the journey.

"Be not sad," spoke his mother: "thy father went to the glorious Tugy mountains and slew an accursed serpent, and now thou must needs go thither likewise. Take not thy swift, stout bow, nor thy war-club, thy far-reaching spear, nor yet thy sharp sword. I will give thee a little whip of the seven silks, which thou must brandish; and I will give thee a magic kerchief. Thy right hand will droop, the light will fade from thine eyes, and the Dragon will begin to drag thee away, and to hurl thee down, and the little dragons to bite thy horse's fetlocks as he trampleth on them. But take thy magic kerchief, lift it to thy white face and wipe thy clear eyes, and thou shalt be stronger than before.—Then draw this whip, braided of the seven silks, from thy pocket, and beat thy good steed between the ears and on his hind legs. With that thy brown will begin to prance, and will shake off the Dragon's brood from his feet, and crush them to the last one. And brandish this silken whip; so shalt thou bend the Dragon to earth and subdue it like a Christian beast; and thou shalt sever its twelve tails, and give it over to speedy death."

So Dobrynya mounted his good steed, and rode to the Tugy mountains and the Dragon's cavern. Twelve days he rode, and ate nothing but a wheaten roll. On the thirteenth day he came to the glorious hills, but the Dragon was not in her cave, and the Prince's royal niece he could not see. Then he began to trample on the little dragons, and they coiled about his horse's fetlocks so that the good brown could no longer leap. He drew from his pocket the little whip of the silks of Samarcand, and beat the good steed between the ears and on his hind legs; the good brown began to prance thereat, shook off all the dragon brood, and crushed them to the very last.

Dobrynya gazed out over the open plain, and lo! the accursed serpent came flying towards him. When she espied him, she let fall from her claws upon the damp earth, the soft, thick grass, the dead body of a hero, and flew straight at Dobrynya.

"Aï, little Dobrynya Nikitich! Why hast thou broken thine oath, and crushed all my little dragons?"

"And aï, thou accursed Dragon!" quoth Dobrynya, "what devils bore thee over Kief, that thou shouldest seize young Beauty Putyatichna? Yield her now without battle or bloodshed."

"Without battle and bloodshed I will not yield the Prince's niece."

So they waged mighty battle all that day until the evening; and the snake began greatly to prevail. Yet Dobrynya, recalling his mother's counsel, wiped his clear eyes and his white face upon the kerchief, and his strength was greater than before. The next day they contended until the evening, and again the third day, so that Dobrynya would have fled before the serpent. But a voice from heaven warned him that if he would fight yet three hours longer, he should overcome the beast.

He fought on, but might not endure the Dragon's blood, so great was the flood thereof. Then he would have left the Dragon, but the voice spoke yet again from heaven: "Tarry yet three hours by the serpent, Dobrynya. Take thy far-reaching spear, smite upon the damp earth, and conjure thy spear: 'Yawn, damp mother earth, in all four quarters, yawn! Suck up the Dragon's blood!' "

When he had done this, and had fought the three hours, he overcame the beast. Recalling his mother's behest, he drew forth his whip of the silks of Samarcand, hewed off the twelve tails, cut the sinuous body into small pieces, and strewed them over the open plain.

After that, he entered the Dragon's deep den, and released the Russian prisoners,—Tzars, Kings and Princes by forties, and of lesser folk many thousands,—and bade them go where they would. But young Beauty, the Princess, he could not find, until he came to the farthest den. There she lay chained with hands outstretched. He released her straight, and led her forth to the white world. Then he mounted his good steed, and setting Beauty upon his right hip, rode out over the plain.

Said Beauty: "For thy great service I would fain now call thee little father, but that I may not do; for thy great deed, I would call thee my own brother, yet now I may not; gladly would I call thee friend and lover, but that thou lovest me not, Dobrynushka."

To her Dobrynya made answer: "Aï, Beauty Putyatichna! Thou art of princely birth, and I am but of peasant stock: it is not possible for thee to call me friend and lover."

As they thus rode over the plain, they came upon the traces of a horse, great clods of earth cast up, so that one might sink in the hollows, even to the knee. Dobrynya followed and found Alyosha Popovich in the way.

"Ho there, Alyosha Popovich!" cried he: "take the Princess Beauty, and bear her in honour to Vladimir, our Fair Sun Prince in royal Kief, and thy head shall answer to me for her." And this Alyosha performed.

When he had thus sent away Beauty, Dobrynya followed again after the tracks, and came upon a hero in the open plain, riding, in woman's garb, upon a fair and goodly horse.

"Eh!" quoth Dobrynya; "this is no hero, but a bold damsel-errant, some maid or wife, forsooth!" Therewith he rode after the warrior-maiden, and smote her upon her turbulent head with his mace of damascened steel. But the warlike virgin sat her good steed firmly, wavering not nor glancing back. Dobrynya sat his good steed in terror, and departed from that bold polyanitza: "Plainly," quoth he, "Dobrynya's valour is as of yore, but his strength is not the strength of other days."

Now there stood, near by in the plain, a damp oak, six fathoms in girth. This Dobrynya smote with his mace, and shivered into atoms; and he marvelled greatly.

"Of a truth," he said, "Dobrynya's might is as of old, but his courage is not the courage of earlier days!"

Then he again rode in pursuit of the bold warrior-maid, and smote her honourably upon her tempestuous head.—She wavered not, glanced not behind. But Dobrynya was sore amazed, and tested his might upon a damp oak of twelve fathoms, and shivered it in splinters. Thereupon, Dobrynya waxed wroth, as he sat his good steed, and rode after the bold virgin-warrior a third time, and smote her with his mace.

Thereat she turned and spoke: "Methought the Russian gnats were biting, but lo! 'tis the Russian hero tapping!"

Then she seized Dobrynya by his yellow curls, twisted him from his good horse, and dropped him into her deep leather pouch, and rode her way over the open plain.

At length her good steed spoke: "Aï, thou young Nastasya, Mikula's daughter, thou bold warrior-maid! Two heroes I cannot carry. In might that knight is thine equal, and the courage of that knight is as twice thine."

Quoth young Nastasya Mikulichna: "If the hero be very aged, I will cut off his head; if he be young and well pleasing in my sight, I will call him friend and lover; if he please me not, I will set him on one of my palms, and press him with the other, and make a pancake of him."

Then she drew him forth from the leather pouch, and liked him well. "Hail, dearest Dobrynya Nikitich!" quoth she.

"How knowest thou me, bold virgin knight? for thee I know not."

"I have been in Kief town, and have seen thee, Dobrynushka; but thou couldst by no means know me. I am daughter to the Polish King, young Nastasya Mikulichna, and I roam the open plain, seeking an adversary. If thou wilt take me for thy wife, Dobrynya, I will grant thee thy life. And thou must take a great oath; if thou swear it not, I will make of thee an oat-cake."

"Leave me but my life, young Nastasya, and I will take that great oath, and I will take also the golden crown with thee."

So they took the oath, and set out for Kief town, to courteous Prince Vladimir. Dobrynya's mother came to meet them, inquiring: "Whom hast thou there, Dobrynya Nikitich?"

"Ah, Afimya Alexandrevna, thou honourable widow my mother! I bring my enemy, young Nastasya Mikulichna; I am to take the golden crown with her."

Then they went to Prince Vladimir, and entered his banquet hall, where Dobrynya did reverence to all, and in especial, to the Prince and Princess.

"Hail, Fair Sun Vladimir of royal Kief!"

"Hail, Dobrynya Nikitich! Whom hast thou there?"

Thereupon Dobrynya told him all; Nastasya was received into the Christian faith, and they took the golden crowns. Courteous Vladimir made them a great feast for three days; and thereafter they lived happily for a space.[575]

Special Offer

Would you like to learn more about folklore and mythology? Sign up for our periodic newsletter and also get updates about book releases and promotions. As a thank you, follow this link to receive a FREE supplement to our "Spirits and Creatures" book series. From time to time, we'll change this free gift. The first installment is about a malicious water spirit: Vodyanoy or Vodnik. Discover where he comes from, how to protect yourself from him, how to make him "somewhat" happy, and more. Written in a conversational way, it will engage you, the reader. Illustrations and stories help provide you with an overall picture of this spirit.

Link to download: https://storyoriginapp.com/giveaways/11590b3e-e201-11e9-b12f-f38cdb616e11 or https://bit.ly/2XHovX8

If you'd like to read more dragon fairy tales, check out our book called *Dragon Tales*, available at https://books2read.com/dragon-tales.

About the Author

Ronesa Aveela is "the creative power of two." Two authors that is. Nelly, the main force behind the work, the creative genius, was born in Bulgaria and moved to the US in the 1990s. She grew up with stories of wild Samodivi, Kikimora, the dragons Zmey and Lamia, Baba Yaga, and much more. She's a freelance artist and writer. She likes writing mystery romance inspired by legends and tales. In her free time, she paints. Her artistic interests include the female figure, Greek and Thracian mythology, folklore tales, and the natural world interpreted through her eyes. She is married and has two children.

Rebecca, her writing partner was born and raised in the New England area. She has a background in writing and editing, as well as having a love of all things from different cultures. She's learned so much about Bulgarian culture, folklore, and rituals, and writes to share that knowledge with others.

Connect with us at www.ronesaaveela.com!

Ronesa's Books

Fiction
Mystical Emona: Soul's Journey
The Unborn Hero of Dragon Village
Zmeykovo (Bulgarian version of *The Unborn Hero of Dragon Village*)
La profezia del Villaggio del Drago (Italian version of *The Unborn Hero of Dragon Village*)
O Herói por nascer da Vila do Dragão (Portuguese version of *The Unborn Hero of Dragon Village*)
Dragon Tales

Nonfiction
Light Love Rituals: Bulgarian Myths, Legends, and Folklore
The Wanderer – A Tear and A Smile: Reflections of an Immigrant
Skitnikut – usmivki I sulzi: Rasmisleniata na edin bulgarski emigrant (Bulgarian version of *The Wanderer*)
A Study of Household Spirits of Eastern Europe
A Study of Rusalki – Slavic Mermaids of Eastern Europe
A Study of Dragons of Eastern Europe

Children's short stories, activity & coloring books
Baba Treasure Chest series
The Christmas Thief
The Miracle Stork
Born From the Ashes
Mermaid's Gift
Baba Treasure Chest: A Collection of Modern Bulgarian Tales (contains all four short stories)

Coloring Books
Mermaids Around the World
More Mermaids Around the World
52 Fascinating Mermaid Legends (both mermaid coloring books combined)
Little Zoi

Cookbook
Mediterranean & Bulgarian Cuisine: 12 Easy Traditional Favorites

Reviews

We hope you've enjoyed this book, and that its illustrations and words have inspired you. We would appreciate your gift of a review. Good or bad, we'd love to hear your honest thoughts.

Artist Profiles

Dmitry Yakhovsky, whose illustration graces this book's cover, has received education at the Academy of Art in Minsk, Belarus. He mostly works for authors and publishers all over the world to illustrate books in both digital and traditional ways but is also regularly commissioned for smaller projects. Dmitry writes and illustrates his own books. Examples of this are the graphic novel series "The Shadow of the Cross" and two coloring books for adults which were all published by the British publisher MadeGlobal and two historical graphic novels set in medieval Netherlands published by the Dutch publisher Pear Productions. He is a winner of a big comic contest in the Netherlands. Dmitry is besides this specialized in portrait and landscape paintings which are usually done in oil paint or watercolor and regularly exhibited.

Facebook: https://www.facebook.com/entaroart/
DeviantArt: https://www.deviantart.com/entar0178

Nelinda is the artistic side of Ronesa. Not only does she have thousands of ideas for stories about her Bulgarian heritage, but she is a talented artist. You can see more of her work at www.nelindaart.com.

Keazim Issinov was born in the village of Sadovets, Pleven region, on April 16, 1940. He graduated from the National Art School in 1960, and in 1968 graduated from The National Academy of Art, the class of Prof. Nenko Balkanski in Painting. After graduation he worked as a restorer at the Institute of National Monuments of Culture. In 1969 he started work at the National Research Institute of Psychology and Neurology as an art teacher. During his fifty years of creative work, the author has won many awards and participated in Bulgaria and abroad in many events, connected with charity.

2005: Awarded Artist of the Century in the competition Millennium "1001 Reasons to Love the Earth" held in the Netherlands.

2015: Awarded by the Ministry of Culture the Order "Golden Age."

Although Keazim's thematic range includes a series of paintings dedicated to the great masters of European art, as well as to man's connection with nature, his priority remains christian art, in particular icon art. It has left its mark on the inner light they emit, in the density of brown and fiery red, in the silvery and blue-green tones of the landscapes as a whole, typically giving off its colorful magical polyphony. The retrospective of Keazim's work once again explains his nickname of "enthusiastic pantheist," standing out even more in today's naked and orphaned by ideas, dreams and utopias, world.

Facebook: https://www.facebook.com/issinov

Plamen Dinkov was born in 1957 in Blagoevgrad and spent his childhood and school years in Vratsa, where his love for art and woodcarving was born for the first time. He lives and works in Sofia. Initially, he was also involved in metal plastics and artistic processing of metal in the Association of Masters of Folk and Artistic Crafts, but slowly woodcarving pushed everything aside. For forty years, he has been doing what he loves the most. He learned everything in carving on his own. He even made his first tools himself. It wasn't easy. He had to discover the intricacies of the craft on the go, but it brought him great satisfaction and gave him the opportunity to build his own style. The artist works for the audience, but the great thrill, love, intoxication for him is before, in the sleepless nights when the next work is born in his mind and in the days when it slowly comes out of his hands. His art has been bought and is available all over the world—Italy, Greece, France, Spain, Germany, Russia, America, etc. He's proud, of course, of his woodcarving crosses purchased and donated during the visits of Pope John Paul II and King Juan Carlos of Spain to Bulgaria in 2002 and 2003. Most of his works, though, are in Bulgaria, in private collections and homes. He has notebooks and notebooks full of ideas for new things. There are a lot of ideas—there is so little time. If God said so, Plamen would fulfill as many of them as he could. Finally, a question that a person often asks himself: Was he happy? Yes, he is a happy, extremely happy person. He does what he loves and lives in a world full of beauty and love.

Facebook: https://facebook.com/PLAMEN-DINKOV-WOODCARVING-345970847843/

Website: http://dinkovwoodcarving.com

Valentin Yotkov has been recognized as one of the world's leading experts in the ancient metal techniques of Chasing and Repousse. He has devoted his life and artistic career to reviving these techniques in art metal.

Mr. Yotkov's training began during the late seventies in his homeland of Bulgaria, where he apprenticed with some of the most accomplished Master Silversmiths.

Trained in the "Old world" apprenticeship system of Europe, at the age of twenty-two he became the youngest member in the history of the National Silversmiths Guild of Bulgaria. Three years later he was elected the President of the Guild.

Valentin has received numerous prestigious awards including two gold medals for highest artistic achievement in metal smithing. He is the recipient of the 2011 FSG National Metalsmith's Hall of Fame award. He has also been selected as one of the top fifty artists in New York and featured in the book Made in New York. His artwork can be found in private collections in more than twenty countries. Mr. Yotkov was also featured in the Japanese television documentaries World Heritage and Great Masters of the Arts.

Today Valentin resides in the United States where in 1994 he founded the Valentin Yotkov Studio with locations in Marlboro, New Jersey, and Bulgaria, Europe. The studio is recognized as the only school in the country specializing in Chasing and Repousse instruction.

Mr. Yotkov has developed a unique teaching method that allows students to easily learn and understand the technique. More than 1,900 students, professional jewelers, and metal smiths from around the world have attended his classes. Among them are members of the Tiffany & Co.'s silverware department as well as the Metropolitan Museum of Art's Restoration and Conservation department.

Besides teaching at his own school Mr. Yotkov has conducted over 250 workshops at different facilities around the world.

Website: http://www.valentinyotkov.com/site/studio.htm

Bibliography

Abbott, George Frederick. *Macedonian Folklore*. Cambridge: University Press, 1903. https://hdl.handle.net/2027/uc1.$b98052.

Actualno.com. "Пирин – селото, в което змейове крадат невести" [Pirin – the village where zmeĭove steal brides]. October 28, 2013. https://www.actualno.com/travel/pirin-seloto-v-koeto-zmejove-kradat-nevesti-snimki-news_4016.html.

Alexander, Alex E. "The Death of the Epic Hero in the Kamskoye Poboishche Bylina." *Slavonic and East European Review* 50, no. 118 (1972): 1-9. http://www.jstor.org/stable/4206483.

All About Dragons. "Zmej." http://allaboutdragons.com/dragons/Zmej.

Allegro. "Legendy Polskie. Film SMOK." November 30, 2015. https://www.youtube.com/watch?v=1J_Y12RqeLM.

Anarchelariu. "The Myth of the Hero slaying the Dragon as found in the Romanian Song Iovan Iorgovan." August 9, 2010. https://anarchelariu.wordpress.com/2010/08/09/the-myth-of-the-hero-slaying-the-dragon/.

Annie. "Самодиви, змейове и изобщо нашите си митове" [Samodivi, zmeĭove and our myths in general]. June 8, 2008. http://www.beinsadouno.com/board/forums/topic/4922-самодиви-змейове-и-изобщо-нашите-си-митове/.

Atil. "Змейове и хали (аждерки) в българския фолклор" [Zmeiove and hali (azhderki) in Bulgarian folklore]. June 12, 2016. http://atil.blog.bg/history/2016/06/12/zmeiove-i-hali-ajderki-v-bylgarskiia-folklor.1457442.

Atlantic Religion. "The Celtic otherworld in Romanian folk belief." June 1, 2014. https://atlanticreligion.com/2014/06/01/the-celtic-otherworld-in-romanian-folk-belief/.

Aveela, Ronesa. *Light Love Rituals: Bulgarian Myths, Legends, and Folklore*. Bendideia Publishing, 2015.

———. *A Study of Household Spirits of Eastern Europe*. Bendideia Publishing, 2018.

Avilin, Tsimafei. "Meteor Beliefs Project: Belarussian meteor folk-beliefs." *WGN, Journal of the International Meteor Organization* 34, no. 4 (2006): 119-123. http://articles.adsabs.harvard.edu//full/2006JIMO...34..119A/0000119.000.html.

———. "Meteor Beliefs Project: East European meteor folk-beliefs." *WGN, Journal of the International Meteor Organization* 35, no. 5 (2007): 113-116. https://aviti.livejournal.com/2427.html.

———. "Meteor Beliefs Project: More Belarussian meteor folklore." *WGN, Journal of the International Meteor Organization* 37, no. 1 (2009): 48-50. https://aviti.livejournal.com/1630.html.

Baeva, Vikhra, ed. *Змей. Змеица. Ламя и Хала. Сборник с фолклорни текстове* [Zmeĭ, zmeitsa, lamia and hala: Collection of folklore texts]. Sofia: Iztok-Zapad, 2016.

Belaj, Juraj. "Around and below Divuša: The Traces of Perun's Mother Arrival into Our Lands." Sacralisation of Landscape and Sacred Places – Proceedings of the 3rd International Scientific Conference of Mediaeval Archaeology of The Institute of Archaeology. Zagreb: Institut Za Arheologiju (2018): 69-92. https://www.academia.edu/38520448/Around_and_below_Divu%C5%A1a_The_Traces_of_Perun_s_Mother_Arrival_into_Our_Lands.

Benovska-Sabkova, Milena. "Митични същества" [Mythical creatures]. November 19, 2007. https://web.archive.org/web/20140501000810/http://detsata.zornitsa.com/?p=21.

Bjeletić, Marta. "Духовна култура Словена у светлу етимологије: јсл. (х)ала" [Non-material culture of the Slavs in the light of etymology: South Slavic (h)ala]. Krakow (2002): 75-82. https://www.academia.edu/11725489/Духовна_култура_Словена_у_светлу_етимологије_јсл_х_ала_Non_material_culture_of_the_Slavs_in_the_light_of_etymology_South_Slavic_x_ala.

———. "Јужнословенска лексика у балканском контексту. Лексичка породица именице хала" [South Slavic lexicon in Balkanic context: The word family of the noun xala]. *Balcanica* 34 (2004): 143–146. https://www.academia.edu/11655958/Јужнословенска_лексика_у_балканском_контексту_Лексичка_породица_именице_хала_South_Slavic_lexicon_in_Balkanic_context_The_word_family_of_the_noun_xala.

Blust, Robert. "The Origin of Dragons." *Anthropos* 95, no. 2 (2000): 519-36. http://www.jstor.org/stable/40465957.

Bnr.bg. "Триумфът на девойките – лазарки" [The triumph of the girls – lazarki]. March 19, 2010. https://www.bnr.bg/radiobulgaria/post/100225689/triumfyt-na-devoikite-lazarki.

Bpatarinski. "Маргарита и летящият момък" [Margarita and the flying boy]. July 28, 2011. http://ugarchin-culture.blogspot.com/2011/07/blog-post_28.html.

Cath. "Лазарките, кумичението и змеят" [Lazarki, kumitsa and zmey]. April 12, 2014. http://occultroom.blogspot.com/2014/04/blog-post.html.

Cigán, Ing. Mgr. Michal. "Anthropological and Philological Analysis of Social and Gender Relations in Indo-European Myths: Priest-King of the Warriors and Witch-Queen of the Others." Dissertation Thesis, Masaryk University, 2016. https://is.muni.cz/th/344582/ff_d/thesis-phd-cigan.txt.

Coxwell, Charles Fillingham. *Siberian and Other Folk-tales*. London: C. W. Daniel, 1925. https://hdl.handle.net/2027/osu.32435017842097.

Curtin, Jeremiah. *Myths and Folk-tales of the Russians, Western Slavs, and Magyars*. London: Sampson Low, Marston, Searle & Rivington, 1890. https://hdl.handle.net/2027/ucw.ark:/13960/t0wq0g13s.

Deunov, Peter. "Материална, реална и идеална любов. Категории на любовта" [Material, real and perfect love: Categories of love]. December 12, 1937. https://triangle.bg/books/1937-09-26-10.1998/1937-12-12-10.html.

Dobrev, Venelin. "Из дебрите на българската митология. Ламята" [From the depths of Bulgarian mythology: The lamia]. September 12, 2015. https://uspelite.bg/iz-debrite-na-balgarskata-mitologiq-zmei-i-zmeitza.

———. "Из дебрите на българската митология. Змей и змеица" [From the depths of Bulgarian mythology: Zmey and zmeitsa]. September 4, 2015. https://uspelite.bg/iz-debrite-na-balgarskata-mitologiq-zmei-i-zmeitza.

Douglas, Cristina. "Once Upon a Time: Understanding Death during Childhood through Fairy Tales." https://www.academia.edu/15602840/Once_Upon_a_Time_Understanding_Death_during_Childhood_through_Fairy_Tales.

Drăgule, Radu. "Analysis of the Connotative and Denotative Meanings of the Term 'Dragon' (Balaur) as it Appears in the Romanian Phytonymy" [In Romanian]. *Journal of Romanian Literary Studies*, no. 10 (2017): 104-111. https://www.academia.edu/34704020/ANALYSIS_OF_THE_CONNOTATIVE_AND_DENOTATIVE_MEANINGS_OF_THE_TERM_DRAGON_BALAUR_AS_IT_APPEARS_IN_THE_ROMANIAN_PHYTONYMY.

Dupnyshko (SBU 8, 67). "Змей обича мома" [Zmey loves a maiden]. https://liternet.bg/folklor/sbornici/minkov_1/47.htm.

Eminescu, Mihai. *Povestiri* [Fairy Tales]. Bucureşti: Socec, 1908. https://hdl.handle.net/2027/hvd.hwleav.

Etymonline.com. "Dragon." https://www.etymonline.com/word/dragon.

Fillmore, Parker. *The Laughing Prince; a Book of Jugoslav Fairy Tales and Folk Tales*. New York: Harcourt, Brace, 1921. https://hdl.handle.net/2027/mdp.39015066624910.

Find Bulgarian Food. "Bulgarian Folklore Calendar, April 12." http://www.findbgfood.com/calendar/calendar-april.htm.

Fol, Valeria. "Проф. Валерия Фол, траколог: Легендите за змейове в Странджа са урок младите момичетата да се пазят от слънцето по време на Горещниците" [Prof. Valeria Fol, thracologist: The legends of zmeiove in the Strandzha are a lesson for young girls to keep out of the sun during the

Dog Days]. By Anna Angelova, Radio "Focus." September 13, 2018. http://m.focus-news.net/?action=opinion&id=47455.

The Folklore Podcast. "Episode 68 - ZMEY. Performed by A Spell in Time." January 29, 2020. https://thefolklorepodcast.weebly.com/season-5/episode-68-zmey-performed-by-a-spell-in-time.

Fontenrose, Joseph. "Appendix 4. Saint George and the Dragon." In *Python: A Study of Delphic Myth and its Origins*. Berkeley: University of California Press, 1959.

Garnett, Lucy Mary Jane. *The Women of Turkey and Their Folk-lore*, vol. 1. London: D. Nutt, 1890-1891. https://hdl.handle.net/2027/bc.ark:/13960/t8x99v99m.

Genov, Anton. "The Symbolism of Caves as a Border Between Worlds in the Conceptions of Ancient Societies." *Knowledge – International Journal* 20.6 (December 2017): 2859-2864. https://www.academia.edu/35480780/THE_SYMBOLISM_OF_CAVES_AS_A_BORDER_BETWEEN_WORLDS_IN_THE_CONCEPTIONS_OF_ANCIENT_SOCIETIES.

Georgieva, Ivanichka. *Bulgarian Mythology*. Sofia: Svyat Publishers, 1985.

Giuglea, G., ed. *Dela Românii din Serbia, culegere de literatură populară* [From the Romanians in Serbia, a collection of popular literature]. București: Tipografia Curții Regale, 1913. https://hdl.handle.net/2027/mdp.39015065634860.

Hapgood, Isabel Florence. *The Epic Songs of Russia*. New York: C. Scribner's Sons, 1916. https://hdl.handle.net/2027/mdp.39015051105214.

Howey, M. Oldfield. *The Horse in Magic and Myth*. London: W. Rider & Son, 1923. https://hdl.handle.net/2027/wu.89092547082.

Hristov, Ivan, Dr. "Змейова сватба – по следите на един мотив в българския литературен модернизъм" [Zmey's wedding – in the footsteps of a motif in Bulgarian literary modernism]. January 7, 2012. https://nauka.bg/zmejova-svatba-po-sledite-na-edin-moti/.

Humphrey, Grace. *Heroes of Liberty*. Indianapolis: Bobbs-Merrill, c1921. https://hdl.handle.net/2027/uiug.30112075047529.

The Idle Woman. "I Am Dragon (Он – Дракон) (2015)." August 12, 2018. https://theidlewoman.net/2018/08/12/i-am-dragon-он-дракон/.

Iliescu, Laura Jiga. "The Ambiguous Dragon: Considerations on Abduction and Marriage in Legends about the Fairs of the Two Lands." *Revista de etnografie si folclor/Journal of Ethnography and Folklore* 1-2. Bucharest, Romanian, Academy Publishing House (2013): 51-63. https://www.academia.edu/11015140/THE_AMBIGUOUS_DRAGON_CONSIDERATIONS_ON_ABDUCTION_AND_MARRIAGE_IN_LEGENDS_ABOUT_THE_FAIRS_OF_THE_TWO_LANDS_in_Revista_de_etnografie_si_folclor_Journal_of_Ethnography_and_Folklore_new_series_1_2_Bucharest_Romanian_Academy_Publishing_House_2013_p_51_63_ISSN_0034_8198.

Imdb. "Butter on the Latch." May 9, 2013. https://www.imdb.com/title/tt2252304/.

Ispirescu, Petre. *The Foundling Prince and Other Tales*. Boston: Houghton Mifflin, 1917. https://hdl.handle.net/2027/mdp.39015043595746.

Israfela. "How is the cosmos perceived according to the Bulgarian folk belief?" February 18, 2018. https://wiccanrede.org/2018/02/how-is-the-cosmos-perceived-according-to-the-bulgarian-folk-belief/.

Ivanov, Mikhail. "Сексуалната сила или Крилатият дракон" [The sexual power or the Winged dragon]. http://www.beinsadouno.com/board/forums/topic/8219-образът-на-змията-в-митологията/?tab=comments#comment-128571.

Jezierski, Edmund. "Smok wawelski," 148-152. In *Ze swiata czarow: zbior basni, podan i legend roznych narodow* [From the world of magic: A collection of fairy tales, tales and legends of different nations]. Warszawa, [1921?]. https://hdl.handle.net/2027/uc1.b5128176.

Jobes, Gertrude. *Dictionary of Mythology, Folklore and Symbols*, vol. 2. New York: Scarecrow Press, 1962. https://hdl.handle.net/2027/mdp.49015002859669.

Karamanov, Georgi. "Прадядо ми змеят" [My great-grandfather, the dragon]. March 14, 2014. https://spisanie8.bg/рубрики/загадки/2379-прадядо-ми-змеят.html.

Kenaz, Iva. *Runes: Magical Codes of Nature*. 2020.

Kępa, Marek. "Traditional Polish Dragon Legend Retold in Short Sci-Fi Movie." December 11, 2015. https://culture.pl/en/article/traditional-polish-dragon-legend-retold-in-short-sci-fi-movie.

Kerewsky-Halpern, Barbara. "Watch out for Snakes! Ethnosemantic Misinterpretations and Interpretation of a Serbian Healing Charm." *Anthropological Linguistics* 25, no. 3 (1983): 309-25. www.jstor.org/stable/30027675.

King James Bible Online. "Bel and the Dragon, Chapter 1." https://www.kingjamesbibleonline.org/Bel-and-the-Dragon-Chapter-1/.

Kmietowicz, Frank A. *Slavic Mythical Beliefs*. Windsor, Ontario: F. Kmietowicz. 1982.

Konobeeva, Nadezhda. "Числовые и цветовые акценты в былине «Добрыня и змей» и мультфильме «Добрыня Никитич и змей»" [Numerical and color accents in the epic "Dobrynya and the Zmey" and the cartoon "Dobrynya Nikitich and the Zmey"]. http://elib.bsu.by/bitstream/123456789/103289/1/Надежда%20Конобеева%20Числовые%20и%20цветовые%20акценты%20в%20былине%20_Добрыня%20и%20змей_%20и%20мультфильме%20_Добрыня%20Никитич%20и%203мей%20Горыныч_.pdf.

Konstantinova, Daniela, trans. "The rainbow: Bulgarian legends and beliefs." April 26, 2012. http://bnr.bg/en/post/100151281/the-rainbow-bulgarian-legends-and-beliefs.

Kovak. "Змеят в българския фолклор и връзката с Рептилите" [The zmey in Bulgarian folklore and the relationship with the reptiles]. November 27, 2016. https://kovaklog.wordpress.com/2016/11/27/змеят-в-българския-фолклор-и-връзката/.

Kramer, Samuel Noah. *Sumerian Mythology, a Study of Spiritual and Literary Achievement in the Third Millennium, B. C.* Philadelphia: The American Philosophical Society, 1944. https://hdl.handle.net/2027/inu.39000005918599.

Kremenliev, Boris. "Some Social Aspects of Bulgarian Folksongs." *Journal of American Folklore* 69, no. 273 (1956): 310-19. doi:10.2307/537147. https://www.jstor.org/stable/537147.

Kuchera, Mikhail Petrovich. "Змієві вали" [Serpent walls]. By Encyclopedia of History of Ukraine. From Kuchera, *Змиевы валы Среднего Поднепровья* [Snake walls of the Middle Dnieper.] K., 1987. http://resource.history.org.ua/cgi-in/eiu/history.exe?&I21DBN=EIU&P21DBN=EIU&S21STN=1&S21REF=10&S21FMT=eiu_all&C21COM=S&S21CNR=20&S21P01=0&S21P02=0&S21P03=TRN=&S21COLORTERMS=0&S21STR=Zmievi_valy.

Kushnir, Dmitriy, translator. *Songs of Bird Gamayun: The Slavic Creation Myth* [ebook]. This source is probably a reconstruction of Slavic mythology of unknown authenticity.

Kursulan. "Змейове, змеици" [Zmeĭove, zmeitsi]. October 14, 2007. http://bulgarian-folklore.com/articles.php?article_id=283. From "Folk Faith and Religious Folk Traditions," D. Marinov, 1994, BAS.

Lang, Andrew. "The Death of Koshchei the Deathless." In *The Red Fairy Book* [ebook].

Liternet.bg. "Морска ламя поголтва Марковото дете, а Марко я разпорва и изважда детето си" [A sea lamia swallows Marko's child, and Marko tears her and takes his child out]. https://liternet.bg/folklor/sbornici/shapkarev_1/15.htm.

———. "Никола и хала семендра" [Nikola and hala semendra]. https://liternet.bg/folklor/sbornici/vekovno/28.htm.

———. "Радка и змей" [Radka and Zmey]. https://liternet.bg/folklor/sbornici/bnt/4/55.htm.

Lord, Albert Bates. "Bulgarian Traditional Literature in its Balkan Setting." *Indiana Slavic Studies* 6 (1992). https://hdl.handle.net/2027/osu.32435056449119.

———. *Epic Singers and Oral Tradition*. Ithaca; London: Cornell University Press, 1991. http://nrs.harvard.edu/urn-3:hul.ebook:CHS_LordA.Epic_Singers_and_Oral_Tradition.1991.

Low, David Halyburton, trans. *The Ballads of Marko Kraljević*. Cambridge: University Press, 1922. https://hdl.handle.net/2027/inu.39000005800714.

MacDermott, Mercia. *Bulgarian Folk Customs*. London: Jessica Kingsley Publishers, 1998.

Magnus, Leonard A. *The Heroic Ballads of Russia*. London: K. Paul, Trench, Trubner, 1921. https://hdl.handle.net/2027/uc2.ark:/13960/t25b0174t.

Majuru, Adrian. "Khazar Jews. Romanian History And Ethnography." https://www.icr.ro/pagini/khazar-jews-romanian-history-and-ethnography.

Malchev, Rossen Rossenov. *Hagiology and Demonology Tensions in the Structure of Folklore Faith* [In Bulgarian]. Sofia: ROD, 2017.

Mallory, J. P. *Encyclopedia of Indo-European Culture*. Chicago: Fitzroy Dearborn Publishers, 1997. https://ia801601.us.archive.org/6/items/EncyclopediaOfIndoEuropeanCulture/Encyclopedia_of_Indo-European_Culture.pdf.

Manning, Clarence A. "The Coming of Marko." In *Marko, the King's Son: Hero of the Serbs*. New York: Robert M. McBride, 1932. http://markokraljevic.uzice.net/01.htm.

Markov, Alexander. "Dragons and Lamias in Bulgarian folklore." May 31, 2013. https://bnr.bg/en/post/100200249/dragons-and-lamias-in-bulgarian-folklore.

Markov, Nikolai. "Демон на лошото време, характерен за Славянската етническа група на Сърбите, Българите и Македонците" [Demon of bad weather, characteristic of the Slavic ethnic group of Serbs, Bulgarians and Macedonians]. Temišvar / Niš (2015): 211-224. https://izdanja.filfak.ni.ac.rs/casopisi/2015/download/1441_29a2669cd76fbb3dbd47db5a23ddc5ec.

McBeath, Alastair, and Andrei Dorian Gheorghe. "Balauri & Zmei – Romanian Dragons." First published in *The Dragon Chronicle* 13 (July 1988). https://www.cosmopoetry.ro/Romanian%20Astrohumanism%207/Pages/romanian_astrohumanism_VII-3.htm.

Mijatović, Chedomil. *Servia of the Servians*. New York: Scribner, 1913. https://hdl.handle.net/2027/uc1.b5094137.

Milev, Geo. "Змей" [Zmey]. https://chitanka.info/text/11310-zmej.

Milosevic, Nikola. "Ala." Translated by Snježana Todorović. http://www.starisloveni.com/English/Ala.html.

———. "Dragon." Translated by Jelena Salipurović. http://www.starisloveni.com/English/Dragon.html.

Moldován, Gergely. *Alsófehér vármegye román népe. Néprajzi tanulmány* [The Romanian people of Alsófehér county: Ethnographic study]. Nagyenyed: Nagyenyedi könyvnyomda, 1897. https://hdl.handle.net/2027/nnc1.1002537877.

Mollov, Todor. "Свети Георги Убива Сура Ламя" [St. George kills tawny lamia]. December 6, 2000. https://liternet.bg/publish/tmollov/georgi.htm.

Morfill, William Richard. *Slavonic Literature*. London: Society for Promoting Christian Knowledge, 1883. https://hdl.handle.net/2027/uc1.$b321353.

Mrdjenovic, N. "Голубачка Ала Клинтонка." 2015. http://politikin-zabavnik.rs/clanci/golubachka-ala-klintonka.

Murray, Eustace Clare Grenville. *The National Songs and Legends of Roumania*. London: Smith, Elder, 1859. https://hdl.handle.net/2027/hvd.hxcquh.

Nandris, Grigore. "The Historical Dracula: The Theme of His Legend in the Western and in the Eastern Literatures of Europe," 109-143. In *Comparative Literature: Matter and Method*. Urbana: University of Illinois Press, 1969. https://archive.org/details/comparativeliter00aldr/page/124.

Oxenford, John. "The Bogies of Bulgarian Song." *Macmillan's Magazine* 34, no. 204 (1876): 547-552. https://hdl.handle.net/2027/hvd.32044092683549.

Paciorek, Andrew L. *Black Earth: A Field Guide to the Slavic Otherworld*. Durham, U.K.: Blurb, 2017.

Panayotova, Rumyana. "Тъмен се облак задава" [A dark cloud is coming]. September 21, 2006. https://web.archive.org/web/20070930185239/http://www.bnr.bg/RadioBulgaria/Emission_Bulgarian/Theme_Folklor/Material/2109_oblak.htm.

Peragraš, Aleksandar. *Ale i bauci: Prilog proučavanju tajanstvenih biča Balkana* [Ale i bauci: A contribution to the study of the mysterious scourges of the Balkans]. Beograd: Naučna knjiga, 1989.

Petkova, Savina. "#DBW A Dragon's Wife: Rewriting the Folklore Tale in Josephine Decker's 'Butter on the Latch'." September 1, 2019. https://screen-queens.com/2019/09/21/rewriting-the-folklore-tale-in-josephine-deckers-butter-on-the-latch/.

Petrovitch, Woislav M. *Hero Tales and Legends of the Serbians*. New York: Stokes, [1915]. https://hdl.handle.net/2027/uc1.$b98107.

PIC. "Легендите са живи! Николина от село Пирин била последната любов на Змея Горяни" [Legends are alive! Nikolina from the village of Pirin was the last love of Zmey Goryani]. May 9, 2017. https://pik.bg/легендите-са-живи-николина-от-село-пирин-била-последната-любов-на-змея-горянин-news655961.html.

Pinkham, Mark Amaru. "The Dragons of Serbia." February 14, 2016. https://www.facebook.com/TheReturnOfTheSerpentsOfWisdom/photos/a.665387323499605/1023438054361195/.

Pluskowski, Aleksander. "The Dragon's Skull: How Can Zooarchaeologists Contribute to our Understanding of Otherness in the Middle Ages?," 109-124. In *Animals and Otherness in the Middle Ages: Perspectives Across Disciplines*. Oxford: Archaeopress, 2013. https://www.academia.edu/24439076/The_dragon_s_skull_Zooarchaeological_perspectives_on_otherness_in_the_Middle_Ages.

Pochivka.blitz.bg. "Това е най-митичното място в цяла България!" [This is the most mythical place in all of Bulgaria!] August 24, 2019. https://pochivka.blitz.bg/pateshestviya/tova-e-nay-mitichnoto-myasto-v-tsyala-blgariya.

Poor, Laura Elizabeth. *Sanskrit and its Kindred Literatures. Studies in Comparative Mythology*. Boston: Roberts Brothers, 1890. https://hdl.handle.net/2027/uva.x030789217.

Potter, Murray Anthony. "The Horse as an Epic Character," 109-139. In *Four Essays*. Cambridge: Harvard University Press, 1917. https://hdl.handle.net/2027/mdp.39015028767104.

Quora.com. "Is the Zmeu dragon of Romanian mythology or Slavic?" https://www.quora.com/Is-the-Zmeu-dragon-of-Romanian-mythology-or-Slavic.

Radenković, Ljubinko. "Митска бића српског народа: (Х)АЛА" [Mythical beings of the Serbian people: (H)ALA]. Liceum 2, Kragujevacm (1996): 11-16. Archived from the original on 2014-04-11. https://web.archive.org/web/20140411193132/http://www.rastko.org.rs/antropologija/ljradenkovic/ljradenkovic-ala_c.html.

Radford, Benjamin. "Dragons: A Brief History of the Mythical, Fire-Breathing Beasts." April 11, 2019. https://www.livescience.com/25559-dragons.html.

Radosavljevich, Paul Rankov. *Who Are the Slavs? A Contribution to Race Psychology*, vol. 1. Boston: R. G. Badger, c1919. https://hdl.handle.net/2027/mdp.39015007018669.

Ralston, William. *Russian Folk-tales*. London: Smith, Elder, 1873. https://hdl.handle.net/2027/uc1.31158010565728.

Reed, Helen Leah. *Serbia: a Sketch*. Boston: Pub. for the benefit of the Serbian distress fund, 1917. https://hdl.handle.net/2027/njp.32101032964841.

Sawyer, Sarah. "Mythic Creature: The Balaur." October 10, 2011. https://www.sarahsawyer.com/2011/10/mythic-creature-the-balaur/.

Severozapazenabg.com. "Змейова сватба в Северозападна България" [Zmey's wedding in northwestern Bulgaria]. December 18, 2017. https://severozapazenabg.com/змейова-сватба-в-северозападна-бълга.

Sheppard Software. "Dragons." https://www.sheppardsoftware.com/Europeweb/factfile/Unique-facts-Europe31.htm.

Shiau, Yvonne. "The Evolution of Dragons in Western Literature: A History." October 23, 2019. https://www.tor.com/2019/10/23/the-evolution-of-dragons-in-western-literature-a-history/.

Siamashka, Volha. "He is dragon (English Version) HD." April 2, 2018. https://www.youtube.com/watch?v=K9yi_DzmNy4.

Silverfox57. "Zmeu." June 29, 2016. https://brickthology.com/2016/06/29/zmeu/.

Simeonova, Gatya. "От митология към история: трансформация на образи (змей, исполин, овластен овек) или закономерна смяна на преобладаващата антроломорфна форма" [From mythology to history: Image transformation (zmey, ispolin, authorized man) or the natural change of the dominant anthropomorphic form]. Venets: *The Belogradchik Journal for Local History, Cultural Heritage and Folk Studies* 4, no. 1 (2013), http://www.venets.org/getfile.php?id=142.

Skendi, Stavro. *Albanian and South Slavic Oral Epic Poetry*, vol. 44. Philadelphia: American Folklore Society, 1954. https://hdl.handle.net/2027/inu.30000118592439.

Slaveikov, Pencho. "Змейново любе" [Zmey's Sweetheart]. https://chitanka.info/text/6625-zmejnovo-ljube.

Slavic Mythology and Tales. "Vile and Rusalki – part 2." https://slavicmythologyandtales.wordpress.com/2020/08/15/vile-and-rusalki-part-2/.

Slavici, Ioan. *Poveşti* [Fairy Tales]. Bucureşti: Minerva,1908. https://hdl.handle.net/2027/hvd.hwlel1.

St. Clair, S. B. G. and Charles A. Brophy. *Twelve Years' Study of the Eastern Question in Bulgaria*. London: Chapman and Hall, 1877. https://hdl.handle.net/2027/hvd.32044018820068.

Stăncescu, Dumitru. *Basme, culese din gura poporului* [Fairy tales, collected from the mouths of the people]. Bucuresci: Haimann, 1892. https://hdl.handle.net/2027/hvd.32044019182302.

Stanciu, N. "Some notes about dragons in Slavic and Romanian cultures." *Bulletin of the Karagand A University*, 2015. https://articlekz.com/en/article/14634.

Stratilesco, Tereza. *From Carpathian to Pindus: Pictures of Roumanian Country Life*. Boston: J. W. Luce, 1907. https://hdl.handle.net/2027/uc2.ark:/13960/t2794b12p.

Strauss, Bob. "Dracorex Hogwartsia." January 21, 2020. https://www.thoughtco.com/dracorex-hogwartsia-1092859.

Tenev, Stanimir. "Валентин Стамов потомък на Змей?" [Valentin Stamov descendant of the Zmey?]. February 21, 2015. https://www.chudesa.net/валентин-стамов-потомък-на-змей/.

———. "Русин камък – пещерата, в която змей отвлякъл мома" [Rusin stone – the cave where a dragon kidnapped a girl]. September 15, 2010. https://www.chudesa.net/rusin-kamak-pesterata-v-koyato-zmei-otvlyakal-moma/.

———. "Змей живял в долмените на Хлябово" [The zmey lived in the dolmens of Khliabovo]. October 18, 2014. https://www.chudesa.net/змей-живял-в-долмените-на-хлябово/.

Thurston, Herbert. "St. George," 453–455. *The Catholic Encyclopedia* 6, New York: Robert Appleton. https://books.google.com/books/download/Catholic_Encyclopedia.pdf?id=BFc_AQAAMAAJ&output=pdf.

Vuković, Milan T. *Narodni običaji, verovanja i poslovice kod Srba: Sa kratkim pogledom u njihovu prošlost Народни обичаји, веровања и пословице код Срба* [Folk customs, beliefs and proverbs among Serbs: A brief look at their past Folk customs, beliefs and proverbs among Serbs]. Belgrade: Sazvežđa (2004): 220. From: Wikipedia. "Ala (demon)." https://en.wikipedia.org/wiki/Ala_(demon).

Walker, Mary A. *Untrodden Paths in Roumania*. London: Chapman and Hall, 1888. https://hdl.handle.net/2027/gri.ark:/13960/t23c36v0w.

Ward, W. H. "The Story of the Serpent and Tree." *The American Antiquarian and Oriental Journal* 20 (1898): 211-226. Chicago: Jameson & Morse. https://hdl.handle.net/2027/uc1.a0002682805.

Warner, Elizabeth. *Russian Myths*. Austin: University of Texas Press, 2002.

Wheeler, Joseph Trank. The *Zonal-belt Hypothesis; a New Explanation of the Cause of the Ice Ages*. Philadelphia: J.B. Lippincott, 1908. https://hdl.handle.net/2027/uc1.b4175758.

Wikipedia. "Wawel Dragon." https://en.wikipedia.org/wiki/Wawel_Dragon.

Wilson, Richard. *The Russian Story Book*. London: Macmillan, 1916. https://hdl.handle.net/2027/mdp.39015002199639.

Wratislaw, A. H., M.A., trans. *Sixty Folk-tales from Exclusively Slavonic Sources*. London: Elliot Stock, 1889. https://hdl.handle.net/2027/uc1.$b282186.

Yearsley, Macleod. The Folklore of Fairy-tale. London: Watts, 1924. https://hdl.handle.net/2027/mdp.39015002220419.

Yosifova, Nadezhda. "Подземен свят! Правнук на змей... говори, за първи път в тв ефир." [Underworld! A great-grandson of a dragon ... talk, for the first time on TV]. August 5, 2018. https://www.dnes.bg/akoshtete-vqrvaite/2018/08/05/podzemen-sviat-pravnuk-na-zmei-govori-za-pyrvi-pyt-v-tv-efir.383949.

Zhelev, Radostin. "The Golden Fruit Bearing Tree." March 9, 2012. https://bnr.bg/en/post/100144653/the-golden-fruit-bearing-tree.

End Notes

1 Blust, "The Origin of Dragons," 520.

2 Blust, "The Origin of Dragons," 521.

3 Blust, "The Origin of Dragons," 519.

4 Simeonova, "От митология към история," 57-58.

5 Ward, "Serpent and Tree," 213.

6 Ward, "Serpent and Tree," 212.

7 Ward, "Serpent and Tree," 213-214.

8 Ward, "Serpent and Tree," 212.

9 Kramer, *Sumerian Mythology*, 78.

10 Kramer, *Sumerian Mythology*, 83.

11 Simeonova, "От митология към история," 58.

12 Ralston, *Russian Folk-tales*, 65-66.

13 Pluskowski, "The Dragon's Skull," 119.

14 Simeonova, "От митология към история," 44.

15 Ward, "Serpent and Tree," 211.

16 Ward, "Serpent and Tree," 211-212.

17 Sawyer, "The Balaur."

18 Sawyer, "The Balaur."

19 Kramer, *Sumerian Mythology*, 30.

20 Georgieva, *Bulgarian Mythology*, 64.

21 Kushnir, *Songs of Bird Gamayun*, chapter 1. This source is probably a reconstruction of Slavic mythology of unknown authenticity.

22 Kushnir, *Songs of Bird Gamayun*, chapter 1.

23 Kushnir, *Songs of Bird Gamayun*, chapter 1.

24 Kushnir, *Songs of Bird Gamayun*, chapter 1.

25 Anarchelariu, "The Myth of the Hero slaying the Dragon." Referencing: Vulcănescu, Romulus. *Mitologie Românească, Bucureşti*, 1987.

26 Kushnir, *Songs of Bird Gamayun*, chapter 2.

27 Belaj, "The Traces of Perun's Mother Arrival," 70.

28 Mollov, "Свети Георги Убива Сура Ламя."

29 Kushnir, *Songs of Bird Gamayun*, chapter 2.

30 Mollov, "Свети Георги Убива Сура Ламя."

31 Anarchelariu, "The Myth of the Hero slaying the Dragon."

32 Mollov, "Свети Георги Убива Сура Ламя."

33 Georgieva, *Bulgarian Mythology*, 30.

34 Zhelev, "The Golden Fruit Bearing Tree."

35 Aveela, *Light Love Rituals*, 9.

36 Georgieva, *Bulgarian Mythology*, 68.

37 Israfela, "How is the cosmos perceived."

38 Israfela, "How is the cosmos perceived."

39 Israfela, "How is the cosmos perceived."

40 Aveela, *Light Love Rituals*, 2.

41 Israfela, "How is the cosmos perceived."

42 Georgieva, *Bulgarian Mythology*, 64.

43 Georgieva, *Bulgarian Mythology*, 64.

44 Georgieva, *Bulgarian Mythology*, 64.

45 Georgieva, *Bulgarian Mythology*, 65.

46 Kenaz, *Runes*, 36.

47 Anarchelariu, "The Myth of the Hero slaying the Dragon."

48 Georgieva, *Bulgarian Mythology*, 23.

49 Baeva, *Змей. Змеица. Ламя и Хала*, 151.

50 Georgieva, *Bulgarian Mythology*, 71, 72.

51 Pochivka.blitz.bg, "Това е най-митичното място в цяла България!"

52 Abbott, *Macedonian Folklore*, 260.

53 Abbott, *Macedonian Folklore*, 260.

54 Abbott, *Macedonian Folklore*, 260.

55 Sawyer, "The Balaur."

56 Strauss, "Dracorex Hogwartsia."

57 Pluskowski, "The Dragon's Skull," 117.

58 Pluskowski, "The Dragon's Skull," 119.

59 Yosifova, "Правнук на змей."

60 Karamanov, "Прадядо ми змеят."

61 Yosifova, "Правнук на змей."

62 Tenev, "Валентин Стамов потомък на Змей?"

63 Simeonova, "От митология към история," 43.

64 Pinkham, "The Dragons of Serbia."

65 PIC, "Легендите са живи!"

66 Tenev, "Змей живял в долмените на Хлябово."

67 Kuchera, "Змієви вали."

68 McBeath, "Balauri & Zmei."

69 Bpatarinski, "Маргарита и летящият момък."

70 Georgieva, *Bulgarian Mythology*, 59.

71 Milosevic, "Dragon."

72 King James Bible Online, "Bel and the Dragon, Chapter 1."

73 Malchev, *Hagiology and Demonology*, 139.

74 Malchev, *Hagiology and Demonology*, 138.

75 Malchev, *Hagiology and Demonology*, 143.

76 Malchev, *Hagiology and Demonology*, 140.

77 Malchev, *Hagiology and Demonology*, 140.

78 Malchev, *Hagiology and Demonology*, 140.

79 Malchev, *Hagiology and Demonology*, 141.

80 Malchev, *Hagiology and Demonology*, 138.

81 Garnett, *The Women of Turkey*, vol. 1, 22.

82 Garnett, *The Women of Turkey*, vol. 1, 22.

[83] Garrett, *The Women of Turkey*, vol. 2, 282.

[84] Garnett, *The Women of Turkey*, vol. 2, 282.

[85] Georgieva, *Bulgarian Mythology*, 66, 67.

[86] Jezierski, *Ze swiata czarow*, 148-152.

[87] Georgieva, *Bulgarian Mythology*, 59.

[88] Simeonova, "От митология към история," 51.

[89] Kmietowicz, *Slavic Mythical Beliefs*, 207.

[90] Kmietowicz, *Slavic Mythical Beliefs*, 206.

[91] Km etowicz, *Slavic Mythical Beliefs*, 207.

[92] Milosevic, "Dragon."

[93] Simeonova, "От митология към история," 51.

[94] Simeonova, "От митология към история," 51.

[95] Simeonova, "От митология към история," 53.

[96] Milosevic, "Dragon."

[97] Fillmore, *Shoemaker's Apron*, 158.

[98] Benovska-Sabkova, "Митични същества."

[99] Maksimović, "The Serbian Dragon: Fact or Fable?"

[100] MacDermott, *Bulgarian Folk Customs*, 65.

[101] Simeonova, "От митология към история," 55.

[102] Simeonova, "От митология към история," 54.

[103] Baeva, *Змей. Змеица. Ламя и Хала*, 347.

[104] Baeva, *Змей. Змеица. Ламя и Хала*, 403.

[105] Fol, "Легендите за змейове в Странджа."

[106] Fol, "Легендите за змейове в Странджа."

[107] MacDermott, *Bulgarian Folk Customs*, 65.

[108] Simeonova, "От митология към история," 59.

[109] Georgieva, *Bulgarian Mythology*, 59.

[110] Simeonova, "От митология към история," 58.

[111] Simeonova, "От митология към история," 61.

[112] Baeva, *Змей. Змеица. Ламя и Хала*, 154.

[113] Simeonova, "От митология към история," 60.

[114] Simeonova, "От митология към история," 60.

[115] Fol, "Легендите за змейове в Странджа."

[116] Georgieva, *Bulgarian Mythology*, 65.

[117] Georgieva, *Bulgarian Mythology*, 41, 59.

[118] Baeva, *Змей. Змеица. Ламя и Хала*, 347.

[119] Georgieva, *Bulgarian Mythology*, 59.

[120] Simeonova, "От митология към история," 61.

[121] Simeonova, "От митология към история," 61.

[122] Simeonova, "От митология към история," 59.

[123] Simeonova, "От митология към история," 62.

[124] Simeonova, "От митология към история," 58.

[125] Tenev, "Русин камък."

[126] Baeva, *Змей. Змеица. Ламя и Хала*, 347.

[127] Dobrev, "Змей и змеица."

[128] Georgieva, *Bulgarian Mythology*, 60.

[129] Baeva, *Змей. Змеица. Ламя и Хала*, 347.

[130] Avilin, "More Belarussian meteor folklore."

[131] Simeonova, "От митология към история," 51.

[132] Bpatarinski, "Маргарита и летящият момък."

[133] Georgieva, *Bulgarian Mythology*, 59.

[134] Baeva, *Змей. Змеица. Ламя и Хала*, 145.

[135] Baeva, *Змей. Змеица. Ламя и Хала*, 128. Recorded by Vihra Baeva from Lyubimka Biserova and Zlata Stoimenova in June 2013.

[136] Baeva, *Змей. Змеица. Ламя и Хала*, 128. Recorded by Vihra Baeva from Lyubimka Biserova and Zlata Stoimenova in June 2013.

[137] Fol, "Легендите за змейове в Странджа."

[138] Simeonova, "От митология към история," 48.

[139] Simeonova, "От митология към история," 55.

[140] Baeva, *Змей. Змеица. Ламя и Хала*, 123.

[141] Kutsulan, "Змейове, змеици." Simeonova, "От митология към история," 49.

[142] Simeonova, "От митология към история," 49.

[143] Kutsulan, "Змейове, змеици."

[144] Simeonova, "От митология към история," 49.

[145] Georgieva, *Bulgarian Mythology*, 59.

[146] Baeva, *Змей. Змеица. Ламя и Хала*, 121.

[147] Simeonova, "От митология към история," 47.

[148] Georgieva, *Bulgarian Mythology*, 41.

[149] Georgieva, *Bulgarian Mythology*, 41.

[150] Georgieva, *Bulgarian Mythology*, 41.

[151] Georgieva, *Bulgarian Mythology*, 41.

[152] Georgieva, *Bulgarian Mythology*, 31.

[153] Georgieva, *Bulgarian Mythology*, 71.

[154] Georgieva, *Bulgarian Mythology*, 71.

[155] Georgieva, *Bulgarian Mythology*, 61.

[156] Georgieva, *Bulgarian Mythology*, 70.

[157] Georgieva, *Bulgarian Mythology*, 60.

[158] Avilin, "Belarussian meteor folk-beliefs," 122.

[159] Avilin, "East European meteor folk-beliefs," 114.

[160] Georgieva, *Bulgarian Mythology*, 60.

[161] Avilin, "Belarussian meteor folk-beliefs," 122.

[162] Annie, "змейове."

[163] Baeva, *Змей. Змеица. Ламя и Хала*, 159.

[164] Simeonova, "От митология към история," 65.

[165] Simeonova, "От митология към история," 65.

[166] Simeonova, "От митология към история," 64.

[167] Simeonova, "От митология към история," 65.

[168] Milosevic, "Dragon."

[169] Baeva, *Змей. Змеица. Ламя и Хала*, 154.

[170] Malchev, *Hagiology and Demonology*, 123.

[171] Dupnyshko, "Змей обича мома."

[172] Baeva, *Змей. Змеица. Ламя и Хала*, 154.

[173] Milosevic, "Dragon."

[174] Avilin, "East European meteor folk-beliefs," 114.

[175] Avilin, "East European meteor folk-beliefs," 114.

[176] Kremenliev, "Some Social Aspects of Bulgarian Folksongs," 317.

177 Simeonova, "От митология към история," 63.

178 Baeva, *Змей. Змеица. Ламя и Хала*, 348.

179 Baeva, *Змей. Змеица. Ламя и Хала*, 347-348.

180 Dobrev, "Змей и змеица."

181 Baeva, *Змей. Змеица. Ламя и Хала*, 347.

182 Morfill, *Slavonic Literature*, 133.

183 Baeva, *Змей. Змеица. Ламя и Хала*, 154.

184 Annie, "змейове."

185 Georgieva, *Bulgarian Mythology*, 62.

186 Pochivka.blitz.bg, "Това е най-митичното място в цяла България!"

187 Baeva, *Змей. Змеица. Ламя и Хала*, 154.

188 Malchev, *Hagiology and Demonology*, 49; 50, footnote 38.

189 Avilin, "Belarussian meteor folk-beliefs," 122.

190 Georgieva, *Bulgarian Mythology*, 61.

191 Georgieva, *Bulgarian Mythology*, 62.

192 Slaveikov, "Змейново любе."

193 Georgieva, *Bulgarian Mythology*, 61.

194 Baeva, *Змей. Змеица. Ламя и Хала*, 159.

195 Milosevic, "Dragon."

196 Dobrev, "Змей и змеица."

197 Deunov, "Материална, реална и идеална любов."

198 Find Bulgarian Food, "Bulgarian Folklore Calendar, April 12."

199 Simeonova, "От митология към история," 60.

200 Simeonova, "От митология към история," 64.

201 Simeonova, "От митология към история," 45.

202 Liternet.bg, "Радка и змей."

203 Georgieva, *Bulgarian Mythology*, 61.

204 Kutsulan, "Змейове, змеици."

205 Hristov, "Змейова сватба."

206 Hristov, "Змейова сватба."

207 Georgieva, *Bulgarian Mythology*, 70.

208 Severozapazenabg.com, "Змейова сватба."

209 Severozapazenabg.com, "Змейова сватба."

210 Severozapazenabg.com, "Змейова сватба."

211 Severozapazenabg.com, "Змейова сватба."

212 Severozapazenabg.com, "Змейова сватба."

213 Severozapazenabg.com, "Змейова сватба."

214 Hristov, "Змейова сватба."

215 Milev, "Змей."

216 Hristov, "Змейова сватба."

217 Hristov, "Змейова сватба."

218 Hristov, "Змейова сватба."

219 Warner, *Russian Myths*, 45.

220 Simeonova, "От митология към история," 54.

221 Simeonova, "От митология към история," 53.

222 MacDermott, *Bulgarian Folk Customs*, 65.

223 Atil, "Змейове и хали (аждерки) в българския фолклор."

224 The Folklore Podcast, "Episode 68 - ZMEY."

225 Simeonova, "От митология към история," 72.

226 Georgieva, *Bulgarian Mythology*, 59.

227 Simeonova, "От митология към история," 58.

228 Simeonova, "От митология към история," 62.

229 Malchev, *Hagiology and Demonology*, 50, footnote 37.

230 Simeonova, "От митология към история," 59.

231 Simeonova, "От митология към история," 59.

232 Simeonova, "От митология към история," 53.

233 Simeonova, "От митология към история," 53.

234 Baeva, *Змей. Змеица. Ламя и Хала*, 154.

235 Avilin, "Belarussian meteor folk-beliefs," 122.

236 Georgieva, *Bulgarian Mythology*, 59.

237 Simeonova, "От митология към история," 54.

238 Simeonova, "От митология към история," 66.

239 Baeva, *Змей. Змеица. Ламя и Хала*, 135.

240 Baeva, *Змей. Змеица. Ламя и Хала*, 135.

241 Baeva, *Змей. Змеица. Ламя и Хала*, 144.

242 Georgieva, *Bulgarian Mythology*, 68.

243 Simeonova, "От митология към история," 66.

244 Baeva, *Змей. Змеица. Ламя и Хала*, 144.

245 Georgieva, *Bulgarian Mythology*, 68.

246 Baeva, *Змей. Змеица. Ламя и Хала*, 146.

247 Discover more about these rituals in my book *Light Love Rituals: Bulgarian Myths, Legends, and Folklore*, 72-77.

248 Cath, "Лазарките, кумичението и змеят."

249 Severozapazenabg.com, "Змейова сватба."

250 Baeva, *Змей. Змеица. Ламя и Хала*, 178.

251 Hristov, "Змейова сватба."

252 Cath, "Лазарките, кумичението и змеят."

253 Georgieva, *Bulgarian Mythology*, 61-62.

254 Georgieva, *Bulgarian Mythology*, 37.

255 MacDermott, *Bulgarian Folk Customs*, 66.

256 Baeva, *Змей. Змеица. Ламя и Хала*, 158.

257 Milosevic, "Dragon."

258 The role of hair in wedding rituals has been covered in more detail in my book *A Study of Rusalki – Slavic Mermaids of Eastern Europe*.

259 Morfill, *Slavonic Literature*, 133-134.

260 Liternet.bg, "Радка и змей."

261 Baeva, *Змей. Змеица. Ламя и Хала*, 162.

262 Baeva, *Змей. Змеица. Ламя и Хала*, 158.

263 Translator comment regarding the meaning of the two words.

264 Baeva, *Змей. Змеица. Ламя и Хала*, 159.

265 Dobrev, "Змей и змеица."

266 Dobrev, "Змей и змеица."

267 Garnett, *The Women of Turkey*, vol. 1, 355-356.
Original source: Dozon, *Chansons Populaires Bulgares*, No. 8.

268 Mcllov, "Мома среща три (два) змея."

269 Dobrev, "Змей и змеица."

270 Baeva, *Змей. Змеица. Ламя и Хала*, 131.
Recorded by Vihra Baeva from Lyubimka Biserova, Zlata Stoimenova and Aunt Nedyalka in June 2013, in the village of Pirin, municipality.

271 Actualno.com, "Пирин - селото, в което змейове крадат невести."

272 Actualno.com, "Пирин - селото, в което змейове крадат невести."

273 PIC, "Легендите са живи!"

274 Baeva, *Змей. Змеица. Ламя и Хала*, 154.

275 Baeva, *Змей. Змеица. Ламя и Хала*, 154.

276 Atil, "Змейове и хали (аждерки) в българския фолклор."

277 Baeva, *Змей. Змеица. Ламя и Хала*, 154.

278 Baeva, *Змей. Змеица. Ламя и Хала*, 165.

279 Baeva, *Змей. Змеица. Ламя и Хала*, 165.

280 Baeva, *Змей. Змеица. Ламя и Хала*, 165.

281 Malchev, *Hagiology and Demonology*, 123-125.

282 Malchev, *Hagiology and Demonology*, 132-134.

283 Georgieva, *Bulgarian Mythology*, 36-37.

284 Georgieva, *Bulgarian Mythology*, 46.

285 Baeva, *Змей. Змеица. Ламя и Хала*, 166.

286 Fochivka.blitz.bg, "Това е най-митичното място в цяла България!"

287 Milosevic, "Dragon."

288 Milosevic, "Dragon."

289 Georgieva, *Bulgarian Mythology*, 70.

290 Atil, "Змейове и хали (аждерки) в българския фолклор."

291 Simeonova, "От митология към история," 47.

292 Malchev, *Hagiology and Demonology*, 61.

293 Malchev, *Hagiology and Demonology*, 61.

294 Malchev, *Hagiology and Demonology*, 61.

295 Malchev, *Hagiology and Demonology*, 56.

296 Kovak, "Змеят в българския фолклор и връзката с Рептилите."

297 Georgieva, *Bulgarian Mythology*, 61.

298 Malchev, *Hagiology and Demonology*, 57.

299 Kmietowicz, *Slavic Mythical Beliefs*, 208.

300 Malchev, *Hagiology and Demonology*, 57-58.

301 Simeonova, "От митология към история," 72-73.

302 Malchev, *Hagiology and Demonology*, 59-60.

303 Malchev, *Hagiology and Demonology*, 59.

304 Malchev, *Hagiology and Demonology*, 60.

305 Garnett, *The Women of Turkey*, vol. 1, 355.

306 Georgieva, *Bulgarian Mythology*, 65.

307 Georgieva, *Bulgarian Mythology*, 60.

308 Baeva, *Змей. Змеица. Ламя и Хала*, 134.

309 Baeva, *Змей. Змеица. Ламя и Хала*, 133.

310 Atil, "Змейове и хали (аждерки) в българския фолклор."

311 Malchev, *Hagiology and Demonology*, 122-123.

312 Georgieva, *Bulgarian Mythology*, 64-65.

313 Georgieva, *Bulgarian Mythology*, 59.

314 Baeva, *Змей. Змеица. Ламя и Хала*, 140.

315 Baeva, *Змей. Змеица. Ламя и Хала*, 126.

316 Baeva, *Змей. Змеица. Ламя и Хала*, 124-126.
Modified translation of the tale recorded in 1970, and includes notes from other sources.

317 Baeva, *Змей. Змеица. Ламя и Хала*, 399.

318 Markov, "Демон на Лошото Време," 221.

319 Bjeletić, "Јужнословенска лексика," 149.

320 Milosevic, "Ala."

321 Radenković, "Митска бића српског народа: (Х)АЛА."

322 Baeva, *Змей. Змеица. Ламя и Хала*, 400.

323 Bjeletić, "Духовна култура Словена," 77.

324 Georgieva, *Bulgarian Mythology*, 66.

325 Simeonova, "От митология към история," 52.

326 Bjeletić, "Јужнословенска лексика," 149, footnote 21.

327 Peragraš, *Ale i bauci*, 64-65.

328 Georgieva, *Bulgarian Mythology*, 63.

329 Bjeletić, "Духовна култура Словена," 80, footnote 13.

330 Baeva, *Змей. Змеица. Ламя и Хала*, 405, 406, 408.

331 Bjeletić, "Духовна култура Словена," 76.

332 Baeva, *Змей. Змеица. Ламя и Хала*, 416.

333 Radenković, "Митска бића српског народа: (Х)АЛА."

334 Baeva, *Змей. Змеица. Ламя и Хала*, 405.

335 Avilin, "East European meteor folk-beliefs," 113.

336 Markov, "Демон на Лошото Време," 218.

337 Peragraš, *Ale i bauci*, 65.

338 Atil, "Змейове и хали (аждерки) в българския фолклор."

339 Baeva, *Змей. Змеица. Ламя и Хала*, 400.

340 Bjeletić, "Духовна култура Словена," 76-77.

341 Radenković, "Митска бића српског народа: (Х)АЛА."

342 Milosevic, "Ala."

343 Markov, "Демон на Лошото Време," 221.

344 Baeva, *Змей. Змеица. Ламя и Хала*, 401.

345 Georgieva, *Bulgarian Mythology*, 63.

346 Milosevic, "Ala."

347 Markov, "Демон на Лошото Време," 215.

348 Baeva, *Змей. Змеица. Ламя и Хала*, 416.

349 Radenković, "Митска бића српског народа: (Х)АЛА."

350 Baeva, *Змей. Змеица. Ламя и Хала*, 408.

351 Radenković, "Митска бића српског народа: (Х)АЛА."

352 Markov, "Демон на Лошото Време," 219.

353 Georgieva, *Bulgarian Mythology*, 25.

354 Georgieva, *Bulgarian Mythology*, 61.

355 Kenaz, *Runes*, 224.

356 Milosevic, "Ala."

357 Markov, "Демон на Лошото Време," 218.

358 Markov, "Демон на Лошото Време," 219, footnote 33.

359 Radenković, "Митска бића српског народа: (Х)АЛА."

360 Bjeletić, "Духовна култура Словена," 80, footnote 13.

361 Radenković, "Митска бића српског народа: (Х)АЛА."

362 Bjeletić, "Јужнословенска лексика," 146.

363 Mrdjenovic, "Голубачка Ала Клинтонка."

364 Radenković, "Митска бића српског народа: (Х)АЛА."

365 Wikipedia, "Ala (demon)." Original source: Vuković, *Narodni običaji, verovanja i poslovice kod Srba*, 220.

366 Petrovitch, *Hero Tales*, 19-20.

367 Panayotova, "Тъмен се облак задава."

368 Baeva, *Змей. Змеица. Ламя и Хала*, 407.

369 Baeva, *Змей. Змеица. Ламя и Хала*, 422.

370 Markov, "Демон на Лошото Време," 219.

371 Panayotova, "Тъмен се облак задава."

372 Radenković, "Митска бића српског народа: (Х)АЛА."

373 Markov, "Демон на Лошото Време," 221.

374 Radenković, "Митска бића српског народа: (Х)АЛА."

375 Liternet.bg. "Никола и хала семендра."

376 Abbott, *Macedonian Folklore*, 266.

377 Baeva, *Змей. Змеица. Ламя и Хала*, 399.

378 Milosevic, "Ala."

379 Baeva, *Змей. Змеица. Ламя и Хала*, 399.

380 Baeva, *Змей. Змеица. Ламя и Хала*, 404.

381 Simeonova, "От митология към история," 54.

382 Baeva, *Змей. Змеица. Ламя и Хала*, 401.

383 Georgieva, *Bulgarian Mythology*, 66.

384 Abbott, *Macedonian Folklore*, 266.

385 Warner, *Russian Myths*, 70.

386 MacDermott, *Bulgarian Folk Customs*, 64.

387 Baeva, *Змей. Змеица. Ламя и Хала*, 409.

388 Simeonova, "От митология към история," 46.

389 Abbott, *Macedonian Folklore*, 255-255.

390 Garnett, *The Women of Turkey*, vol. 1, 170.

391 Baeva, *Змей. Змеица. Ламя и Хала*, 403.

392 Baeva, *Змей. Змеица. Ламя и Хала*, 403.

393 Baeva, *Змей. Змеица. Ламя и Хала*, 402.

394 Baeva, *Змей. Змеица. Ламя и Хала*, 409.

395 Baeva, *Змей. Змеица. Ламя и Хала*, 409.

396 Malchev, *Hagiology and Demonology*, 135, footnote 144.

397 Malchev, *Hagiology and Demonology*, 128.

398 Malchev, *Hagiology and Demonology*, 135.

399 Baeva, *Змей. Змеица. Ламя и Хала*, 556.

400 Abbott, *Macedonian Folklore*, 268-277.

401 Nandris, "The Historical Dracula," 124-125.

402 Anarchelariu, "The Myth of the Hero slaying the Dragon."

403 Moldován, *Alsófehér vármegye román népe*, 187-188.

404 McBeath, "Balauri & Zmei."

405 Nandris, "The Historical Dracula," 124.

406 Murray, *The National Songs and Legends of Roumania*, 41.

407 Moldován, *Alsófehér vármegye román népe*, 184.

408 McBeath, "Balauri & Zmei."

409 Moldován, *Alsófehér vármegye román népe*, 185, 187, 188.

410 Moldován, *Alsófehér vármegye román népe*, 187.

411 Anarchelariu, "The Myth of the Hero slaying the Dragon."

412 McBeath, "Balauri & Zmei."

413 Drăgule, "Meanings of the Term 'Dragon' (Balaur)," 105.

414 Moldován, *Alsófehér vármegye román népe*, 178.

415 Moldován, *Alsófehér vármegye román népe*, 178.

416 Majuru, "Khazar Jews. Romanian History And Ethnography."

417 Moldován, *Alsófehér vármegye román népe*, 179.

418 McBeath, "Balauri & Zmei."

419 Drăgule, "Meanings of the Term 'Dragon' (Balaur)," 104.

420 McBeath, "Balauri & Zmei."

421 McBeath, "Balauri & Zmei."

422 Stratilesco, *From Carpathian to Pindus*, 187-188.

423 Moldován, *Alsófehér vármegye román népe*, 180.

[424] Murray, *The National Songs and Legends of Roumania*, 41-42.

[425] Murray, *The National Songs and Legends of Roumania*, 92-93.

[426] Stăncescu, *Basme, culese din gura poporului*, 245-257.

[427] Moldován, *Alsófehér vármegye román népe*, 190.

[428] Stanciu, "Some notes about dragons in Slavic and Roman an cultures."

[429] Nandris, "The Historical Dracula," 119.

[430] Iliescu, "The Ambiguous Dragon."

[431] Moldován, *Alsófehér vármegye román népe*, 188.

[432] McBeath, "Balauri & Zmei."

[433] Nandris, "The Historical Dracula," 119.

[434] Nandris, "The Historical Dracula," 124.

[435] Ispirescu, *The Foundling Prince*, xiii.

[436] McBeath, "Balauri & Zmei."

[437] Nandris, "The Historical Dracula," 119.

[438] Iliescu, "The Ambiguous Dragon."

[439] Iliescu, "The Ambiguous Dragon."

[440] Iliescu, "The Ambiguous Dragon."

[441] Murray, *The National Songs and Legends of Roumania*, 13-16.

[442] Iliescu, "The Ambiguous Dragon."

[443] Stanciu, "Some notes about dragons in Slavic and Romarian cultures."

[444] Iliescu, "The Ambiguous Dragon."

[445] Iliescu, "The Ambiguous Dragon."

[446] Iliescu, "The Ambiguous Dragon."

[447] McBeath, "Balauri & Zmei."

[448] Iliescu, "The Ambiguous Dragon."

[449] McBeath, "Balauri & Zmei."

[450] McBeath, "Balauri & Zmei."

[451] Giuglea, *Dela Românii din Serbia*, 366-374.

[452] Anarchelariu, "The Myth of the Hero slaying the Dragon."

[453] Anarchelariu, "The Myth of the Hero slaying the Dragon."

[454] Ivanov, "Крилатият дракон."

[455] Potter, "The Horse as an Epic Character," 110.

[456] Potter, "The Horse as an Epic Character," 110.

[457] Potter, "The Horse as an Epic Character," 125.

[458] Warner, *Russian Myths*, 54.

[459] Wilson, *The Russian Story Book*, 294.

[460] Douglas, "Once Upon a Time," 7.

[461] Warner, *Russian Myths*, 55.

[462] Blavatsky, *Isis Unveiled*, vol. 1, 554.

[463] Curtin, *Myths and Folk-tales of the Russians, Western Slavs, and Magyars*, 41.

[464] Moldován, *Alsófehér vármegye román népe*, 185.

[465] Warner, *Russian Myths*, 45.

[466] Moldován, *Alsófehér vármegye román népe*, 187.

[467] Wratislaw, *Sixty Folk-tales*, 137.

[468] Douglas, "Once Upon a Time," 11.

[469] Nandris, "The Historical Dracula," 119.

[470] McBeath, "Balauri & Zmei."

[471] Eminescu, *Povestiri*, 13-15.

[472] Ispirescu, *The Foundling Prince*, xii.

[473] Ispirescu, *The Foundling Prince*, xii.

[474] Eminescu, *Povestiri*, 15.

[475] Slavici, *Povești*, xxx.

[476] Slavici, *Povești*, 12-14.

[477] Slavici, *Povești*, 14-15.

[478] Paciorek, *Black Earth*, 108.

[479] Coxwell, *Siberian and Other Folk-tales*, 880.

[480] Lang, *The Red Fairy Book*, 56.

[481] Lang, *The Red Fairy Book*, 58.

[482] Lang, *The Red Fairy Book*, 58.

[483] Lang, *The Red Fairy Book*, 58-59.

[484] Yearsley, *The Folklore of Fairy-tale*, 138.

[485] Coxwell, *Siberian and Other Folk-tales*, 771.

[486] Coxwell, *Siberian and Other Folk-tales*, 772.

[487] Wilson, *The Russian Story Book*, 303.

[488] Wheeler, *The Zonal-belt Hypothesis*, 341.

[489] Parker, *Laughing Prince*, 144.

[490] Parker, *Laughing Prince*, 144.

[491] Lang, *The Red Fairy Book*, 63.

[492] Wheeler, *The Zonal-belt Hypothesis*, 340.

[493] Wratislaw, *Sixty Folk-tales*, 306.

[494] Thurston, "St. George," 454.

[495] Cigán, *Social and Gender Relations in Indo-European Myths*, 81.

[496] Mollov, "Свети Георги Убива Сура Ламя."

[497] Cigán, *Social and Gender Relations in Indo-European Myths*, 82.

[498] MacDermott, *Bulgarian Folk Customs*, 18.

[499] MacDermott, *Bulgarian Folk Customs*, 18.

[500] Mollov, "Свети Георги Убива Сура Ламя."

[501] Cigán, *Social and Gender Relations in Indo-European Myths*, 81.

[502] Fontenrose, "Saint George and the Dragon," 518.

[503] Mollov, "Свети Георги Убива Сура Ламя."

[504] Mollov, "Свети Георги Убива Сура Ламя."

[505] Malchev, *Hagiology and Demonology*, 48-49.

[506] Baeva, *Змей. Змеица. Ламя и Хала*, 527. This particular song is sung about St. Demitrius, but other songs about St. George have the same result.

[507] Oxenford, "The Bogies of Bulgarian Song," 552.

[508] Georgieva, *Bulgarian Mythology*, 22.

[509] Panayotova, "Тъмен се облак задава."

510 Georgieva, *Bulgarian Mythology*, 117.
511 Konstantinova, "The rainbow."
512 Warner, *Russian Myths*, 20.
513 Warner, *Russian Myths*, 20.
514 Stratilesco, *From Carpathian to Pindus*, 186.
515 Georgieva, *Bulgarian Mythology*, 64.
516 Poor, *Sanskrit and its Kindred Literatures*, 370.
517 Warner, *Russian Myths*, 20.
518 Poor, *Sanskrit and its Kindred Literatures*, 370.
519 Warner, *Russian Myths*, 20.
520 Warner, *Russian Myths*, 20.
521 Georgieva, *Bulgarian Mythology*, 116.
522 Warner, *Russian Myths*, 20.
523 Radosavljevich, *Who Are the Slavs?*, vol. 1, 291.
524 Warner, *Russian Myths*, 69.
525 Wikipedia, "Wawel Dragon."
526 Mijatović, *Servia of the Servians*, 103.
527 Manning, "The Coming of Marko."
528 Reed, *Serbia: a Sketch*, 35.
529 Mijatović, *Servia of the Servians*, 104.
530 Reed, *Serbia: a Sketch*, 35.
531 Low, *The Ballads of Marko Kraljević*, 42.
532 Low, *The Ballads of Marko Kraljević*, 44.
533 Low, *The Ballads of Marko Kraljević*, 175.
534 Mijatović, *Servia of the Servians*, 109.
535 Kremenliev, "Some Social Aspects of Bulgarian Folksongs," 317.
536 Howey, *The Horse in Magic and Myth*, 12.
537 Slavic Mythology and Tales, "Vile and Rusalki."
538 Lord, *Epic Singers and Oral Tradition*, 205.
539 Howey, *The Horse in Magic and Myth*, 12.
540 Potter, "The Horse as an Epic Character," 133.
541 Howey, *The Horse in Magic and Myth*, 12.
542 Reed, *Serbia: a Sketch*, 36.
543 Lord, "Bulgarian Traditional Literature in its Balkan Setting," 173.
544 Lord, "Bulgarian Traditional Literature in its Balkan Setting," 173-174.
545 Liternet.bg, "Морска ламя погълта Марковото дете."
546 Skendi, *Albanian and South Slavic Oral Epic Poetry*, 44.
547 Mijatović, *Servia of the Servians*, 109.
548 Potter, "The Horse as an Epic Character," 135-136.
549 Humphrey, *Heroes of Liberty*, 266.
550 Morfill, *Slavonic Literature*, 162-163.
551 Genov, "The Symbolism of Caves," 2862.
552 Story paraphrased from St. Clair, *Twelve Years' Study*, 56-57.
553 Warner, *Russian Myths*, 68.
554 Radosavljevich, *Who Are the Slavs?*, vol. 1, 298.
555 Radosavljevich, *Who Are the Slavs?*, vol. 1, 298.
556 Magnus, *The Heroic Ballads of Russia*, 47.
557 Wilson, *The Russian Story Book*, 105.
558 Magnus, *The Heroic Ballads of Russia*, 48.
559 Magnus, *The Heroic Ballads of Russia*, 56.
560 Hapgood, *The Epic Songs of Russia*, 148.
561 Magnus, *The Heroic Ballads of Russia*, 50.
562 Hapgood, *The Epic Songs of Russia*, 273.
563 Radosavljevich, *Who Are the Slavs?*, vol. 1, 300-301.
564 Warner, *Russian Myths*, 64.
565 Warner, *Russian Myths*, 69.
566 Warner, *Russian Myths*, 69.
567 Warner, *Russian Myths*, 28.
568 Konobeeva, "Былине «Добрыня и змей»."
569 Warner, *Russian Myths*, 29.
570 Alexander, "The Death of the Epic Hero," 5.
571 Alexander, "The Death of the Epic Hero," 4.
572 Parker, *Laughing Prince*, 139-160.
573 Liternet.bg, "Морска ламя погълта Марковото дете."
574 Baeva, *Змей. Змеица. Ламя и Хала*, 225-226.
575 Hapgood, *The Epic Songs of Russia*, 140-150.

www.ingramcontent.com/pod-product-compliance
Lightning Source LLC
Chambersburg PA
CBHW©42332030426
42335CB00027B/3310